Women in North Korea
From Revolution to Markets

Miryang Youn

Women in North Korea
From Revolution to Markets

Miryang Youn

GOOD
PLUS
BOOK

Preface

It has been seventeen years since I published a book titled *The Policy towards Women in North Korea* (in Korean, 1991). During the past seventeen years, many changes have occurred, shedding new lights into the life of North Korean people. Kim Il Sung, the supreme leader of North Korea, died in 1994. North Korea suffered a great famine during the mid-1990s. One notable aftermath of the famine was a flood of refugees from North Korea to third nations or to South Korea. There were two inter-Korean Summits in 2000 and 2007, many rounds of separated families' reunion events, and many conferences and gatherings of socio-cultural exchanges. All these changes provided outsiders an opportunity to look into the secretive state.

Many friends of mine urged me to revise the aforementioned book in accordance with the newly discovered facts about North Korea. However, for me, the new discoveries were rather reinforcing my argument in the book: Although North Korea claimed to emancipate its women as a part of socialist revolution, its political power succession from father to son reinstated the patriarchal social order and subjugated women to men. My argument remained strong and viable after almost two decades of publication. North Korean women were not emancipated, and the policy towards women in North Korea was not emancipating or gender-specific. Therefore I hesitated to add a mediocre book to the overabundant publications in the bookstores. Another book would be a torture to some and a bore to most readers. However, after I arrived at the Woodrow Wilson International Center for Scholars in Washington DC on April 2006, I realized how little outsiders knew about women in North Korea, and made up my mind. There should be at least one book about North Korean women in English, however boring it might be.

If one were to Google the term "North Korean Women," he or she would mostly find news headlines dealing with trafficking, slave labor, refugees etc. This creates an image of North Korean women as poor, weak, and defenseless. The image, of course, correctly portrays a number of North Korean women in desperation. After the great famine struck North Korea in the mid 1990s, many women fled to China and other neighboring countries to obtain foods. Many women were fallen victims to the human-trafficking and slave-labor. However, not all North Korean women were defenseless victims. Many other women vigorously fought against the famine, and survived. They tilted the barren soils and cultivated grains and groceries. They also bought and sold anything that could be changed into money and food. More women than men became the breadwinner of the family and managed the family to survive the famine. They were strong mothers and bald daughters. They were also new economic forces that drove North Korea to marketization.

This book is a history of North Korean women after the Liberation in 1945 to the present. Whereas my aforementioned book of 1991 was about public policy of North Korea, this book is about women's struggle since 1945. My argument is that women in North Korea have always been an active player, not a passive object, in the making of their life and the North Korean history. While North Korean government attempted to grant women "equality" through legal and social reforms, persistent social customs and economic conditions hampered women to gain equality in reality. It was women's struggles and continuous effort to obtain social recognition and change in gender relations.

North Korea launched a communist revolution during the late 1940s. The North Korean revolution attempted to change the whole society and the status of women. North Korean regime promised equality of men and women, and took measures to mobilize women into society outside of the home in accordance with the Marx-Engels' theory of women's emancipation. During this revolutionary era, from 1945 to 1950, women actively participated in social and political rallies and polls. During the disastrous Korean War women took the machines instead of their soldier husbands and sons, and cultivated the rice fields. Many women became the labor heroes and advanced into the Supreme People's Assembly. The proportion of women in the labor force reached up to a half, and the proportion of women in the People's Supreme Assembly recorded around 20 percent since the 1970s.

After North Korea claimed to complete the socialist revolution and designated Kim Jong Il as heir-apparent in the 1970s, however, North Korea began to lose interest on women's issues, insisting that it had accomplished women's emancipation. Furthermore, the idolization of the Great Mothers, the mothers of Kim Il Sung and Kim Jong Il, demanded women to be loyal to their rulers and husbands. The Confucian tradition was reinstated. Nevertheless, women continued to work outside and inside of the home for the sake of their family and themselves. Women also opened a small but significant path to market by opting for "unemployed" Domestic Workshops instead of mandatory job assignments. Becoming the member of Domestic Workshops were rather highly rewarding, because they were allocated with consumer goods that the workshops were producing. In an economy of chronicle shortage of consumer goods, the access to consumer goods was not a bad deal. By the end of 1980s, contrary to the state statistics, seventy percent of married women in rural areas became "unemployed."

During the 1990s when North Korea's GDP was reduced by half, many women became the breadwinners of the family, since their husbands were practically unemployed. They cultivated vegetables in their small backyard, produced small handcrafts, or bought and sold goods that they obtained illegally by trading with the Chinese across the border. It was mostly women who kept their family alive. It was women who introduced markets to North Korea from the grass-roots. In a sense, it was women who made the regime muddle through during the economic debacle. As the economic crisis resulted in the increase of women's role in supporting their family, women's attitudes and consciousness regarding men and society began to change.

I did not visit North Korea until I had first published the aforementioned book. Only after the historical Inter-Korean Summit in 2000, I had many opportunities to visit North Korea. Although I was a member of government delegation that usually engaged in political affairs, I was naturally inclined to watch women in North Korea, mainly because I had experienced discrimination as a woman, and also because I wanted to examine my book through the reality.

I was amazed by the scene of farming women. During the spring farming season, the workers who were stooping down and manually planting rice in the field were all women. The only man I could see was standing far away, probably inspecting the field. Sure, I thought, work that needed to be done by stooping down was so menial that it did not suit men. Menial work should be done by women. It was what I heard so often from many women refugees from North Korea.

Even before I visited North Korea, I encountered many female refugees among whom some escaped from the North as early as the 1970s. While I continued to watch the refugees, I realized significant changes in their attitudes corresponding to the period of their escape. Women who fled the North during the 1970s and 1980s kept the typical "virtues of Korean women" that meant to be polite, complaisant, and submissive to men. They often insisted that "women should be feminine." However, women who escaped after the late 1990s, after the period of the so-called "Arduous March," tend to be more assertive and to have a strong will to survive. They were survivors.

This book is to argue the active role of women throughout the history of North Korea. Women were directed or suggested to choose what the regime desired them to do. Women's response, however, was not always in accord with the regime's intention. Women's conscious or unconscious choices wove their lives and social conditions, as well as unwittingly changed the regime's path from time to time. I hope this book could contribute to enhancing the understanding of North Korean women who are perseverant survivors and adamant warriors.

This book is organized in chronological order. I divide the time span into three periods: from Korean Liberation in 1945 to the end of Korean War (1945~1953); from the post-war rehabilitation to the brink of the "Arduous March" (1953~1989); and during and after the "Arduous March" (1990~present).

The first period was the most dynamic and turbulent. It was the era of revolution. It was the era of passion and zeal for the abolition of the old order and the construction of new nation. The pure passion for change shaped the first state.

The question of when the second stage began would be not so easy. The War and post-War rehabilitation period together would make an independent period. Or, the post-War era could be included in the first phase of the North Korean revolution. However, I observed, there had been more circumstance-driven tactical decisions than strategic decisions regarding women since the end of the War. Women's legal status, in a sense, was almost fully settled in 1946 with the Sex Equality Law. No other legislation afterwards enhanced women's lot much further.

The last period was during the Arduous March. There could be another controversy when the Arduous March actually began. However, following a joint study project carried out by Sejong Institute, I designate the year 1989 as the beginning of the Arduous March. I was involved in a three-year project on North Korean society, "Continuities and Changes in North Korea," by the North Korean Research Center, Sejong Institute in Seoul during 2004-2005. The project yielded a seven-book series in 2006.[1] Seven scholars who were

---

1 See Sejong Institute, *Bukhanui Sahoe Munhwa* 북한의 사회문화, Sejong Yungoo Chongsoe 7 (Seoul: Hanul, 2006).

engaged in the socio-cultural part of the study had a lengthy discussion about the periodization of North Korean change, and finally agreed on the year 1989 as the beginning of the Arduous March. At least articles dealing with social and cultural changes in the seven books had the year 1989 as the criterion.

I have quoted many testimonies in this book. The sources of the testimonies are existing publications and interviews. For the early stage of North Korean regime, I mostly relied on historic documents and publications, because there were only few defectors from North Korea who were able to testify women's conditions until the late 1980s. For the lives of women during the Arduous March, I mainly relied on materials of in-depth interviews with refugees from North Korea, because there were a flood of refugees from North Korea during the 1990s. Many NGOs in South Korea systematically carried out interviews and regional surveys targeting the refugees. Many scholars concerning North Korea also published a variety of books containing their in-depth interview results with the refugees. The list of books that contain interview materials is provided in Appendix 2.

In addition, for the above-mentioned joint study project, Sejong Institute carried out an in-depth interview series for three years. Each interview was carried out once a week, with some exceptions, for eight hours a day. Four to seven scholars of different disciplines met one refugee each week and recorded the whole interview with the refugee's consent. I heavily relied on the interview results. I attach the list of those interviewees and the date of interview in Appendix 1.

For Romanization of Koreans, I have followed the Standard Romani zation System of the National Institute of the Korean Language [국립국어원].[2]

---

2 The automatic Romanization engine is available at the homepage of the National Institute of the Korean Lan-

However, there are some exceptions:

- For Kim Il Sung and Kim Jong Il I have followed the North Korean practices in their official publications and translations such as the *Works* of Kim Il Sung and Kim Jong Il.
- For the North Korean place names and ideological terminology (e.g. *Juche*) I also have followed the North Korean practices.
- For the North Korean publications, I followed the Library of Congress romanization, for the sake of the retrieving the books from libraries.
- I have placed the family name last in Korean names except Kim Il Sung, Kim Jong Il, Kim Jong-Suk and Kang Ban-Sok.
- Ihave inserted a hyphen between the two elements of personal names of Koreans, except Kim Il Sung, Kim Jong Il, and author's own.

Table of Contents

Table of Contents

Chapter I

Introduction

1.1 Korean Culture on Women

Confucianization of the *Chosun* Dynasty

Until the end of the *Koryo* dynasty (918~1392), women in Korea enjoyed relatively equal rights with men: they had property rights, equal rights to inheritance with male siblings, the rights to divorce and marry, and partial parental authority in case of divorce. The *Silla* Dynasty had three (BC 57~AD 935) Queen-monarchs among its 56 monarchs. Many royal women were remarried during the Three Kingdom period and *Koryo* dynasty. Men and women enjoyed considerable freedom to associate each other. Incest and adultery were frequent without much stigma: an aunt could marry her nephew; and sometimes two sisters shared one husband. At least one queen remarried to the brother of her deceased husband, which allowed her second husband to succeed to the throne in the Koguryo kingdom (BC 37~AD 668). During the *Koryo* dynasty, women's remarriage was widely practiced and accepted. Men and women often bathed together in the open stream, with their clothes lying along the bank.[1] Women shared the right and duty of ancestor worship, as well as the right to the headship of the family.

However, the establishment of the *Chosun* dynasty in 1392 led to Confucianization of Korea, which deprived women of most legal rights. During most of the *Chosun* Dynasty women were legally subordinated to men. Women were confined at home, and their conditions were determined by the Confucian family sys-

---

1 Richard Rutt, *James Scarth Gale and His History of the Korean People*, re-quoted from Yung-Chung Kim, *Women of Korea: A History from Ancient Times to 1945* (Seoul: Ewha Woman's University Press, 1976): 83.

tem. The major characteristics of the family system of the *Chosun* Dynasty were:[2] 1) Only the paternal line relatives were regarded as relatives; 2) Social class and rights were transmitted only from fathers to sons; 3) The sole authority in the family rested with the father who held control over the children; 4) Marriages were allowed only with those outside the (paternal) blood clan; 5) First-born males held the right to lineal succession.

In this family system, women were denied legal competence in the right to choose whether or who to marry or divorce, the parental authority, and the contract rights. Women also lost the right to perform ceremonies for ancestor worship. All the power within the family rested in the hands in the male head of household. Women were also denied parental authority, even for a widow with children. The parental authority was given to the head of the family who might be the uncle, brother or cousin of the deceased husband.

However, women were allowed to keep the right to inheritance under the law. In the *Kyungguk Taejon*, the Basic Law of the *Chosun* dynasty, male and female offspring were both entitled to inherit their father's property, including land and servants.[3] The inherited property of the wife was under joint ownership of the couple. The dowry property was to return to her father upon her death. However, in practice, the head of the husband's family exercised the sole ownership of the property, and seldom retuned the dowry to the father of the deceased wife.

All the family members were recorded in *Hojuk*, the family registry. Males were recorded in full names, but female members were only recorded as birth and death, or marriage-away. A new bride was recorded to the in-laws' family registry by her natal family name only. The family registry system was originally appli-

---

2 Yung–Chung Kim: 89.

3 Yung–Chung Kim: 101–102.

cable only to nobles. However, during the turbulent years of the late *Chosun* dynasty when Japanese pirates invaded Korea in the 16th century, many commoners and even the lower orders began to make their own family registry. The family registry soon became the main means of social identification, making the family more powerful over the individual.

The *Chosun* Dynasty published the *Samgang Haengsil-Do* [삼강행실도: Three Principles of Virtuous Conduct] in 1432. This book collected many exemplary cases of "virtuous women" and presented them as a guide to all Korean women. All women should learn about the exemplary women, and endeavor to be like them.

The Rule of Obedience to Three Men

The Neo-Confucianism that dominated the *Chosun* dynasty was reinforced by the teachings of Zhu Xi, especially his emphasis on the *Three Cardinal Principles and Five Ethical Norms*. The *Three Cardinal Principles* are loyalty to the ruler, filial piety, chastity of women. The *Five Ethical Norms* are justice between ruler and subjects, closeness between father and son, order between elders and youths, distinction between husband and wife, and trust between friends. These principles all emphasized hierarchy and relationship rather than equality and impartiality, and as a result, legitimized discrimination against women. Women were regarded as inferior, so they had to rely on and obey men. The *Rule of Obedience to Three Men* demanded women to obey three men in their lives: their fathers during their childhood, their husbands during marriage and their sons after the death of their husbands.

Before marriage, a girl should remain virgin at all circumstances. Girls' virginity and married women's chastity were regarded more important than their life itself. In order to protect girls' virginity, boys and girls were separated since the age of seven. Boys and girls of age seven and above were not allowed to be seated in a room together. Even being seen outsiders were regarded to taint the chastity. Women, except for servants and the lowest class, were not to be seen to the outsiders: women could not stroll in their garden or venture out during the daytime except under strict conditions like receiving royal visitors or seeing off and greeting members of their family; when outside women were expected to wear a long veil to cover their face and body.

The fathers arranged marriages for their daughters. The bride was to meet the groom for the first time at the wedding ceremony. However, even at the wedding ceremony, the bride could not see the groom because her eye-lids were shut with honey. For wedding ceremony, the bride was to be prepared with honey on her eye-lids, a jujube in her mouth, and small padded cotton in her ears. This preparation meant to warn the bride not to see any misbehavior of her husband and her in-laws; not to speak anything against the will of her husband and in-laws; and not even try to hear, and therefore respond, bad things spoken or done to her by her husband and in-laws during marriage. It symbolized the plight of married women, which was summarized in the phrase, "Blind for three years, Dumb for three years, and Deaf for three years." A newly married woman was assumed to behave like a blind for first three years, a dumb for next three years, and a deaf for another three years. Obedience and endurance were the virtues that women should follow.

Women's virtue lay in women's lack of, or their tremendous ability to suppress, sexual desire and jealousy: Husbands were allowed to have as many concubines as they could afford, while wives had to accept the concubines with "virtuous" smile. A Woman's failure to obey her husband or in-laws could result in her expulsion from the family. The infamous *"Seven Evils"* of women that gave men the right to desert their wives on seven grounds were: failure to bear a son, disobedience to parents-in-laws, adultery, jealousy, larceny, garrulousness, and hereditary diseases.

The only consolation for women was the existence of the *"Three Cases of Non-Expulsion,"* which prohibited expelling the wife even when the wife committed one or several of the *"Seven Evils."* The *Three Cases* were: when the wife had performed the three-year mourning rituals for the deceased parents-in-laws; when the wife had managed to save the family from poverty and amass a fortune; and when the wife had nowhere to go.

Despite the family oppression, the lives of the first wives were far better than those of concubines or secondary wives. Secondary wives and concubines had to endure disdain and humiliation by the first wives, by the family members, and by society. Their children were also destined to be despised and discriminated against. In Korea, every person was required to register in a family register that records all lineages. All the events of life of the family members including birth, death, and marriage were recorded in the family register. Since having a concubine was not regarded as a marriage, the names of concubines were not recorded. Those children from concubines were recorded as bastards, and later married to children of concubines of other families. The children of concubines had to call their fathers "Sir" or "Master." They were often well-fed and educated, but not allowed to take national examinations. Some of them managed to remain rich after their fathers' death, but most were poor and unhappy because of their bastard status, which was sometimes considered lower than a commoner.

After her husband's death, a woman should, at least in theory, obey to her eldest son. In practice, it means that, even when she had to support the family by herself, the head of the family should be the father-in-law or her son. All important decisions were to be made by the head of the family. By marriage, a woman came to belong to the husband's family forever. It also means that a woman had to have only one husband in her life; remarriage was viewed as losing chastity which in any circumstance was regarded as worse than death.[4]

Remarriage for widows was prohibited in 1485 by law. Sons of remarried widows, including the sons from their first marriages, could not apply for the state examination, which was the only way to become a government official and obtain wealth and social privilege. This rule alone was powerful enough to force most widows to give up remarriage.

Sacred Motherhood, Praised Innocence

The most important role of women was to bear and rear the children, particularly sons. Although the ideal woman in Korea was a *"Wise Mother, Virtuous Wife* [현모양처]", as in other Asian societies, the Korean version put an overwhelming emphasis on motherhood. While *"Virtuous Wife"* implied mostly obedience and compliance to husband and in-laws, *"Wise Mother"* required loving, caring, discipline, dedication and sacrifice. There are many anecdotes of *"Wise Mothers"* to this day.

The mother of Sok-Bong Han (1543~1605), one of the most famous mas-

---

4 It is the rule of obedience to *Three* men, not three kinds of men. Multiple husbands would make more than three men involved in a woman's life.

ter calligraphers in Korea, was widowed very early without inheritance. She supported her family by making and selling rice cakes. She made the rice cakes during the night, and sold them in the market during the day. Despite living in poverty, she insisted her son to continue his study in the city. One day Han claimed that he mastered calligraphy and returned home. His mother asked him to write in the dark without candle light, while she cut rice cakes. When the candle was lit, Han saw his writing was illegible, while his mother's cakes were beautifully cut all in same size and shape. He realized what his mother wanted to tell: mastery was not just writing well in favorable condition only; mastery required to overcome the most hostile conditions; his study and calligraphy was far short of mastery. Therefore he resumed his study, perfected calligraphy, and created his own style. His mother's quiet lesson and wisdom led him to be a great master. The instruction of Han's mother was repeatedly praised during the *Chosun* Dynasty.

The story of Han's mother contained a few "educational" values: she kept her chastity as a widow; she was strong enough to shoulder all the hardships of supporting her children by herself; she brought up her children with strict discipline; and she was wise enough to influence and instruct the children to excel. If a widow remarried, she surely ended up ruining her children's future. If a widow was unable to support and educate the children, she also failed her children. A widowed mother was also demanded to be stern and strict in discipline, because a child could be easily spoiled without the guidance of father. Han's mother was stern enough to conceal her love and persuade her son to leave home to continue his study.

Another exemplary mother was the mother of Seo-Bong Hong (1572~1645). Hong's mother became a young widow after only two years of marriage. She never married again, of course. She was born to a noble family, and read more books than ordinary noble men. Because both her natal family and the Hong's paternal family were rich, she could provide Hong with almost everything except father. The absence of the father worried her of the possibility of spoiling her son. She determined to set a strict discipline, and instructed him with a switch. However, she always kept the switch in a large piece of silk like a treasure. When a maid asked her the reason, she answered: "My son will be a great man for the nation. I sometimes had to hit him with the switch for lecture. This switch is an educational tool for his future greatness. Therefore this switch is valuable."[5]

Like the mother of Han, the mother of Hong was chaste, wise, and disciplinary. The mothers of Han and Hong were the symbol of chastity, perseverance, discipline and wisdom. Korean women were taught to be just like these mothers. In return, the children were expected to obey to their mother as much as to their father. The mother was entitled to her children's filial duty as her husband.

While wise motherhood was honored, intelligence or wisdom of a woman about the outside world was detested. Since virtuous women were confined at home, women were supposed to be innocent of the outside world. An intelligent woman would be disapproved of arrogance, or in some extreme cases deserted by the husband and in-laws. A wise woman should, therefore, pretend to be innocent, or rather ignorant.

Although the mother of Hong was very erudite and intelligent, she never attempted to reveal her knowledge. When her younger brother urged her to

---

5 Si-Rim O, *Sin Saimdang kwa Chanyo Kyoyuk* 신사임당과 자녀교육 (Seoul: Minyesa, 1986): 207–211.

utilize her knowledge for the public, she reprimanded him, saying: "A woman should be good at homemaking rather than at books. The reason why I am indulged in reading is only to educate my children in the future."[6]

An anecdote of Shin Saimdang, one of the most famous female intellectuals, poets and artists of *Chosun* dynasty, also displays the social demands on women. Shin was talented in poetry and arts. An eight fold screen composed of her paintings is registered an important cultural property in Kangwon Provence in Korea. Some of her poets are also introduced Korean textbooks. She usually remained taciturn when her in-laws were around. At a family gathering, her parents-in-law asked her why she was keeping silent during the meeting. Shin answered that the reason of her silence was because she was a woman staying at home and ignorant about anything outside. Despite her wisdom, she pretended to be ignorant and remained silent at home. Shin is still regarded the most respectable woman in Korea.

Women's Social Activities

As innocence was one virtue of women, women were denied of education. Only a small number of noble women were educated within their home, mostly by their fathers and sometimes by private tutors. Even when they were educated and intelligent enough to excel men, women were not allowed to reveal their talent. Many talented female writers ended their lives in misery.

The most prominent woman was Ho Nansolhon (1563~1589), who was

---

6 Si-Rim O, Sin Saimdang kwa Chanyo Kyoyuk 신사임당과 자녀교육 (Seoul: Minyesa, 1986): 208-209.

an excellent poet and the sister of a famous writer Ho Kyun. She was praised for her poetic genius at the age of eight. She was married to a Kim at the age of fifteen. Her husband was against her writing and deserted her. She died at the age of twenty-seven. Her poems were later sent to China by her brother, and published in China and Japan.

However, there were three groups of professional women in Chosun: the *Kisaengs* who were courtesans and entertainers; the *Moodangs* who were shamans; and medical doctors and nurses. They lived outside of the social norms, and exerted their influences to other people, sometimes to national matters.

Most of the famous female writers came from the *Kisaeng* group, the Korean equivalent of Japanese Geisha. The *Kisaengs* were socially despised but highly intelligent female entertainers. They were supposed to be beautiful and good at literature, singing and dancing. They were also expected to be able to engage in intelligent conversation with their clients. They were nicknamed as "Hae-O-Hwa (flowers that understand literature)." Since they existed outside the boundaries of Confucian teachings, their writings were accepted and often highly regarded. While oppressing their wives' intelligence at home, men were at liberty to enjoy the company of many intelligent courtesans outside of the home. Among the most famous *Kisaeng* poets were Hwang Jinee (1516~1559), Mae-Chang (1573~1610) and Hong-Rang (n.a.). Their poems outlived their time and became the treasures of Korean literature.

Shamanism has been regarded as the core of the Korean religious belief. Throughout the history, many established religions such as Buddhism were introduced, and soon assimilated and transformed into a new shamanistic variation. Buddhism in Korea became so shamanistic that most Buddhist temples have one or two shamanist buildings, like *Chilsunggak* [칠성각] where the spirits of sacred Seven Stars reside. Even Christianity in Korea today is under the strong influence of shamanism, leading many church goers to pray for an instant reward from the Holy Spirit. In Korea, *Moodang* [무당] originally referred to a female shaman. Male shaman was called *Paksu Moodang* [박수무당]. The *Moodang* had three major functions: to contact with the spirits; to heal the sick; and to prophecise. Although the *Chosun* Dynasty tried to replace shamanism with Confucianism, the government also maintained an office of shamanist practices, reflecting the people's strong inclination towards shamanism. The *Moodang* exerted a great influence on the national and individual decision makings. When women were supposed to be kept in the home without their voice, the *Moodang* was an extraordinary group of female professionals.

The *Chosun* dynasty had to develop a female group of medical practitioner since the *Chosun* dynasty emphasized the segregation of the sexes as moral discourse. When women of royal family became ill, they had to call a woman doctor. Therefore the government first established a system of training women medical practitioner in 1406.[7] Since the traditional medical practices in Korea included diagnosis, herb medicine and acupuncture that required a certain degree of knowledge in Chinese characters, girls chosen for medicine received an intense education on reading books and practicing the art of medicine. In a sense, they were the genuine professionals and exerted influence through their patients to some degree. One female doctor, Dae-Janggeum (birth and death dates unknown), became the head of the attending physicians to King Joong-Jong (1506~1544).

---

7 Yung-Chung Kim: 134.

1.2 Colonization of Korea (1910–1945)

Enlightenment Movement

During the 18th and 19th centuries, the *Chosun* Dynasty suffered from domestic instability and international interferences: Kings died young, some without heir, leaving the court in political conspiracies and struggles; Western forces were rapidly advancing to East Asia; Japan was fast growing and demanding the opening of the dynasty. In 1876 *Chosun* was forded to open its door to Japan and to other foreign nations, becoming a prey for the imperial forces.

During the last days of *Chosun*, the "woman question" was raised by many nationalist intellectuals. Facing the crisis of losing national independence, many Korean intellectuals regarded the subjugation of women as one aspect of Korean backwardness and advocated for women's rights and education. For strengthening of the nation, many intellectuals aspired of women's education and opened girls' schools.

Foreign Christian missionaries were first to open women's schools. The first ever women's school in Korea was opened by Mrs. Scranton, a missionary, in 1885.[8] From 1885 to 1909, the Christian missionaries established forty women's schools nationwide.[9]

The *Tokrip Hyuphoe* [독립협회: Independence Club, 1896~1899], the most

---

8 She opened the Ewha Hakdang, which became the most prestigious women's university in Korea today, the Ewha University.

9 Sung-Hee Sohn, Gwanrip Hansung Yuhakgyoui *Sullip gwajonggwa Gyogwa Gwajong Yungoo* 관립 한성고등 여학교의 설립과정과 교과과정 연구(Seoul: MA Thesis at the Ewha University, 2004): 19-20.

famous nationalist organization, advocated equality between men and women in all spheres of social life, with particular emphasis on education. Its newspaper, *Tokrip Shinmun* (The Independent), often published articles advocating sexual equality and equal educational opportunities for men and women.[10] Under the influence of the *Tokrip Hyuphoe*, many nationalist intellectuals joined the Enlightenment Movement. They perceived education as the ultimate national resource. Under the slogan *"Knowledge is Power"* they established numerous schools, public and private, registered or underground, for men and women. Immediately before and after Japanese colonization all the nationalist newspapers emphasized the importance of women's education. Soon many noble Korean women gathered together to run women's schools by Koreans themselves. The first Korean run women's school was opened in 1898.[11] By 1910 at least fifteen women's schools were run by Koreans in Seoul area alone.[12]

Women's confinement at home was also criticized. Women's employment was advocated. The first employer of women was the government, which employed women at the royal mint in 1900. Fifteen girls were selected through competitive examination.[13] They were the forerunners of modern career women in Korea. In the next year, a newly established textile company in Seoul began to employ men and women. Since then, textile and tobacco companies became the major work place for women.

---

10 Vipan Chandra, *Imperialism, Resistance, and Reform in Late Nineteenth Century Korea: Enlightenment and the Independence Club* (Berkeley: Institute of East Asian Studies, University of California, 1988): 107.

11 Sung-Hee Sohn: 23.

12 Sung-Hee Sohn: 30.

13 Yung-Chung Kim: 272.

Nationalists also supported women's organizations, many of which were established in connection with the nationalist movement. The Christian churches were also the first to organize women, mostly for purpose of missionary works. The *Chanyanghoe* [찬양회: Praising Club] was born in 1898 in support of women's education, which succeeded in establishing thee first women's school run by Koreans. Following the *Chanyanghoe*, many women's organizations were formed on local or national basis. These organizations sought to expand women's education and raise national consciousness among women. Basically, however, the characteristics of the organizations were nationalist, not feminist or women-centered. Many women activists advocated women's education because women were the mothers of new generation and a half of national health.

The nationalist movement provided legitimacy for women's education and activities outside of the home. There could have been a bitter struggle for women's education, if the nationalists had not supported it. Also, women's activities outside of the home might have been ridiculed and suppressed. However, it was for the sake of national cause. During the colonial period, women's organizations and activities were supported and legitimized by most Koreans because the leaders of the women's movement "rightfully (*sic*)"[14] perceived national independence as the supreme goal of their activities. The enlightenment movement was mainly for national cause. So was the advocacy for women's education and activities outside of the home.

---

14 Yosup Chung, *Hankuk Yusong Woondong-Sa* 한국여성운동사(Seoul: Iljogak, 1971): 7.

Colonial Rule

Despite desperate efforts by the nationalists and the royal court, *Chosun* fell into a colony in 1910. It became the rice bowl of Japan and essentially a one-crop country in exports. Natural resources that were necessary to complement but not to compete with Japanese production were developed, usually under Japanese ownership and management. Industrial and communication facilities were built in order to promote the Japanese exploitation of Korea and to support the Japanese war machine.

In the first decades of colonial rule, the Japanese carried out a heavy-handed "military policy (*budan seiji*)" that was based on coercion: the governor-general was a military man who headed the Japanese army stationed in Korea; all the police wore uniforms and carried swords; and even teachers were armed at classrooms. The Japanese strengthened central bureaucratic power, destroying the old balance of power between the ruler and the aristocracy, and minimizing the local autonomy. Korean newspapers were shut down; and the freedoms of speech and the right to assemble were abolished.

The "military policy" caused strong resistance from Koreans. On March First 1919, a nationwide mass protest against Japan swept the Korean peninsula: at least half a million Koreans took part in protest during March and April at more than six hundred different places. The protests were suppressed with bloodshed: according to Japan's official records, only 553 people were killed and over 12,000 arrested, but Korean nationalist sources put the totals at 7,500 killed and 45,000 arrested.[15]

15 Bruce Cumings, *Korea's Place in the Sun: A Modern History* (New York: WW Norton, 1997):154–155.

Stunned by strong Korean resistance and foreign condemnation, the Japanese authority changed its colonial policy into the so-called "cultural policy" (*bunka seiji*)." The "cultural policy" relaxed some restrictions, allowing Koreans to publish Korean newspapers and to form organizations. Many nationalist and communist organizations were born during the 1920s as part of many disguised resistance activities.

During the 1920s Japan aimed to make Korea into a rice-bowl for the Japanese. With a rapid growth in the Japanese population, coupled with increasing industrialization, there was a food shortage in Japan. Thus the Japanese decided to use Korean rice as their food source: by 1933 more than half of the annual rice crop was being sent to Japan. While the share of agricultural output in the Korean economy fell to 50 percent in 1941, from 84.6 percent in 1912, rice exports to Japan continuously increased. By the end of 1930s the average Japanese consumed almost twice much rice as the average Korean, who had to supplement their diet with millet, maize and barley, mostly imported from Manchuria.[16]

The colonial authority also tried to transform the northern part of Korea into a logistical base for invasion into the continent, and developed a few industrial bases. In 1939-1941, the manufacturing sector made up 29 percent of industry, of which heavy industries such as machines, chemicals, and metals constituted 46 percent.[17] For the sake of continental invasion, the colonial authority disproportionately located heavy industry in the north, and light industry and agriculture in the south. Almost 80 percent of all heavy industry bases were

16 Woo-keun Han, *The History of Korea*, tr. by Lee, Kyung-shik (Seoul: Eulyoo-Gak, 1970): 480.

17 Eui-Gak Hwang, *The Korean Economies: A Comparison of North and South* (Oxford: Clarendon Press, 1993): 16-18.

located in the north.

After the Manchurian invasion in 1937, Japanese leadership returned to its hard-line policy, and sought to organize every aspect of Korean life to serve the war. To some extent, Japanese leadership pursued a cultural way of ethnic cleansing: Korean language, Korean custom and Korean names, in fact everything Korean, were to be abolished: Japanese became the official language of the government and the courts; the *Shinto* religion was deemed as a mandatory belief; and every family was compelled to change its name to a new Japanese name. Through the use of spies, police and the military, the Japanese governors were able to hold a tight rein over all aspects of Korean life. In addition to the Japanese military presence in Korea, a horde of Japanese bureaucrats came to Korea: by the 1940s, around 246,000 Japanese served in Korea as government employees and professionals to rule 21 million Koreans. By comparison, the French ruled 17 million Vietnamese people with 2,920 administrative personnel and about 11,000 troops.[18]

Few Koreans were given opportunities to gain higher education or high-level experience in responsible jobs. Those Koreans who rose to important positions in government, industry, and the military were usually regarded as collaborators with the Japanese by the Korean people.[19] Intellectuals were forced either to fight against the colonial power and become political criminals, or to "collaborate" with Japan. Those with large landholdings were required to "vol-

---

18 Bruce Cumings: 153.

19 The trauma of colonization and the "collaborators" were so deep in the memory of Korean people that Korean politicians were often fallen victims of the "past digging" because of the "collaborative" family history. The Ro Moo-Hyun Administration established the "Presidential Committee of the Clearance of the Past" to investigate the past human rights abuse cases, including the collaboration cases of the Japanese colonial period.

untarily contribute" a large portion of their property to the colonial power in order to keep the remaining land. This situation later led landowners to be named
as collaborators.

Conditions of Korean Women

With regard to women, the colonial authority adopted many laws and regulations that denied equal rights of women. The governor-general proclaimed
the *Regulation of Civil Relations in Chosun* [조선민사령] in March 1912,
which adopted the laws and customs of the *Chosun* dynasty with a few changes
following the Japanese Civil Code. The Article 11 of the *Regulation of Civil
Relations in Chosun* stipulated that in accordance with Korean custom, wom-
en were denied the right to the headship of the family. As to the ownership of
property, the husband had the right to own the common property and to manage
and use the wife's possessions, while the wife was not allowed to share the
husband's possessions. The wife had no right to inherit the deceased husband's
property, except when there was no male heir in their family. When the head of
the family died without a male heir, the property could be inherited by female
members in the following order: his grandmother, his mother, his wife, and last-
ly his daughters. Even in this case, married daughters were deprived of the inheritance right since they were regarded as outsiders by marriage.[20] The Korean
custom that prohibited marriage between persons of the same surname remained
in force. Women were not allowed to file for divorce, while men were allowed

---

20 Yung-Chung Kim: 267.

to divorce and commit polygamy. There was a judicial precedent in 1918, however, that made the demand for divorce possible for both husband and wife. A woman's right to remarriage, which was legally pronounced in 1894 when a reformist group took power in the ailing *Chosun* dynasty, was re-enforced.

The colonial authorities revised the *Regulation of Civil Relations in Chosun* in 1921, 1922 and 1939, and gradually introduced the Japanese culture with the family system. The revised Regulation of 1921 provided for divorce by trial. The legal grounds for divorce were stipulated as double marriage, adultery, ill-treatment or insult, imprisonment for more than three years, and disappearance for more than three years. These stipulations provided some protection for women from arbitrary desertion. In the case of adultery, however, the law discriminated against women: an adulterous man was to be punished only when he had an affair with a married woman while a woman could be punished whether the man was married or not. The Regulation also restricted women's parental authority: a mother had to get an agreement from the family council when she stood proxy for her minor child in activities that affected property and financial situations of the child. Since a wife was denied inheritance from her deceased husband, the restriction of a mother's authority on financial matters meant that other male members of the family were in full control of the widowed mother and the children.

In 1922, the Regulation prescribed the principle of monogamy and abolished the custom of secondary wives and concubines. Concubinage and polygamy were declared illegal. A marriage was to be concluded only when it was legally registered. The Regulation also provided for divorce by agreement, which became effective when the couple agreed to divorce and reported it to the head of their county or city of their residence. However, the *Chosun* custom of requiring parents' consent to divorce was still enforced. With the 1939 revision of the Regulation, the Japanese custom of adopting their son-in-law as successor of the head of the family was introduced. Korean custom allowed adoption for succession only when the adoptee originally had the same surname – hence belonged to the same paternal lineage.

During the colonial rule, women's employment in industries increased as Korea was industrialized. In 1910, the colonial authority reported that 151 small to medium sized factories were operating with a mixed workforce of 8,203. By 1919, the number of factories had increased to 1,900 with a total workforce of 48,705.[21] In 1922, women consisted of 20.4 percent of the total workforce of 9,849; by 1936, 33.3 percent of the workforce was women, numbering 50,550.[22]

The working conditions of Koreans were typical example of colonial exploitation. While only 0.3 percent of Japanese workers were required to work more than 12 hours a day, 46.9 percent of Koreans had to work for that long (Table 1.1).

---

21 Tokanfu, *Tokanfu tokei nenpo* (Annual Statistical Report of the Residency-General of Korea 1910. Re-quoted from Theodore Jun Yoo, *The Politics of Gender in Colonial Korea: Education, Labor, and Health 1910-1945* (Berkeley: University of California Press, 2008): 110-111. It was only after 1922 that female workers were separately reported in statistics.

22 Theodore Jun Yoo: 111.

Table 1.1) Working Hours in Korea and Japan

Working Hours	Korea	Japan
Less than 8 Hours	0.8 %	1.4 %
9–10 Hours	28.7 %	45.3 %
11–12 Hours	11.0 %	43.7 %
More than 12 Hours	46.9 %	0.3 %

Source: Hosokawa Karoku, *Shokuninshi*, Tokyo, 1941, p.353; re-quoted from Choi, Hochin, *The Economic History of Korea: From the Earliest Times to 1945*, p.292

Female workers were overcrowded in light industries such as textile and food-processing factories: female workers constituted 63.4 percent of the textile industry and 89.9 percent of the silk-reeling sector in 1921.[23] Light industries pay less than heavy or mining industries. Moreover, the proportions of female workers were larger in vulnerable groups like minors and the elderly than in young adult group. Particularly, the number of female minors was far larger than male minors in most cases (Table 1.2). The motive behind employing female minors became obvious when the disparity of average daily wages between men and women and between minors and adults is taken into account. Female minors received less than a third of the wage of male adults (Table 1.3). This disparity based on sex and age was more compounded by colonial exploitation. Koreans received about half of the wages compared to their Japanese counterparts. The wage of Korean female minors was a sixth of that of Japanese male adults among factory workers.

---

23 Theodore Jun Yoo: 111.

Table 1.2) Employees by Age and Gender (1929)

Industry	Workers below 16			Workers 16 to 50			Workers over 50		
	Male	Female	%(Fe)	Male	Female	%(Fe)	Male	Female	%(Fe)
Textile									
Silk-reeling	74	3,805	98.1	667	5,234	88.7	1	20	95.2
Cotton Fabric	80	661	89.2	898	1,277	58.7	1	1	50.0
Silk Fabric	6	36	85.7	113	341	75.1	0	0	–
Knit Fabric	250	80	24.2	707	257	26.6	6	3	33.3
Cotton ginning	31	36	53.7	706	1,694	29.4	13	22	62.8
Subtotal	441	4,618	91.3	3,091	8,803	74.0	21	46	68.6
Food-processing	275	664	70.7	18,383	1,947	9.5	306	204	40.0
Chemical	176	146	45.3	4,614	3,995	46.4	141	6	4.0
Lumber	128	23	15.2	2,942	36	1.2	29	1	3.3
Ceramics	224	7	3.0	5,120	373	6.8	108	4	3.5
Printing	271	4	1.4	3,778	64	1.6	31	0	0.0
Machinery	163	0	0.0	3,813	1	0.0	53	2	3.6
Metal	223	0	0.0	2,452	18	0.7	46	0	0.0
Gas/Electric	0	0	–	815	0	0.0	13	0	0.0

Source: "Breakdown of Jobs by Age and Gender," in Theodore Jun Yoo, *The Politics of Gender in Colonial Korea: Education, Labor, and Health 1910-1945* (Berkeley: University of California Press, 2008): 112. Proportion of female workers was added by author.

Table 1.3) Average Daily Wage (June 1931, in yen)

Nationality	Factory Workers		Mine Workers	
	Korean	Japanese	Korean	Japanese
Male (Adults)	0.85	1.87	0.54	1.64
Male (Minor)	0.30	0.50	0.33	0.40
Female (Adults)	0.46	0.85	0.29	0.57
Female (Minor)	0.29	0.74	0.23	–

Source: Kojyooyobi Kosen ni okeru Rodosha Jyoku Chosa, p.84 and p.87; re-quoted and rearranged from Choi, Hochin, *The Economic History of Korea: From the Earliest Times to 1945*, p. 245.

Undeniably Korean women were exploited by sex, age and nationality. This situation generated many anger and despair among Korean female workers, which led to the industrial disputes by women.

Furthermore, numerous Korean women were fallen victims to the military sex-slavery system, as so-called "comfort women." The comfort women or military comfort women (*jugun-ianfu*) is a euphemism for women who were forced to provide sex in military brothels established by the Japanese military during the WWII. There is no way to determine exactly how many women were forced to serve as comfort women, but it is estimated to be between 80,000 and 200,000 women, about 80 percent of whom were Korean.[24] Others came from China, Taiwan, Thailand, Vietnam, Singapore, Dutch East Indies, and other Japanese occupied territories.

24 Jonghee Sarah Suh, Human Rights and Humanity: The Case of "Comfort Women," The ICAS Lectures No. 98-1204-CSSb, December 4, 1998, http://www.icasinc.org/lectures/cssl1998.html

In the early stage of the war, Japanese authorities recruited comfort women from Japanese volunteers who were already prostitutes. However, these "legitimate" sources soon dried out, and the military turned to deception, fraud, and kidnapping from outside Japan. The military authority deceivingly offered many Korean girls factory jobs or manual labor services, or simply kidnapped girls. These victims of deception and kidnapping ended in sexual slavery. A single comfort woman would be raped a dozen to forty times a day, often resulting in injury to sexual organs. Beating and physical torture were common. In the event of pregnancy, forced abortions or killings of the pregnant women were also common.

Many women were murdered or committed suicide during their enslavement. Some were released before the war ended, usually due to ill health. At the end of the war some "comfort women" were summarily killed, some died in combat at the frontlines, while others were simply left stranded. Survivors faced severe hardship whilst attempting to make their way home, some died in transit. There are accounts of women who assimilated into the countries they were taken to. Some survivors returned to their home countries but rarely to their hometowns. On return, the women often kept silent about what happened to them, for many "rape and brutalization were but a prelude to a life of suffering. The view that a raped woman is a defiled woman dies hard everywhere in Asia," and resonates in other parts of the world too. The location of shame upon the violated woman is a thread that links the experiences of "comfort women" to other victims of sexual abuse in war, peace, at home and elsewhere across the world.[25]

---

25 Amnesty International, Still Waiting After 60 Years: Justice for Survivors of Japan's Military Sexual Slavery System, ASA Index 22/012/2005, October 28, 2005, http://web.amnesty.org/library/Index/ENGASA220122005

After the war, the Japanese military abandoned comfort women where they were stationed, leaving many women far away from their homeland, sometimes thousands of miles away from their country. For Korean girls who valued chastity and virginity more than life, sexual slavery was the worst possible stigma. Many Korean girls gave up the hope to return home, ending their lives in misery and loneliness in a foreign country.

Development of Women's Organizations

During the colonial period, many Korean nationalists fought against the Japanese colonial forces, either in arms or underground, or in disguise. Some nationalists turned to education and enlightenment to strengthen the national power. Others turned to communism as a way of anti-Japanese struggle.

After the Koreans experienced an organized resistance through the March 1st Anti-Japanese Protest, the Koreans began to form many organizations during the 1920s, making the decade as the "Decade of Organizational Flood." These organizations focused on enlightening the people and raising the nationalist consciousness. Among these organizations, women's organizations were most conspicuous. Therefore some people determined that "the most radically advanced group is the women" during the 1920s.[26] According to the newspapers of the time, the number of women's organizations that were formed in 1920 was more than 30; and it reached up to 130 by 1923. In accordance with the appeal of the *Independence Club*, more than 70 women's organizations were engaged in ed-

---

26 Hankuk Yusung Yungooso, *Hankuk Yusung-Sa*한국여성사 (Seoul: Poolbit, 1992): 113.

ucation and enlightenment movement.[27] Among them, the *Chosun Association for Women's Education* [조선여자교육협회] succeeded in establishing a women's school after raising fund by organizing a series of lecture trip throughout the nation.[28] Many other local organizations also opened lectures and operated night schools for women's education and enlightenment.

During the 1920s, the number of women workers increased in the textile and light industries. However, the working conditions, as were mentioned, miserable and discriminating against women. This environment gave the communists good opportunities. They tried to organize trade unions and succeeded in igniting many industrial disputes as part of the anti-imperialist struggle. Many women workers actively participated in the industrial disputes, consisting of almost 80 percent of the participants. In many cases, including Women Workers' Strike in Kyungsung Rubber Factories (1923) and Women Workers' Strike in Rice Milling Factories (1923-1924), the leaders and participants to the strikes were women only.[29] The Women Workers' Strike in Kyungsung Rubber Factories was organized by the cooperation of women working in four rubber factories in Seoul (named as Kyungsung at the time). This strike led to the organization of the first all-women labor organization of Korea, the Women's Trade Union of Kyungsung Rubber Industry, in 1923.[30]

Women workers' performance in the industrial disputes contributed to enhancing the status of women in the communist movement and led to the es-

27 Hankuk Yusung Yungooso: 114.

28 Hankuk Yusung Yungooso: 115.

29 Hankuk Yusung Yungooso: 130–133; Hyo-Je Lee, *Hankukui Yusung Woondong: Oje-wa Onul* 한국의 여성 운동: 어제와 오늘 (Seoul: Chung-Woo, 1989): 107–116.

30 Hyo-Je Lee: 120.

tablishment of the first communist women's organization, the *Korean Women's League* [조선여성동우회], in 1924.[31] Under the leadership of Jong-Myung Chung, Jong-Sook Huh and Se-Jook Joo, the *Korean Women's League* declared that "women's liberation movement should work towards transforming the capitalist economic system into the socialist one in line with the proletariat class struggle."[32] Encouraged by their successes, the communists established the Korean Communist Party in April 1925, only to experience extreme persecution, continuous arrests of its members, and then forced dissolution of the party in 1928.

While the communists were active among the working women, other women's organizations were gradually losing momentum since the mid-1920s. In the liberal side, most women's organizations were linked to the Christian groups that were inherently conservative in the perception of women's role, which restricted the development of women's activities. While they were concentrating on the hygiene and the savings campaigns, those efforts were unrealistic for the absolute majority of the poverty-stricken Korean women.[33] The communists, however, also faced limitation because the number of female workers was so small compared to the more than 80 percent of Korean women engaged in agriculture. Further, the *Korean Women's League* was split into the socialist *Korean Women's League* and the liberal *Korean Union of Women's Liberation* [조선여성해방동맹]. They confronted with each other, making the women's activism weakening.

---

31 Hankuk Yusung Yungooso: 140–141.

32 Hyo–Je Lee: 123.

33 Hankuk Yusung Yungooso: 148.

The Japanese resumed oppressing the freedom of association and expression of the Koreans since the late 1920s, as Korean organizations tried to expand their nationalist activities. In the wake of the intensified oppression, many nationalist leaders were either imprisoned or forced to exile, threatening the existence of their organizations. This situation made women's organizations aware of the importance of solidarity. When two famous nationalist activists, Sin-Duk Hwang and Hyun-Kyung Lee, returned from Tokyo and joined the *Korean Women's League*, women's organizations came to move fast to form a unified body. Their efforts resulted in the establishment of the *Geunwoo-Hoe* [근우회: The Association of Working Friends, 1927-1933] as the unified organization of Korean women.

At the time of the establishment of the *Geunwoo-Hoe*, Korean organizations were suffering from internal conflicts and ideological division, because the Japanese had been tactfully maneuvering to transform Korean nationalists into "reformists" under the mask of the "cultural politics." As a result, some nationalist leaders turned into "autonomists" and tried to persuade Koreans to give up the struggle for independence. Many nationalists who rejected this idea and severely criticized the autonomists became to be referred to the so-called "leftist nationalists." Facing the resumed oppression from the Japanese during the late 1920s, the "leftist nationalists" and the communists collaborated with each other and formed a unified socialist organization, *the Singan-Hoe* [신간회: The New Pillar Club, 1927-1931].

While *the Singan-Hoe* was fiercely waging a war against the autonomists, the *Geunwoo-Hoe* was a little indifferent to the conflict between the socialists and the national autonomists.[34] The *Geunwoo-Hoe* focused on abolishing the discrimination against women. It demanded to introduce the principle of equal pay for equal work and the limited working hours. It also advocated prohibiting night shift and hazardous work for women and minors. At the same time, it was actively engaged in nationalist protests by sending investigation squads to girl's schools or provinces where anti-Japanese protest incidents occurred.[35] However, the *Geunwoo-Hoe* was forced to dissolve in 1933, without official liquidation, due to the aggravated oppression from the Japanese authorities.[36]

However, the experience of organizing the *Geunwoo-Hoe* led Koreans to accept the concept of national organization of women. It later contributed to the success of the Women's Union in North Korea.

1.3 Kim Il Sung and Women

A Short Biography of Kim Il Sung

After the March First Independent Struggle and the conclusion of the World War One, many nationalists turned into communists. It was reminiscent of the Chinese experience. The Versailles Conference approved the Japanese rights in East Asia. Chinese intellectuals were dismayed by the Versailles Conference and turned to Marxism and the lessons of the Bolshevik revolution of

34 Hankuk Yusung Yungooso: 149.

35 Hankuk Yusung Yungooso: 163-170; Hyo-Je Lee: 123-125.

36 Hankuk Yusung Yungooso: 170-176.

1917. The Chinese Communist Party (CCP) was organized in 1920.

Similarly, inspired by the success of the Bolshevik revolution, Koreans first organized a communist-oriented political party in exile, at Khabarovsk in 1918. This party developed into the *Koryo* Communist Party in 1921 in Shanghai. Some Korean students in Japan also formed a study group on communism in 1921. Inside the Korean peninsula, some intellectuals contacted the idea of class oppression, and organized a laborer's association in 1920. All these trends accelerated the development of a communist party.

Dae-Sook Suh argued that very few Korean communists understood the meaning of the concept of bourgeois capitalist exploitation of the proletarian masses, and almost no one had pondered the effect of communism as a political ideology for Korea in comparison and in competition with other political principles.[37] Although his criticism to Korean communists was severe, many have viewed that Korean communism was born more for independence than for class struggle.

It was these historic backgrounds that Kim Il Sung shaped his idea on independence, revolution and women's emancipation. Kim Il Sung was born in 1912 in a village near Pyongyang. His father was an enlightened intellect, and engaged in small scale anti-Japanese activities. Although North Korean official publication denies, his parents were Christians, and he was for a while raised by the maternal grandparents who were Presbyterian.

Kim Il Sung first enrolled to a Manchurian elementary school, but was soon sent to the maternal grandparents in Pyongyang. He enrolled in the *Changdok* School in Pyongyang in 1923 and learned Korean language and culture.

---

37 Dae-Sook Suh, *The Korean Communist Movement 1918~1948* (Princeton: Princeton University Press, 1967): 52.

He returned to Manchuria in 1925, and completed his elementary education in Manchuria. In 1926, he enrolled in a secondary school in Huadian, Manchuria, which was established by some Korean nationalists. North Korea claims that Kim was soon expelled from this school because he formed an anti-Japanese organization, "League for Abolition of Imperialism" [타도 제국주의 동맹], alias TD [ㅌㄷ], in 1926.[38] After leaving the school, Kim and his family moved into Jilin. In 1927 Kim again enrolled in a Chinese private school (Yuwen Middle School) that was described as the most progressive in the city.[39]

Many researchers on Kim Il Sung suggested that he had contacted Marxism-Leninism for the first time during the Yuwen Middle School period because there was a communist teacher who was a member of Chinese Communist Party.[40] In the posthumous memoir of the teacher, Kim Sung-Ju –an alias of Kim Il Sung– was mentioned as a bright, daring leader of Korean nationalist students.[41]

During the Yuwen School period Kim appeared for the first time in an official document of the Japanese authorities. In May 1929, the Japanese Consul General of Jilin reported that Kim Sung-Ju, a Yuwen Middle School student,

---

38 However, A Japanese scholar, Haruki Wada, has disputed to the claim. He suspected Kim had to move to Jilin because of poverty after his father died. Wada pointed out that until 1972 there was no mention of the "League for Abolition of Imperialism" among North Korean publications. Whatever was the truth, North Korea has firmly established the claim that he was expelled because of the "League for Abolition of Imperialism" since 1972. The date of the alleged anniversary of the League became one of must-remember historic events in North Korea. On the anniversary every year, North Korea runs an article or holds a meeting to commemorate the event. See, Haruki Wada, *Kin Nichisei to Manshu Konichi senso* (Tokyo: Heibonsha, 1992), pp.30-32

39 Bradley K. Martin, *Under the Loving Care of the Fatherly Leader: North Korea and the Kim Dynasty* (New York: St. Martin's Press, 2004): 22.

40 Haruki Wada: 34-35; Bradley K. Martin: 27-28.

41 Haruki Wada: 35-36.

organized the "Korean Communist Youth Association."[42] His anti-Japanese struggle came to be his career that autumn, at the age of seventeen with his imprisonment in 1929. He was released from prison in May 1930, and never returned to complete his middle school. His schooling lasted for less than eight years. Therefore, he had hardly any opportunity to sophisticate his thoughts into a profound philosophy or elaborate fundamental principles.

Upon his release in 1930, Kim Il Sung spent two years in a small Manchurian village with his mother. He joined the Chinese Communist Party (CCP) in 1931, and fought against the Japanese forces as a middle level commander of the united Chinese guerilla army in Manchuria. Although in middle level, he was one of the highest leaders among Koreans. His major guerilla activities were with the CCP-led Northeast Anti-Japanese United Army (*Dongbei Kangri Lianjun*, NEAJUA) around between 1934 and 1940.[43]

He obtained a huge fame as "General Kim Il Sung" among Korean people as well as among Japanese authorities in June 1937 when he and his guerilla unit waged a surprise attack on a Japanese colonial police station in Bochonbo. Bochonbo was a small village inside of the Korean peninsula near the Yalu River. His group succeeded in pillaging and destroying the police station. Although the success of Kim's unit was rather moderate, it gave a deep impression to Korean people. The *Dong-A* Ilbo bannered this attack for several days. Even the Japanese forces took the attack very seriously and came to keep watch on Kim Il Sung. This incident and the resulting fame became one of the most valuable

---

42 Haruki Wada: 43–44.

43 Charles K. Armstrong, The North Korean Revolution, 1945–1950 (Ithaca: Cornell University Press, 2003): 28; Adrian Buzo, *The Guerilla Dynasty: Politics and Leadership in North Korea* (Boulder: Westview Press: 1999): 8.

resources of Kim Il Sung when he returned to Korea after the Independence.[44] Korean people were waiting for him with profound respect, which in the end led Kim Il Sung to the head of the new state.

In 1939, the Japanese forces crushed the NEAJUA and its activities in Manchuria. In late 1940, Kim Il Sung and his guerilla unit crossed the Soviet border to "raise the Northeast anti-Japanese struggle to a new level,"[45] and joined the Soviet camp. Although retreating and joining the Soviet camp seemed a clear defeat to many, some argued that saving his guerilla unit from total destruction was also an evidence of his leadership. He stayed in Russia until the Liberation, and returned to Korea with his comrades in October 1945.

There have been controversies surrounding the extent and the characteristics of Kim Il Sung's guerilla warfare. North Korean official publications tend to exaggerate the successes and the meaning of the guerilla activities. Many others discount the importance of his activities. Nevertheless, several points are clearly close to the facts: Kim Il Sung voluntarily chose anti-Japanese guerilla struggle as the way of his life; although his ideas on communism or class struggle might be unsophisticated, he believed in communism and acted as a communist; and he rose quickly as a guerilla fighter to become a partisan commander through bloody battle and prominent performances as leader. These facts later affected the politics and the status of women in North Korea.

---

44 Haruki Wada: 331–332.

45 Yang Zhaoquan, "Comrades Kim Il Sung," quoted in Charles K. Armstrong: 32.

Kim Il Sung' Idea On Women' Emancipation

It is almost impossible to analyze the North Korean system without reading and understanding Kim Il Sung's works. Publication and interpretation of the so-called "Kim Il Sung's works"[46] have been the declaration of policy intentions of North Korean leadership of the time. His works have been revised and re-edited several times according to the changes in political setting. For this reason, some North Korean watchers rely on reading the North Korean official publications, not because they fully trust the materials, but because they can discern the differences between the past and present and recognize the policy intentions behind the sentence.

Kim Il Sung was reported to advocate women's rights and accepted several tens of women in his guerilla unit as warrior. His wife Kim Jong-Suk was one of the women warriors. Alleged his words reveal that, like many other Korean intellectuals of the time, his advocacy for women's right was related more to the national Independence than to class struggle. He was recorded to mention on the rights of women during the guerilla period.

If Korean women want to gain true freedom and rights in every aspect of political, economic and social life, they should first abolish the feudal and colonial regime. In order to abolish the feudal and colonial regime, women must drive out the Japanese colonial invaders and accomplish national Liberation and Independence. For this, women should participate in the anti-Japanese Liberation struggle and fight

---

46 The so-called Kim Il Sung's works were mostly his speeches to the public. The names of the speech writers were never revealed. Some speeches published during 1950s were revised decades later according to the idolization of the Kim family. See Un Rim, *Bukhan Kim Il Sung Wangjo Bisa* 북한 김일성왕조 비사 (Seoul: Hankuk Yangsheo, 1992): 102–114.

arms-in-arms with men.[47]

His idea of sexual equality was first fully stated in one of his earliest ad-dresses after Liberation. On October 25, 1945, he gave a lecture to women offi-cials in Pyongyang. Under the title of *"The Present Internal and International Situation and the Tasks of Women,"*[48] he compared women to a wheel of a wagon, and demanded women to take an active part in nation-building. He pro-claimed that women could be emancipated through participation in nation-build-ing as workers and as revolutionaries.

In order to achieve this responsible yet honorable task of nation-building success-fully, those with money should contribute money, those with strength - strength, and those with knowledge - knowledge; and all people, young and old, men and women, should rise up as one man. This is where the masses of women should play a great role.

A very important task confronts the women in building a new Korea. It can be said that the women who account for half our population play a role equitable to one wheel of a wagon in the work of nation-building. If the wagon is to run smoothly, its two wheels must rotate normally. Like this, if our nation-building is to meet with success, the women must play a great role together with the men..... An im-portant guarantee of attaining women's emancipation is their active participation in nation-building.

.....

Bound through the centuries by feudal ethics, Korean women had to isolate them-selves from social activities to remain cooped up in their homes, and lived a bitter life held in contempt and humiliation of every kind. If our women are to extricate

---

47 *Choson Chungang Yongam* [DPRK Central Yearbook] 1970 (Pyongyang: Choson Chungan Tongshinsa, 1970): 194. Translation by author.

48 Kim Il Sung, *Works 1*: 324–331.

themselves from this old position and achieve social emancipation, they must join in the work of nation-building.

At present some women hesitate to take part in nation-building, saying "What good can we women do? If we women put ourselves forward, nothing will come of it." Moreover, some women sneer behind the backs of other women engaged in social work. This is not an attitude worthy of liberated Korea. Unless they do away with this wrong attitude, they can never bring about their own social emancipation.

We are now fighting to building a new, democratic society. Our work of nation-building is at the same time a great revolutionary work to free the women from their double and treble fetters and social inequality of all kinds. Only by participating in the work of nation-building can they extricate themselves from their own situation.

In congratulating address to the founding of the women's magazine, *The Korean Women* [조선녀성] in September 9, 1946, Kim Il Sung reiterated his view on women's emancipation by urging women to participate in the production fronts as well as in the political and cultural fronts.

The women who constitute a part of society can achieve complete emancipation only if they strive with no less devotion and awareness than men to solve the problem arising on the productive fronts of the factories and countryside and on the political and cultural fronts. This is the only way to be followed by the women of Korea.

We are well aware that women were treated like slaves in feudal relationship. They were excluded from economic, productive and all other social activities under the feudal system. If a women's organization claims emancipation apart from economic and productive activities and all other social activities related to them directly or indirectly, such an organization will eventually turn into a rich women's club.[49]

---

49 Kim Il Sung, *Works 2*: 353–355.

Later, he explained that urging women to engage in social work was not because of a shortage of the labor force. On the contrary, the state was taking pains to provide social conditions for women. Women were benefiting by the state effort to bring them into social activities, not the opposite.

> We draw women into society not because we are short of manpower. Frankly speaking, at present women engaged in public activity bring not so much benefit to the state as that the latter gives the former. In order to let women work out in society, nursery schools and kindergartens have to be built at a large state expense....
>
> In addition, we have built many schools everywhere and provide the school children with clothing and school things at cheap prices so that the women may work in society without worries for the education of their sons and daughters..... The working women are also provided by the state with the paid maternity leave and with adequate welfare service facilities. The sate even ensures them time for feeding their babies.
>
> Thus, to let the women launch forth into society and take up jobs, the state and the public bear heavy burdens and have many things to provide for them.[50]

His argument that he and the communists exerted themselves to mobilize women for the sake of women was to some extent grounded on truth. Women have been working outside of the home throughout the history, in the farms and in the family businesses. However, women's work has mostly been unpaid and regarded supplementary. While women were confined at home, they did the household chores without payment. Women's confinement at home sustained the exploitation of women. Women's work outside of the home was in fact about the payment for the work done by women. If North Korea needed more

---

50 Kim Il Sung, *On the Revolutionization and Working-Classization of Women* (Pyongyang: Foreign languages Publishing House, 1974): 7–8.

manpower, keeping women at home and appropriating as unpaid supplementary workers would cost less than providing social conditions.

His addresses also emphasized that women should participate in the productive labor outside of the home in order to destroy the old social customs. He perceived women's participation in social work as a part of socialist revolution, breaking-up the rule of women's confinement at home. As Kim pointed out, the biggest obstacle to mobilizing women into social labor lay in the Korean attitude towards labor itself. Furthermore, women's labor outside the home was barred and despised by women themselves.

> In order to achieve complete social emancipation for the women and provide them with equal rights with men, we must eradicate the remnants of Japanese imperialism and feudal conventions and build a truly democratic society. Bringing about women's social emancipation and sex equality is part of the anti-imperialist, anti-feudal democratic revolution. Moreover, it has a great bearing on the fulfillment of the tasks at higher stages of the revolution.[51]

> Formerly labor was frowned upon as the meanest thing whereas living idly on the labor of others was considered something to be admired. This is a bad idea implanted by the exploiting classes. Under the people's government, labor is sacred and honorable in the true sense of the word.[52]

> Formerly the Korean women were barred from state affairs or political activity. Consequently, many housewives still tend to hold the erroneous view that state affairs are for the men and that all that is required of women is to do the cooking

---

51 Kim Il Sung, "On the Future Tasks of the Women's Union," *Works* 2: 184–185.

52 Kim Il Sung, *Works* 2: 192.

and washing and raise the children at home. True, they should attend to household work. But if they are occupied only with housekeeping and excluded from state affairs, they cannot be truly equal with men.[53]

However, all in all, his addresses reveal that the basic theory behind his pledge was straight forward traditional Marxist: if women participate in the work outside of the home and be independent, they will be emancipated. There is no way conflicting interests between men and women.

Since Marx's works did not directly deal with women's oppression, Marxist theories on women have been based primarily on Engels' work, *The Origin of the Family, Private Property and the Sate (1884).*[54] In this work, Engels argued that women's oppression has not always existed, but that it began with the first private property and class society, for it was only then men's desire to pass property to their known heirs motivated them to control women. This motive caused the antagonism between men and women in monogamous marriage and the "first class oppression" of the female by the male. This motive would disappear with the overthrow of capitalism, when women would no longer be economically dependent on men; and the socialization of housework and child care would liberate them from domestic chores. The way forward for women, therefore, is to participate in labor outside the home as working class, and at the same time to fight alongside working class men for the revolutionary transformation of society. This position ruled out any idea that the interests of working men and women might conflict, that women can have group interests cutting across class

---

53 Kim Il Sung, *Works* 2: 194.

54 Friedrich Engels, *The Origins of the Family, Private Property and the State : In the Light of the Researches of Lewis H. Morgan* (1884), in Karl Marx and Frederick Engels, *Collected Works*, Vol.26, August 1882~December 1889 (New York: International Publishers, 1990):129–276.

line, or that gender relations might have an independent dynamic of their own.

Like traditional Marxism, Kim Il Sung always instructed women to engage in social work in order to be independent and liberated. He never explained why and how social activity would ensure women equality. He also never questioned for the possibility of conflicting interests between the sexes. This lack of comprehension on the possibility of conflicting interests between men and women led him to announce that "women were liberated fully in North Korea" while women were still suffering from abuse and many old social customs.

Kim Il Sung's idea on women's oppression is of a stark contrast with Mao Tse-tung in the sense that Kim never recognized the specific oppression of women by men. China and Korea had very similar experiences of suffering during the 19th and early 20th centuries. Both shared Confucian culture, lagged behind in modernization during the 19th century, and suffered from the advances of imperialist forces. Particularly, the two cultures on women were almost identical.

Similar to Korea, China was dominated by the teachings of Confucius and his disciples which had been the ruling ideology in China since the 2nd century BC. Women were to take no part in public affairs: the *Book of Rites*, a Confucian classic, reads "a man does not talk about affairs inside (the household), and a woman does not talk about affairs outside."[55] Daughters were at the mercy of their fathers to be married off. Poor fathers sold daughters to rich families as maids or concubines. Since Confucianism never explicitly forbade men to have concubines, having multiple concubines was rather a norm for affordable Chinese men. The destiny of maids or concubines was just like that of livestock: they were sold again and again at the owner's will. Marriage was in principle

---

55 Elizabeth Croll, *Feminism and Socialism in China* (New York: Schocken Books, 1978): 13.

arranged between the parents: the bride and groom could see the other's face only after their wedding ceremony. Women could be expelled by the husbands and in-laws on many grounds, but not the other way around. The only way for women to be freed from an unhappy marriage was death. Many women committed suicide either because of the brutal husband and in-laws, or the prospect of forced marriage. Mao Tse-tung's first article dealing with the woman question was published immediately after a girl's suicide in 1919 because of the arranged marriage.[56]

All these conditions were shared by both Korean and Chinese women. Perhaps the fact that Korean women did not suffer from foot binding while Chinese women did was one of few noticeable differences between the two. It was not surprising that, therefore, many Chinese intellectuals also perceived the conditions of women in the context of Chinese evils. When many Chinese intellectuals launched the New Culture Movement in 1911, they also addressed themselves to the "woman question (*fu-nu wen-ti*)": they wrote about the reform of the family system, marriage and divorce, social child-care, women's suicide, suffrage and so on. The intellectuals and the communists strongly advocated women's rights.

For Chinese communists, mobilization of women became a necessity as well as a principle during the Civil War and the Long March. Women were expected to engage in productive labor in place of their soldier-husbands. Women were also expected to join in the Women Guards who defended villages themselves, or in the Women's Aid Corps who rescued and nursed the wounded, and

---

56 Roxane Witke, "Mao Tse-tung, Women and Suicide," *Women in China: Studies in Social Change and Feminism*, ed. by Marilyn B. Young (Ann Arbor: Center for Chinese Studies, The University of Michigan, 1973): 7–32.

provided necessities to the soldiers. Some women were also recruited as warriors.[57] Either for necessity or for principle, women's mobilization into society became the norm. In particular, Mao paid much attention to the status of women. He recognized specific women's oppression by men, and tried to address the problem. He once wrote:

A man in China is usually subjected to the domination of three systems of authority: (1) the state system (political authority), ranging from the national, provincial and country government down to that of the township; (2) the clan system (clan authority), ranging from the central ancestral temple and its branch temples down to the head of the household; and (3) the supernatural system (religious authority) ranging from the King of Hell down to the town and village gods belonging to the nether world, and from the Emperor of Heaven down to all the various gods and spirits belonging to the celestial world. As for women, in addition to being dominated by these three systems of authority, they are also dominated by men (the authority of the husband).[58]

By contrast, Kim Il Sung never mentioned the dimension of women's oppression by men. This trait later led him to the claim that he succeeded in emancipating women in North Korea, while women were still expected to be subordinated to men. This fact also resulted in a great deal of differences in the status of women in China and North Korea. Nevertheless, Kim Il Sung was regarded more in favor of sexual equality than other Korean revolutionary leaders, even

---

57 Kang Keqing was the most prominent woman warrior, who led the troops in battle during the Long March. She was also the wife of Zhu De. See Elizabeth Croll: 185–222.

58 Mao Tse-Tung, "Report on an Investigation of the Peasant Movement in Hunan" (March 1927), *Selected Works 1* (Peking: Foreign Languages Press, 1967): 44.

compared to other guerilla units.⁵⁹

Later, his idea of women's liberation was summarized in the slogan of *"revolutionization and working-classization of women (making women the revolutionary and the working class*: 여성의 혁명화, 노동계급화)." Women were emphasized to become the working class first. When imperialism and feudalism were rampant, women had also to fight against these forces. When imperialism and feudalism were overcome, women should continue to fight for socialist revolution that demanded collectivist mind and labor loving attitude. In short, under the principle of the equality between the sexes, women should be mobilized into the society in order to perform whatever the regime demands women to do at that time.

59 Charles K. Armstrong: 92–93. Armstrong argues that Kim Il Sung and his guerilla group were more in favor of gender equality than the Yanan group.

Chapter II

North Korean
Revolution and Women
(1945~1953)

2.1 Formation of North Korean System

Political Division

After WWII, the Soviet army marched into the northern part of the Korean peninsula, whereas US troops occupied the southern part. As in Eastern
Europe, the Soviet occupation authorities, the Soviet Civil Administration,[1]
worked closely with North Korean communists to establish a regime modeled
after the Soviet Union. The North Korean communists, most of whom had
fought against the Japanese on foreign territory as guerillas and returned to Korea with the Soviet army after Liberation, succeeded in establishing people's
committees as local self-governing bodies. People's committees then formed the
North Korean Provisional People's Committee (PPC) in February 1946 as the
first country-wide autonomous governing body, effectively dividing the Korean
Peninsula into two nations. The communists managed to elect Kim Il Sung as
the PPC Chairman, paving the way to communist rule. Kim Il Sung was not a
handpicked Soviet puppet, but the famous and respected "Hero of anti-Japanese
Struggle, General Kim Il Sung" of Korean people. He gained his way to the top
position by uniting his guerilla comrades under his leadership in the party, by
allying with Soviet-aligned Koreans for a while, and then by creating a powerful
army under his own leadership in 1948.[2]

---

1 The Soviet Union realized that matters in Korea required a huge amount of civil relations activities. The
Soviet Union therefore named the occupation authorities as the Soviet Civil Administration, and provided it
with the authority equivalent to a North Korean state in October 1945.

2 Bruce Cumings, *Korea's Place in the Sun: A Modern History* (New York: WW Norton & Company, 1997):
227.

In Seoul, the Korean Communist Party (KCP), which had been established in 1925 and then dissolved in 1928, was reorganized in October 1945 by domestic communists who had continued their underground struggle against Japan within Korea during the colonial period. Recognizing the legitimacy of the Korean Communist Party, Kim Il Sung formed the North Korean Communist Party (NKCP) as a branch of the KCP. Kim Il Sung was elected as the First Secretary of the NKCP, and pushed forward to establish a variety of social organizations. The first was the Democratic Women's Union, followed by the Democratic Youth Union, the Peasants' Union, and the Workers' Union. These organizations, along with political parties, were brought together into a Democratic National United Front in July 1946 with the slogan "all-out mobilization for nation-building."

Although widely recognized as the legitimate Head Quarter of national communist party, the KCP in Seoul suffered heavily from the partition of Korea. The US occupation authorities were suspicious of the party, so they suppressed its activities and arrested its leaders. The leaders of the KCP soon fled to North Korea, losing its power base. Taking advantage of the situation, Kim Il Sung took steps to sever the NKCP from the KCP, and merged with a small party into the Worker's Party of North Korea (WPNK) in August 1946. After the partition of Korea became a fait accompli, the Worker's Party of North Korea officially merged with the KCP to form the Worker's Party of Korea (WPK) in June 1949. After the merger, the domestic communists were slowly persecuted and driven out by Kim Il Sung and his partisan comrades.

In the meantime, the PPC carried out an extensive land reform and nationalization of major industries and promulgated the *Labor Law for Workers and Office Employees and the Sex Equality Law*. In the course of these social reforms, the communists eliminated all non-leftist political opposition. Small parties incorporated into the united front became the mere transmission belts for the communist party. Large landowners and capitalists were dispossessed and persecuted as pro-Japanese traitors. By the end of 1946, freedom of the press ceased to exist with all newspapers covering essentially the same news. Nevertheless, the communists managed to avoid massive slaughters of their enemies, such as those carried out in the USSR in the early 1930s. Landowners and capitalists were allowed to flee to the South, or to live in other counties.[3]

The PPC was succeeded by the North Korean People' Committee (NKPC) on February 22, 1947, dropping the term "provisional" and thus cementing the division of the country even further. The NKPC adopted a one-year plan for *National Economic Rehabilitation and Development* in 1947, calling for 92 percent growth in industrial production. A year later the plan was declared "splendidly over-fulfilled."[4] Indeed, the one-year plan was a great success, which gave the communists credibility for ruling the country. The NKPC also prepared new elections, made arrangements for the proclamation of a North Korean nation, and passed its power to the first formal government of the Democratic People's Republic of Korea (DPRK). The DPRK came into official statehood on September 9, 1948 with Kim Il Sung as the Premier.

From the beginning, the DPRK was in a far more favorable economic condition than the Republic of Korea. First, almost 80 percent of all heavy industry bases were located in the north. During the colonial period, the Japanese tried to build a logistical base for invasion into the continent, and developed a few in-

3 Bruce Cumings: 232.

4 Kim Il Sung, *Works* 4 (Pyongyang: Foreign Languages Publishing House, 1980): 60.

dustrial bases in the northern part of Korea. For the sake of continental invasion, the colonial authority disproportionately located heavy industry in the north, and light industry and agriculture in the south. Second, the north held approximately 80 percent of all of the mineral deposits on the peninsula. It had an abundance of iron ore, copper, lead, zinc, uranium, and manganese. Therefore, North Korea accounted for 65 percent of Korean heavy industry, including the development of hydroelectricity, the mining of raw materials, and the production of chemical fertilizers.[5] After the founding of the state, it continued to exert itself in social reforms and economic development with enormous success.

It also rapidly built up its military. Both a border constabulary and the People's Army were established in 1946. The army, equipped with Japanese rifles, numbered 20,000 by the end of that year. When the Soviet army began to withdraw from North Korea in February 1948, it turned over limited quantities of weapons, including a few tanks and aircrafts. From 1948 to 1950 North Korea ground forces had an estimated strength of 135,000 men.[6]

Drawing on its economic and military superiority over the South, the DPRK initiated an all-out war against the South in June 1950, which lasted for three years. The Korean War ended in an armistice in 1953, resulting in neither victory nor defeat for either side. It caused much devastation of the peninsula. There were millions of casualties, separation and displacement of millions of families, and long-lasting, intense hostility.

---

5 Amy K. Nash, *North Korea* (Philadelphia: Chelsea House Publisher, 1999): 99.

6 Robert K. Sawyer, *Military Advisors in Korea: KMAG in Peace and War* (Washington DC: Department of the Army, 1962): 104–105.

Social Revolution

Since his partisan period, Kim Il Sung had always promised to build a class-less (socialist) independent nation in Korean peninsula. Liberation provided him with a huge space to implement his ideas on socialism and national independence. Furthermore, the Soviet sponsorship somewhat forced him to pursue more socialist programs.

Immediately after Liberation, Kim Il Sung addressed the communist military and political cadres on the task of communists. In his address, *On Building the Party, State and Armed Forced in the Liberated Homeland* (August 20, 1945), he suggested the first task of the communists should be first to establish the communist party that would be the "general staff of the Korean revolution and vanguard."

> At the present stage the most important and historic task before the Korean communists is that of founding the Korean Communist Party, which will be the General Staff of the Korean revolution and the Vanguard detachment of the working class.
>
> ...
>
> The Korean Communist Party must in no way be an organization for only a few communists. It must be a mass political party which is deeply rooted in the workers, peasantry, and other working masses. It must become the experienced General Staff of revolution which organizes and leads the construction of a new Korea. Therefore, we must rapidly expand the Party ranks with excellent people from among the workers, peasants, and progressive intellectuals.[7]

---

7 Kim Il Sung, *Works* 1: 225–241.

He also diagnosed North Korean society as colonial and semi-feudal, and analyzed that the Korean people were still confronted with the task of carrying out an anti-imperialist, anti-feudal democratic revolution. Based on this analysis, Kim advocated for establishing a "democratic people's republic," or "democratic people's regime," which represented the interest of the entire Korean people. To build a democratic people's republic, the communist party must organize a "democratic national united front" that embraced "various strata of the democratic forces such as the broad masses of peasants, intellectuals and conscientious national capitalists." The PPC was, by North Korean definition, the first "democratic people's regime" that successfully carried out anti-imperialist, anti-feudal revolution before true socialist revolution.[8]

This position was different from the orthodox "people's front" that centered on the exclusive concept of "proletariat." Kim reckoned that the anti-imperialist, anti-feudal revolution called for a *coalition* of broader masses rather than the exclusive proletariat. Similar to Mao, Kim had realized the limitation of the "proletariat" in an overwhelmingly agricultural society, and thus pursued united front tactics and emphasized national unity over class conflict since his guerilla days.[9] Based on his united front tactics, he pushed on mobilizing a variety of masses such as workers, peasants, women and youth to form social organizations.

Within several months after his address, the communist party and mass organizations began to mobilize the entire people into categories of workers, peas-

---

8 Seung-Hyo Ko, *Bukhan SahoeJooui-ui Baljon Yungoo: Gu Irongwa Silje* 북한 사회주의의 발전 연구: 그 이론과 실제, trans. by Han-Min Kim (Seoul: Chung-sa, 1988): 15.

9 Charles K. Armstrong, *The North Korean Revolution, 1945-1950* (Ithaca: Cornell University Press, 2003): 59.

ants, youth and women. At the same time, the categories of the organizations became the social identities for the whole population of North Korea, which appeared in a multitude of forms - legal documents, job applications, and other records. Organization became part of the social identity for North Koreans.[10] It was the process of creating a new social order that would overturn the existing social hierarchy. The old social hierarchy categorized people into the nobles, the commoners, and the servants or slaves. The concept of woman, worker, or peasant as a category with specific and distinct interest was unfamiliar to Koreans. Redefining people into different categories or identities was to abrogate the old social order altogether and to remake the people. It was a genuine revolution.

The North Korean Women's Union was the first mass organization to be created. On November 15[th,] 1945, the Women's Union was inaugurated with Park Jong-Ae as the Chairwoman. The Workers' Union was organized two weeks later, on November 30. The Peasants Union was formed January 31st, 1946. The Democratic Youth Union concluded the flood of mass organizations on February 17th, 1946.

In addition to redefining the people, the PPC carried out social reforms that would destroy the material bases of the old social order. The first was land reform. Kim Il Sung and his partisan comrades had already adopted a decision on the land reform in October 1945, two months after Liberation. According to the *Decision on the Land Problem*, which was adopted at the first Enlarged Executive Committee Meeting of the Central Organizing Committee of the NKCP, all the lands, forests, rivers, ponds and lakes, and all irrigation facilities that were formerly owned by the Japanese imperialists and reactionary pro-Japanese

10 Charles K. Armstrong: 71-74.

landowners were to be confiscated without compensation.[11]

However, the PPC adopted a more radical approach to land reform and moved forward to abolish the private ownership of land. The *Law on Agrarian Reform*[12] of March 5, 1946, aimed to "abolish the landownership of the Japanese and of the Korean landlords and the tenant system" (Article 1). The law enumerated kinds of the land to be confiscated not only as the land owned by Japanese state, individuals and organizations, or by "traitors," but also as the land owned by the landlords who possess more than 5 *chongbo*,[13] or who rent out all of it, and as the land which was continually rented out, regardless of its size (Article 2~4). Moreover, landowners who were confiscated their land had to leave their home county. Confiscated land was distributed to peasants according to their labor capacity, but was banned from being sold or bought, rented out or mortgaged.

Despite the radical approach and the problems of displacing of the landowners, land reform was a surprising success: in less than a month 50 percent of North Korean land was expropriated and then allocated to farmers who had no land. Almost a half million households, comprising nearly three million farmers, that had never owned land before received land.[14]

Before the land reform, there was a great disparity in land ownership: the richest 4 percent of the households owned almost 58.2 percent of the land, while the poorest 57 percent of the households owned a meager 5 percent of the

---

11 Kim Il Sung, *Works* 1: 315–317.

12 Kim Il Sung, *Works* 2: 91–94.

13 *Chongbo* is one of Korean units for land. 1 *Chongbo* is larger than 8 acres and close to 3ha.

14 Myung-Rim Park, *Hankuk Jonjaengui Balbalgwa Giwon II: Giwongwa Wonin* 한국전쟁의 발발과 기원 II: 기원과 원인 (Seoul: Nanam, 1996): 196-198.

land.[15] Farmers without land had to rely on tenancy. In 1940 independent farming households comprised 18 percent, while tenant households including tenants
with small lands were 74.6 percent of all households in Korea.[16] The rent for tenancy was higher than 30 percent of the yield, sometimes over half. The rent for
tenancy was more often than not the cause of the grudge against the landowners,
and sometimes led farmers to starvation. By the end of Japanese colonial rule,
two thirds of tenant households suffered from "spring poverty," in which the
households had consumed all their harvests by the end of the winter and had to
endure the long spring season in hunger.[17]

The impact of land reform was far-reaching. First, a large number of nobles and large landowners fled to the South with their property documents, be-
lieving that they would regain their land. This flood of voluntary displacement
strengthened the communists' grip on power by removing potential dissidents
without much bloodshed. Second, by allocating land to women, the North Korean government introduced the concept of equality to the people, and made room
for the mobilization of women into the labor force outside of the home. Third,
by allocating lands to poor peasants who had never owned their land before, the
nascent North Korean regime secured the support of the peasants who constituted the largest part of the population. When the Korean War broke out in 1950,
most peasants of North Korea fought genuinely for the regime in order to keep
their land. In fact, the North Korean government propagated land reform as a
means of defeating and liberating people from the evils of the large landowners

---

15 *Choson Chungang Yongam* 조선중앙연감 1949 (Pyongyang: Choson Chungang Tongshinsa, 1949): 71.

16 Hochin Choi, *The Economic History of Korea: From the Earliest Times to 1945* (Seoul: The Freedom Library, 1971): 265.

17 Hochin Choi: 267-268.

and nobles so vigorously that today many youngsters of North Korea are still afraid of the possibility of a return of past landowners, making them less susceptible to the outside influence of "bourgeois culture."

While consolidating supports from the poor peasants through land reform, the PPC pushed to organize workers. The PPC promulgated the *Labor Law for Workers and Office Employees*[18] in June 1946. This law aimed to eliminate the vestiges of colonial exploitation and to radically improve the material conditions of workers, and established the principles of eight hour working day (Article 1), equal pay for equal work (Article 7), maternity protection measures (Article 14~17), and a compulsory social insurance system (Article18), all of which were the demands of the workers during the colonial period.

During the colonial period, the Japanese had developed a few heavy industrial bases in northern Korea. However, the industrial workers constituted only 4 or 5 percent of the total population by the end of the colonial period. Among its 26 million inhabitants, only 550,000 worked in manufacturing or industry, 180,000 in mines, and all others in agriculture in 1943.[19]

The communists nevertheless pursued to appropriate labor organizations that had been in existence since the colonial period. As unions and labor leaders emerged from underground, the communists organized the North Korean Federation of Trade Unions (NKFTU) in November 1945. This organization incorporated all wage-earners including artisans, white collar workers as well as blue collar workers. The PPC cooperated with the NKFTU in the legislation of the labor law, securing support from the workers. The PPC also provided a sense

---

18 Kim Il Sung, *Works* 2: 242–247.

19 Hochin Choi: 291.

of privilege for the "workers" who had been oppressed and despised in Korean history. A survey by US military during the Korean War estimated that, despite some disillusionment, the majority of workers supported the North Korean regime in 1950.[20]

The PPC also carried out nationalization of major industries with ease in August 1946. At the time of Independence, most of big industries were owned by the Japanese. In 1938, companies owned by Koreans numbered up to 740, almost comparable to 804 of the Japanese owned. However, the total sum of capital of Korean companies was only a seventh of that of Japanese ones.[21] According to the report to the first Supreme People's Assembly in 1949, well over 90 percent of the industry in North Korea was in Japanese hands.[22] With the nationalization law, more than 1,000 industries, over 90 percent of all industries in the North, came under state control.[23]

The PPC and the communists, in a remarkably short period of time, were moving fast forward to create a new society through forging a new identity system as well as land reform and nationalization of industries. In order to complete the social reform, however, the women's issues that encompass half of the population should be resolved as well. The policy towards women was to be taken as a part of the creation of a new socialist society.

20 Charles K. Armstron: 91.

21 Hochin Choi: 288–289.

22 Kukto Tongilwon, *Choigo InminHoeui Jaryojip* 1최고인민회의 자료집 1(Seoul: Kukto Tongilwon, 1988).

23 Charles K. Armstrong: 156.

2.2 Legislation for "Sex Equality"[24]

Enactment of the *Sex Equality Law*

As soon as the establishment of the PPC, Kim Il Sung pronounced to guarantee equal rights of men and women in the *Twenty Points Platform*,[25] in which policy directions on twenty major issues of the newly formed government was addressed on March 23, 1946. The fifth of the "Twenty Point Platform" stipulated equal rights of people in every sphere of social life including politics, economy, and other living conditions, irrespective of sex, religion, or wealth.

> 5. To grant equal rights in political and economic life to all citizens, irrespective of sex, religion or property status;

Equal right for women was also introduced in the Program of the Workers' Party of North Korea[26] in August 29, 1946. When the Worker's Party of North Korea was inaugurated, officially severing from the Korean Communist Party, the party program promised to carry out thirteen clauses of reformist tasks, among which 3 clauses explicitly mentioned of women.

> 6. To introduce an eight-hour working day for the factory and office workers, social insurance, and equal pay for women as for men;

---

24 Since North Korea officially translated the law on gender equality as the *"Sex Equality Law,"* I used the word "sex equality" as an equivalent to gender equality.

25 Kim Il Sung, *Works* 1: 113–115.

26 Kim Il Sung, *Works* 2 (Pyongyang: Foreign languages Publishing House, 1980): 351–352.

7. To grant the equal right to elect and to be elected to Koreans of 20 years of age and upwards, irrespective of property, status, education, religious belief, and sex;

9. To grant women equal political, economic and legal rights with men, abolish the remnants of feudalism in family relations and customs, and give state protection to mothers and children.

According to North Korean official publication, these pledges for equal rights of women were a logical result of Kim Il Sung's ideology on women's emancipation. He has been always the advocate for women's emancipation. His pledge for women's emancipation first appeared in 1935, when Kim fled to Manchuria and allegedly organized several partisans units fighting against Japan. One of the partisan groups was called the *Association for the Restoration of Fatherland* [조국광복회], organized in 1935. Kim Il Sung instructed the partisans with *"Ten Point Program"* which included guaranteeing equality between the sexes and enhancing the social status of women.

7. To abolish the caste system which divides the nobles [양반] and the common people [상민], and other inequalities; to ensure equality based on humanity irrespective of sex, nationality or religion; to improve the social position of women and respect their personalities;[27]

Although this program was an empty promise because of the lack of material ground for implementation, the idea of gender equality was modern. This provision was a further development from the Ten Point Political Program[28]

---

27 Kim Il Sung, *Works* 1 (Pyongyang: Foreign languages Publishing House, 1980): 113.

28 When Chinese communists under the leadership of Mao Tse-Tung established the Kiangsi Soviet Republic in 1931, they announced the Ten-Point Political Program. The Fifth clause of the Program vowed the improvement of conditions of workers, eight hour work days, reduced working hours for

of the Kiangsi Soviet Republic of China, which promised the improvement of conditions for female workers. Despite the fact that China and Korea shared the experiences of Confucian culture and colonial invasion, the political program of the two communist groups varied. While the pledge of equality by Kim Il Sung was for the whole people including women, political program of Mao was rather restricted to the working people. This difference again came from Kim Il Sung's position on the united national front tactic.

He repeated the promise of gender equality again and again after the Liberation. The most tangible result of his repeated promise was the legislation. The first legislation regarding women was the *Sex Equality Law* [남녀평등권에 대한 법령] on July 30, 1946.[29] Aiming "to overthrow the old feudal relationship between the sexes and to incorporate women fully into the economic, cultural, social, and political life," this law was composed of a preamble and nine clauses: women have equal rights in every domain of the state, political, economic, social, and cultural life (§1); women have equal rights in employment, social insurance, and education (§3); women have the right to choose to marry or divorce, and the right of child custody (§4-5); concubinage, polygamy, and prostitution were prohibited (§7); women have equal rights to inherit property and to demand a share of property in the case of divorce (§8); and all the laws and decrees by the Japanese colonial authorities became invalid on the day of proclamation of the law (§9).

Albeit very short and concise, this law was clearly aiming to overthrow

---

minors as well as the improvement of conditions for female workers. "The Ten Point Political Program," Harvard-Yenching Library, Chen Cheng Collection, FC 551~FC 571 *Shisou zi liao shi gong fei zi liao* 1~21, Reel #10; FC 560, Record #33.

29 Kim Il Sung, *Works* 2: 290-292..

the old family system, and gave women full rights with men as the first step. In order to mobilize women into society, the rule of women's confinement at home was to be rejected, and women's right to choose to marry was to be granted. The specific provisions of free marriage and divorce and the mother's rights in case of divorce were to repudiate the old order. Women were allowed to file for divorce, child-custody and child-allowance from their husbands, which had been inconceivable to Koreans. While their Southern sisters were still discriminated under the old *Regulation of Civil Relations in Chosun* [조선민사령], North Korean women were, at least under the law, treated as equal with men.

North Korea explains that "it rendered the principles of the family laws as equality between husbands and wives; special protection for mothers and children; monogamous marriage by free consent of the couple; and state protection and assistance for the education of children."[30] These principles denied concubinage and male headship of the family.

In order to enforce the law, North Korean leadership announced the *Enforcement Regulation for the Sex Equality Law*[31] [남녀평등권에 대한 법령 시행세칙] on September 14, 1946. This regulation was basically to establish the principle of marriage by law. It stipulated that marriage was to be concluded when the couple by their free will wrote out the marriage application form and appeared in person to the People's Committee of the city or county to submit the form, and when the People's Committee legally admitted the form (§8-1). The wedding ceremony and registering in the family register were not regarded as the legal proof of marriage.

---

30 Il-Ho Cho, *Chosun Gajokpup* (Pyongyang: Gyoyuksa, 1958): 26-33.

31 Kuksa Pyunchan Wiwonhoe, *Bukhan Gwangye Saryojip V: Pupjepyun* 북한관계사료집V: 법제편 (Seoul: Kuksa Pyunchan Wiwonhoe, 1987): 856-857.

The *Enforcement Regulation* also provided the right of wives to own and manage their property independently from their husbands. The Article 4 stipulated, "Women have equal rights with men to own and manage their property"; and Article 7 stated, "The property belonged to one party before the marriage remain to be the sole property of the party. But the property accumulated during the marriage will be the common property of the couple." Hence, the wife's property right was confirmed.

However, codifying the principles does not always guarantee the realization of equality. Most North Korean men still kept their concubines and women remained at home. In many cases, concubines were rather scared to be independent because they did not have any means to support themselves and their children born to them. The possibilities for former concubines to remarry or to be employed were very slim, if any. It was the same for any divorced woman. Therefore, the *Sex Equality Law* and the *Enforcement Regulation* remained in paper for some years.

In order to abolish concubinage and other forms of feudal marital customs, the PPC formulated another law, the *Law of Abolition of the Persistent Feudal Customs* [봉건유습 잔재를 퇴치하는 법령] on January 24, 1947.[32] Consisted of only four clauses, this short law specifically aimed at breaking feudal marital customs. Those who received or paid fortune for the purpose of marriage were to be punished. That was because almost all the concubines were sold, and most of forced marriages were arranged with money.

However, already existing concubine relationships had to be tolerated. As was mentioned before, concubines had no future outside the relationship.

---

32 *Bukhan Gwangye Saryojip V*: 791.

Therefore, if a concubine decided to stay within the relationship she was to be excused, for the sake of her and her children. Both the *Sex Equality Law* and the *Law of Abolition of the Persistent Feudal Customs* were to abolish concubinage for the future, not for the past. The "feudal relationship" persisted until the end of the Korean War when the devastation erased almost everything.

The DPRK Constitution of 1948[33] also confirmed the guarantee for equality between the sexes in Articles 11-12, and 22-23: all people have equal rights in every sphere of life such as political, economic, social, and cultural (§11); all people aged 20 and above have the right to elect and to be elected (§12); women have equal rights with men in every sphere of life (§22); marriage and the family are protected by the state (§23). The Constitution also guaranteed equality to children born outside of wedlock:[34] Parents had the same duty towards children born outside of wedlock as towards children born within the wedlock (§23). This article reflected the pain and misery of many children born from concu-

---

33 Daeryuk Yunguso, *Bukhan Pupryungjip* I 북한법령집 1 (Seoul: Naewoe Tongshinsa, 1990): 2-13.
⟨ Excerpt from Constitution of the DPRK ⟩
Article 11) All the citizen of the Democratic People's Republic of Korea have equal rights in all spheres of state, political, economic, social and cultural life, irrespective of sex, nationality, religion, technology, property and knowledge status.
Article 12) All the citizen of the Democratic People's Republic ages 20 and over have the right to elect and to be elected to any sovereign organ, irrespective of sex, nationality, family background, religion, the length of abode, the status of property and knowledge.
Citizens serving in the People's Army of Korea have equal right with other citizens to elect and to be elected to sovereign organs.
Those who have been deprived of the right to vote by the court judgment, those with mental illness and those who are pro-Japanese shall not have the right to elect and to be elected.
Article 22) Women have equal rights with men in all spheres of state, political, economic, social and cultural life.
Article 23) Marriage and the family are protected by the state.
Parents have the same duty towards the children born outside of the wedlock as those who are born in wedlock.

34 Most countries also guarantee equality for the children outside of the wedlock, but by the marriage law or child welfare law.

bines. Equal rights for women were recognized by Constitution and other laws for the first time in history for North Korean women.

Abolishing the Old Family System

As the *Sex Equality Law* explicitly declared, Kim Il Sung and his guerilla comrades aimed to abolish the old family system. They regarded the old family system as the yoke that was particularly oppressive to women and thus needed to be dismantled. In particular, the communists focused on abolishing the family registry system.

As was explained in Chapter One, Introduction, every person had been required to register in a family registry that recorded all paternal lineages. Basically, paternal lineage was recognized as relatives. Maternal lineage and wife's relatives were only partially recognized. All the events of life of the family members including birth, death, and marriage were recorded in the family registry. A marriage was concluded and in effect as soon as a bride was included in the groom's family registry. There was no other registration requirement for legal effect of marriage. If a wife was expelled from her husband's family, her name would be crossed out in the family registry. The power of the family registry and the control of a family over an individual were far stronger than the power of the state over an individual.

The family register system was originally applicable only to nobles. However, during the turbulent years of the late *Chosun* dynasty when Japanese pirates invaded Korea in the 16th century, many commoners and even the lower orders began to make their own family register. The family register soon became the main means of social identification, making the family more powerful over the individual.

If the state was to create a new identification system for the people, the influence of the family and the family registry were to be neutralized. Therefore, Kim Il Sung and the communists introduced the principle of marriage by the law, limiting the effect of the family registry only to private (family) matters.

On August 9, 1946 the PPC announced the Resolution No.57, *Resolution on the Issue of Citizen's Card* [북조선임시인민위원회 결정 57호, 공민증에 관한 결정서], which introduced new Identification Cards for all people aged eighteen and above, irrespective of sex. By this resolution, the family registry began to lose its legal hold on individuals. Also, women were regarded as individual persons, not a subject person to husband or a father. This ID card system developed into a new public registration system in 1955, replacing the traditional family register system.

In an attempt to overthrow the old family system North Korea also attempted to make marriage easily breakable. While the *Sex Equality Law* stipulated the right of women to free divorce in general principle, the *Enforcement Regulation* simplified the divorce procedure to the extent that a simple piece of paper to report the divorce would legally break the marriage. Article 10 of the *Enforcement Regulation* read as: "When the married couple agrees to discontinue the conjugal relationship, the couple shall have divorce by sending the divorce by consent form to the People's Committee and its being accepted." Article 11 of the Regulation provided the procedure of divorce by the court, when the couple could not reach an agreement.

Divorce by consent was so easy that an illiterate wife could be divorced without her knowledge. In fact many party leaders deserted their old ignorant wives in this way, and married young intelligent socialists. This "paper divorce" and easily breakable marriage turned out to be disadvantageous to women, not to men. It was not good for socialist morality either. Some argued that the dismantlement of the family would ruin morality, and could lead to the dissolution of society.

Facing these problems, the Supreme Court first took an initiative by issuing the *Guiding Directive for the Divorce Procedure* [이혼소송을 해결함에 관한 지도적 지시] on March 7, 1950. While basically recognizing the right to divorce, the Supreme Court asked the courts to take into account of the strengthening the family, consolidating the conjugal relationship, and the education of the minor children born to the couple in divorce cases. The Directive was in fact demanding to restrict divorce.

Later, the government decided to abolish divorce by consent in the Cabinet Resolution No.25, *Regulation on Abolishing the Divorce by Consent* (March. 8, 1956) [내각결정 25호, 협의이혼절차를 폐지하고 재판이혼에만 의하게 하는 규정]. Every divorce should thereafter be decided by the court. North Korea explained that this change was necessary "because among the past marital relations, the undesirable ones were already destroyed by the revolution and the progress of democracy, and because people should struggle against imprudence of divorce in the socialist marriage system."[35] Since then, divorce in North Korea has been regarded as evidence of imprudence and rashness.

These changes in marriage regulation, first liberalizing divorce then restricting it, are resonating of the Soviet Union experience. In the Soviet Union, some of the earliest decrees were to provide economic independence of women.

---

35 Il-Ho Cho: 133.

The Decree on Land provided the equal right for women to use and own land. By other decrees a wife was no longer obliged to reside with her husband or to accompany him if a change of job meant a change of residence. Abortion was legalized in 1920, and divorce was simplified to the extent of the so-called "postcard divorce" that a dissatisfied spouse would simply notify the authorities that the marriage was over, and if the other party was not physically present, a postcard would break the news. The major intent of the simple divorce was to free millions of women who had been married off against their will under traditional patriarchal procedures.

It proved to be catastrophically counterproductive. Women lost the protection they previously had against abandonment with children. Millions of Russian men took advantage of the simple divorce: 14 percent of Soviet marriages ended in divorce in the early 1920s which was twice as high as that of Germany at that time.[36] When a couple with children divorced, the court was to decide the amount of child support. However, even when the court decided in favor of the mother, it often proved impossible to collect the child support from the father.

When Stalin obtained power, he found that the traditional conservatism and discipline of individual family units were useful in reinforcing its social and economic policies. In 1936, the Stalinist Constitution and subsequent new legislation reinforced the traditional role of the family, restricting women's rights to independence and mobility. Divorce became very difficult to obtain as well as expensive to afford. There were massive increases in the payment required to register a divorce. Also, unregistered marriages were no longer recognized, reviving the distinction between legitimate and illegitimate children. Only after

36 Barbara Alpern Engel: 154.

Stalin's death, judges began to respond favorably to the request of divorce.

The changes in marriage laws in the Soviet Union and North Korea indicate that "liberating women from the inequalities in the...family life"[37] was much to do with mobilization of women into the social labor. Both countries had not considered the impact of their measures on women. When an unexpected outcome occurred, North Korea hurriedly returned to restrict divorce, not addressing the inequality in the family and in the divorce process. Restricting divorce was easier than addressing the inequalities directly.

Comparison with South Korean Situation

Although the efforts of the North Korean leadership to establish the principle of "Sex Equality" and abolish the old family system had been motivated to a great extent by political reasons, legal reforms for enhancing women's status in North Korea during the early period were very progressive and thorough compared to those in South Korea.

While the communists in North Korea moved fast to enact new laws, including the *Sex Equality Law*, and immediately nullified previous laws as early as in 1946, the occupation authority in South Korea accepted all the previous (Japanese) laws as valid until the first Constitution of the Republic of Korea (ROK) was adopted in 1948. The first Constitution promised sexual equality unconditionally (Article 5) and declared that any previous law remained in force unless it contradicted the provision of the Constitution (Article 127). However,

37 At the Preamble of the *Sex Equality Law*. See Appendix 1.

the laws that contradicted the Constitution also remained in force because enactment of new laws was procrastinated for several years.

The first Civil Code of South Korea was adopted in 1957, and came
into force in 1960. Until 1960, therefore, the *Regulation of Civil Relations
in Chosun* [조선민사령] by the Japanese colonial authority remained in force.
Since the *Regulation of Civil Relations in Chosun* denied wives' legal capacity
in contract or property and restricted mothers' parental authority, women were
legally subject to their husband. In the case of divorce, women were denied
child-custody. Even when her husband passed away, a mother was denied parental authority over her children in property and financial matters. The head of a
family, who must be male, exercised the sole authority over the family.

The first Civil Code of 1960 was more like a minor amendment to the
Regulation of Civil Relations in Chosun than a new law. Women were denied
of the rights to the headship of a family, to parental authority, and to the family
property. The Civil Code gave the sole parental power to the father (§909). Only
when a child had no father, or the father was unable to exercise parental power
for any reason, the child's mother with whom the child was residing exercised
parental power (§909-2). If a divorced mother or a widow remarried, she was
not granted parental authority over the children born to her during her previous
marriage, even after the father of the children died (§909-5). In fear of losing
children, many women endured abuse, violence and infidelity of their husbands
and gave up remarriage. A wife could own her property. However, any property
of which the title was uncertain was assumed to the property of the husband
(§830-2). The husband exercised the sole power over the couple's property. In
the case of divorce, a wife was denied of any right to the property of the couple.
Sons and male descendants took precedence over daughters and female descen-

dants in inheritance rights (§1000). The family register system which had been the backbone of the patriarchal familial relationship and was abolished in North Korea in 1955 remained in force (§778~799; §980~996).

During the course of the enactment of the Civil Code, leaders of the women's movement in South Korea gathered together to protect women's rights. Under the leadership of Tae-Young Lee, who was the first woman judge in the Korean history, eight women's organizations including YWCA and the Association of Housewives of Korea submitted the *"Petition for the Enactment of Civil Code"* to the National Assembly in 1953. When their petition was not reflected in the new Civil Code, those leaders of women's organizations began to wage a campaign for the amendment of the Civil Code since 1958.

In 1962 when the military junta was in control, the women's organizations submitted a proposal for the amendment of the Civil Code and the establishment of the Familial Court. In response to the proposal, the military junta established the Familial Court in 1963. In 1972, YWCA, the Council of the Women's Organizations of Korea and the Korea Legal Aid Center for Family Relations co-sponsored a Lecture Meeting for the Amendment of the Family Law. After the Lecture Meeting, sixty-one women's organizations came together to form the *Coalition for the Amendment of the Family Law* in June 1972. This *Coalition* presented the *"Ten Amendments Program"* that demanded amendment of the Civil Code in ten discriminating provisions. The ten discriminating provisions included: the family register system; the definition of relatives that held legal efficacy in inheritance; the marriage prohibition between the parties whose surname and origin are the same; the sole ownership of the husband over the couple's property; (the lack of) a wife's right to the property of the couple in the case of divorce; (the lack of) procedure of divorce by agreement; the sole parental power of the father; forcing women to become the (legal) mother to their husbands' children born to other women; the male precedence in inheritance over female; and (the lack of) a reserved portion of inheritance for the wife in the case of the death of the husband.[38]

It took more than four decades to amend the ten discriminating provisions. Despite outcries from the women's organizations, the male-dominated National Assembly, the South Korean parliament, did not pay attention to the *"Ten Amendment Program,"* because the number of women in the parliament was negligible, remaining in single digit numbers until 1996 election, with only one exception of 1973 parliament. The exceptional 9th National Assembly (1973~1978), of which women representatives numbered twelve out of 219 members (5.48%) was the best opportunity for the women's movement. The *Coalition for the Amendment of the Family Law* presented a draft bill in 1973 in accordance with the *Ten Amendments Program*. The draft bill was proposed to the National Assembly in 1975 by the miniscule number of the woman parliamentarians.

In 1977, the National Assembly passed a bill to amend some of the ten provisions. The 1977 amendment changed the Civil Code in five issues: the family property of which the title is uncertain is assumed to be the joint property of the spouse (§808); divorce by agreement requires confirmation procedure by the Familial Court (§836-1); both parents share the parental power (§909); an inheritance shall be divided by equal proportion among the heirs who have the same precedence regardless of sex (§1009); and a legal portion of inheritance for the wife of the deceased is reserved (§1112~1118).

---

38 Hyo-Je Lee, *Hankukui Yosongwoondong: Ojewa Onul* 한국의 여성운동: 어제와 오늘 (Seoul: Chung-Woo, 1989): 252-258.

The remainings of the *"Ten Amendment Program"* were debated for another decade. In 1989 the Civil Code was modified again. Women became entitled to be the head of a family (§991). The wife's and the husband's relatives had the same legal rights upon the couple. Maternal and paternal lineages also had the same legal effect. In divorce cases both spouses had the roght to claim a share of property regardless of whether he or she had contributed the accumulation of property by employment (§839). Custody of the children was to be decided by the divorce agreement (§837). After four decades of struggle, the discriminatory clauses in the Civil Code were mostly revised.

The *Labor Standards Law* of 1953, the first and the basic labor law of South Korea, was discriminating against women, too. It deliberately missed the principle of equal pay for equal work, providing opportunities to enterprises to exploit female workers. The Law also allowed the enterprises to have the discretion to determine working conditions by agreement with the employees. Accordingly, many enterprises inserted such clauses as women's early retirement and dismissal upon marriage to the work contract.

Upon the outcry by the women's organizations, the government enacted a new law for gender equality at work. The *Gender Equality Employment Act* of 1988 came to challenge the practices of the discriminatory work agreement. This new law also had many pitfalls, and was subjected to many amendments for genuine equality at work.

In order to keep pace with North Korean legal equality granted by the *Sex Equality Law*, many South Korean women had to struggle for almost five decades. It shed lights to the progressive nature of North Korean legislation during the early period. Although North Korean legislation did not guarantee equality in reality, all these laws were the announcement of the government's and the communists' will to build a socialist society. During the early period of the re-gime, Kim Il Sung and the communists made all-out efforts to promulgate laws that would stimulate and sustain the social revolution in North Korea. Even with some faults, the *Sex Equality Law* and the *Labor Law* were decades ahead of the South Korean counterparts.

2.3 Reform measures for "Sex Equality"

Creation of the Women's Union

Kim Il Sung urged women to form a mass organization to achieve unity. In his aforementioned address, *The Present Internal and International Situation and the Tasks of Women*, he emphasized the importance of women's organiza-tion.

Today one of the important tasks facing the women is to promote in everyway the setting up of a mass democratic organization of women. If women are to fulfill their responsible duties well, they must have their own mass democratic organiza-tion. Only when they form a democratic organization and are united in it, will they be able to contribute to the building of a new country by united efforts and grow up into fine workers through democratic education and organizational training. However great their enthusiasm for nation-building and whatever bold efforts they make, the women will not succeed in accomplishing their tasks for nation-building and their own social emancipation unless they are all united in an organization. Therefore, a women's democratic organization should be formed as soon as possible to achieve this unity.[39]

With the strong support of the communist party and the Soviet occupation authorities, the Democratic Women's Union of North Korea (DWUNK) was inaugurated in November 1945 as the first mass organization in North Korea. Workers' organization followed suit. The first Chairwoman of the Women's Union, Park Jong-Ae, was one of the most famous trade union leaders during the colonial period, and later served as Minister of Agriculture from 1957-1962.

In May 1946 the Women's Union held its first conference and adopted a seven point platform. In this platform, the Women's Union praised Kim Il Sung and the PPC for guaranteeing the right of women to vote and to hold office and declared that it would exert itself to establish a democratic regime in North Korea.

Platform of the Democratic Women's Union in North Korea (May 9, 1946)[40]

1. To unite all the democratic women and to concentrate the whole capacity of us on building the Democratic People's Republic in Korea based on the Twenty Point Platform of General Kim Il Sung;

2. To support the decision of the North Korea Provisional People's Committee on guaranteeing women equal rights to elect and to be elected, and to fight to present this honor for all Korean women;

3. To fight for the elimination of all the fascists, pro-Japanese and national traitors that are scheming to destroy our democracy;

4. To fight for enhancement of Korean culture and for a healthy development of politics and economy;

---

39 Kim Il Sung, *Works* 1: 330.

40 *Choson Chungang Yongam* 1949: 91.

5. To actively participate in every cultural movement and industrial rehabilitation task in order to eradicate illiteracy and improve the living conditions of women;

6. To demand the state for the protection of women;

7. To endeavor to abolish the feudalist customs and superstitions.

As the platform suggests, the Women's Union faithfully echoed the political program of the communist party. In a nascent regime, the Women's Union was expected to play crucial roles in mobilizing women into the society, dismantling the old system, and creating a new system

Many women responded to the call. 600,000 women joined the Women's Union by July 1946.[41] The membership of the Women's Union was almost doubled by September 1947, reaching up to 1.15 million.[42] The total population of the Korean peninsula was recorded as 26 millions in 1942.[43] The population of North Korea in the 1940s was estimated 10 to 11 million. It means that a tenth of the whole population, probably a fifth of the female population and even larger proportion of adult women, became the member of the Women's Union in two years. Even though there could have been a coercive environment for participation, the speed of pulling women out of the long confinement was astonishing.

The successful organization and expansion of the Women's Union was attributable to two factors: first, the concept of women's organization was legitimized by the nationalist movement during the colonial period; second, the rapid change, or the social revolution, after the Independence made people susceptible to any unfamiliar events. After all it was the hour of the revolution.

---

41 Kyung-Hye Lee: 24.

42 Kwang-Woon Kim, *Bukhan Jongchisa Yungu 1: Gundang, gunkuk, gunkunui yuksa* 북한 정치사 연구 I: 건당, 건국, 건군의 역사 (Seoul: Sunin Publishing, 2003): 205.

43 *Choson Chungang Yongam* 1949: 19.

The Women's Union proved to be the foremost advocate of social reforms and played an indispensable role in land reform and passing many new laws. Members of the Women's Union visited factories and farms and explained the current political situation, the evils of feudalism and capitalism, the class consciousness, the ridiculousness of superstition to women. The union succeeded in mobilizing a huge number of women into elections and social campaigns: the union sent 27,500 members to the explanation fair for land reform; and sent 881,761 members for the Labor Law campaigns.[44] This success gave the Women's Union a strong political base within the party and the National United Front. As a constituent organ of the National United Front, the Women's Union had the right to nominate representatives to the people's committees of all level. As a result, many women were elected as the representatives of all levels of people's congresses. Political representation of women became less unusual in North Korea.

When North Korea occupied Seoul during the Korean War, the DWUNK merged with its South Korean counterpart to become the Democratic Women's Union of Korea (DWU) in 1951. The DWU was the driving force in the mobilization of women into the labor force during the War, and boasted of its great contribution to nation building and war efforts. Park Jong-Ae was awarded the Stalinist Medal in 1951 for her contribution to the war efforts.

---

44 Myung-Rim Park: 205.

Providing Child-Care Facilities

Women's work outside of the home was subject to many conditions, of which the first was the issue of child-care. At the time of Independence, however, there had been only 56 kindergartens for pre-school education, but no nursery for very young children in North Korea.[45] In his Welcoming Address for the first conference of the Women's Union in 1946, Kim Il Sung mentioned the necessity of public child-care in enabling women to participate in social life. Since the nascent state did not have means to provide child-care facilities, he asked the Women's Union to set up and operate small-sized nurseries.

> If we are to encourage many women to take part in social life, we must take steps to bring up the children under public care. When women are going to join society, school-age children offer no big problem because they go to school, but the pre-school children present a problem. We shall be able to accommodate the children in nurseries and kindergartens someday when the national situation permits it. As a matter of fact, I should like to have nice buildings erected right now to raise children under public care, but the present circumstances do not allow us to build all the nurseries and kindergartens we need at once. Apart from the difficult economic situation of the country, we haven't enough cadres to manage them, either....
>
> The Women's Union would do well to organize and run many small-scale nurseries and kindergartens. I doing so, you will gain experience and in the meantime the state will take measures to build nurseries and kindergartens in factories and farm villages.[46]

In response, the Women's Union had opened a nursery in Pyongyang with

---

45 *Minju Choson* (The party organ of the WPK), 1953.6.1.

46 Kim Il Sung, "On the Future Tasks of the Women's Union," *Works* 2: 184–195.

modern bedrooms, baths, and playground in March 1947.[47] The nursery was named as the 3.8 Nursery in honor of the International Women's Day (March 8th). After Kim Il Sung visited it in September 1947, he urged the state and companies to establish nurseries and kindergartens throughout the country. The 3.8 nursery became run by the state and later changed its name into Kim Jong-Suk Nursery in April 1988. This nursery is still regarded as the best in North Korea. It is open to foreign visitors as an exemplary facility.

Soon after the North Korea Provisional People's Committee (PPC) was inaugurated, it paid attention to child-care issues. It first attempted to increase kindergartens to accommodate children at the age of six years. In December 1946, the PPC Resolution No.133 decided to establish one-year kindergarten (preschool) classes as an annex to elementary schools.[48] Before the Resolution was implemented, however, the provisional regime developed into the North Korea People's Committee (NKPC) in February 1947. The new regime decided to institutionalize a separate kindergarten system by the NKPC Resolution No.49.[49] The kindergartens were open to children between the ages of three to six years, and were supposed to function as preschool education institution.

At the same time, the NKPC made efforts to create nurseries in order to enable mothers with very young children to work outside of the home. The Order No. 3 of the Bureau of People's Health[50] announced that the state and society should establish and run nurseries for working mothers in June 1947. This Order also stipulated the principles of nursery establishment including the number of

---

47 Kyung-Hye Lee: 118.

48 Kyung-Hye Lee: 120.

49 Kyung-Hye Lee: 120

50 *Bukhan Gwangye Saryojip V*: 616-617.

children per nursery governess, the accommodation capacity per nursery, facility requirements, and qualifications for employees. Nurseries were taking care of children between the ages of 35 days to three years. A governess should be allocated between 18 to 20 children. A governess should have at least one among three qualifications: a medical nurse; a graduate of a special school for nursery governesses; or a teacher of kindergarten or elementary school. Nursing hours were 8 to 24 hours a day.

The Health Bureau formulated the Regulation No. 3[51] at the same time. The Regulation No.3 provided the organizational guide for nurseries, elucidating the jurisdiction of the power to appoint and dismiss the employees, the job description, and minimum number of employees. Every nursery was required to have at least one medical nurse, one part-time doctor, and other office workers and assistants in addition to nursery governesses. After the inauguration of the DPRK, the nursery regulations were developed into the Order No.1 of the DPRK Ministry of Health in February 1949.[52]

The leaders of the WPK realized that at least some temporary facilities for child-care were in urgent need in order to mobilize women during spring farming season. Therefore, the Central Committee of the WPK decided to set up seasonal nurseries in rural areas in May 1947 by a Party resolution.[53] The Women's Union again responded quickly, and improvised nurseries and kindergartens by utilizing vacant rooms and buildings and mobilizing experienced mothers to

51 Bukhan Gwangye Saryojip V: 615

52 Miryang Youn, Bunhakui Yusung Jongchak 북한의 여성정책 (Seoul: Hanul, 1991): 83; Naegak Gongbo 1949, January–June (Pyongyang: Chosun Minjujui Inmingonhwaguk Naegak Samoucho): 207–209.

53 Decision at the 35th Meeting of the Standing Committee of the Central Committee of the WPK (1947.5.20). Jae-Han Kim, Orini Boyuk-Gyoyang Gyunghom 어린이 보육교양 경험 (Pyongyang: Sahoe Gwahak Chulpan-Sa): 23.

take care of children. The Women's Union also ran moving nurseries.

Until the North Korean regime was fully established and equipped with economic capacity in the 1970s, the Women's Union had taken a large share of responsibilities to provide child-care support for working mothers. As the result of the efforts by the government and the Women's Union, the number of kindergartens increased to 109, accommodating 8,056 children by the end of 1949. The number of nurseries also reached up to 104, accommodating 7,000 in 1949.[54] The number seems miniscule, considering 11 millions of population. However, the concept of kindergartens and nurseries for workers, not for the wealthy and powerful, was alien in Korea. This new concept came to be spread among the people and soon accepted as normal from the very small beginning.

Affirmative Social Reforms

Since every attempt to change the existing social order involved women, the half of the populace, the communists and the PPC carried out social reforms with special arrangement for women. Providing women with full legal rights alone required legislators to consider women in every legislative procedure. The communists of North Korea indeed meticulously incorporated women's issues in most reforms and legislations.

Land reform of 1946 was the first to change women's status in society: it distributed land to women, not in tandem with their husbands but in their own right. The core distribution criterion for land was the labor capability of the

---

54 *Minju Chosun* (The party organ of the WPK), 1953.6.1.

household. Therefore, if a household had many working age members, it received more land. The criteria were age and sex. Thus, women of a certain age could receive land in their own legal capacity. Although the methods and the results of land reform in North Korea are still controversial because of the expropriation and forced displacement of landowners, recognizing women as persons with legal capacity remains one of the most important achievements of the land reform.

Table 2.1) Criterion for Land Distribution

Score	Male	Female
1	18–60 year olds	18–50 year olds
0.7	15–17 year olds	15–17 year olds
0.4	10–14 year olds	10–14 year olds
0.3	61 year old and above, under 9	51 year old and above, under 9

Source: Democratic United Front, *Chosun Haebang Nyunbo* [조선해방년보], Moonwooin Seokwan, Seoul, 1946, p.413

Land reform also provided women with the possibility of economic independence. If a widow of 50 years old had two children aged ten and seventeen, she could get 2.1 points, and receive enough land to support her family, albeit with hard labor. Therefore, land reform became the first milestone for the furtherance of women's rights in North Korea. However, the land ownership was soon abolished when all the arable land were nationalized and collectivized in 1958.

The Labor Law for Workers and Office Employees of 1946[55] also stipulated the principle of equality at work: equal pay for equal work regardless of sex, which had not been even heard of in Korea; maternity protection measures that included maternity leave, light job assignment for pregnant women, and the right for working mothers to breast feed. In South Korea, by contrast, the principle of equal pay for equal work was not pronounced in a law until as late as 1987. Even though it was a political gesture, since there was no means of implementing it at that time, North Korea's Labor Law of 1946 was clearly ahead of its time

The Establishment of Education System began in May 1946. The PPC first set to publish the textbook for various levels of schools. The PPC set up the *Supervisory Committee for National Textbook Publishing* [교과서편찬사업 감찰위원회] to select the writers, plan the structure of the books, supervise the contents, and approve the publication of books. The communists put textbook publication as a very high priority, and controlled every phase of the publication.

---

55 *Bukhan Gwangye Saryojip V*: 685–688.
⟨ Excerpt from the Labor Law for Workers and Office Employees ⟩
Article 1. To introduce an eight hour working day for factory and office workers in all the enterprises and offices by the state, social organizations, consumers' cooperatives and individuals.
Article 7. To pay an equal wage to the workers who do equal work with equal techniques, irrespective of their age and sex.
Article 14. To provide women workers and office employees in all enterprises and offices with maternity leave, 35 days before and 42 days after the birth.
Article 15. To allow a pregnant woman who needs to do lighter work for reasons of health to be transferred to easier work from the sixth month of pregnancy until she takes the maternity leave, and to pay her on the basis of the average wage for the last six months.
Article 16. A working woman with a baby one year of age is allowed to have a 30-minute feeding break twice a day, during which she will be paid her average wage.
Article 17. It is prohibited to put pregnant or nursing women on overnight or night work.
Article 18. To introduce a compulsory social insurance scheme for the workers and office employees of all enterprises, offices and economic branches as follows
b. To grant allowances to women on maternity leave;
e. To allow pensions to those families who have been deprived of their breadwinners.

The publications were completed by the end of 1946, almost within a half year.

At the same time, the PPC also established a national university. The PPC decided to name the university as Kim Il Sung University in honor of "General Kim Il Sung, the hero of Chosun nation, who fought against the Japanese imperialists for our liberation."[56] The university opened in September 1946, four months after the decision to establish a national university. The university admitted students with appropriate school diploma and strong progressive democratic inclination, regardless of sex. The PPC continued to establish a College for Teachers, many technical colleges, and a Central School for Cadres of the Workers' Party of Korea. All the colleges and schools admitted women as well as men. The proportion of female students in higher education has not been presented. However, until 1949, the number remained miniscule. In the case of the Central School for Cadres of the Worker's Party of Korea, the number of females was 15 among 141 graduates at the first graduation.[57]

---

56 *Bukhan Gwangye Saryojip V:* 682–683.

57 In the Photo Album of the First Graduates on of the Central School for Cadres of the Workers Party of Korea, pictures of 141 students including 15 women were printed. *Rodongdang Chungang Dang Hakgyo 1950 Nyun 2Nunsaeng Che-1-Hoe Jolup Ginyum Sajinchop* [로동당중앙당학교 1950년 2년생 제1회 졸업기념 사진첩: Photo Album of the First Graduates of the Central School for Cadres of the Workers Party of Korea]. National Archive and Record Administration, Record Group 242. Captured Enemy Documents (North Korea). 190-34-16/2~17/5, Box 13.

2.4 The Responses of Women

Participation in Politics and Social Campaigns

Women responded eagerly to the call for participation in nation-building and social revolution. Women joined the Women's Union with amazing speed and fervor. Although it was the Women's Union who made action plans and guidance for women, the success of the Women's Union was subject to the efforts and zeal of its membership. If women had not been active in social campaigns and political rallies, the influence and the growth of the Women's Union must have been very limited. Therefore it was women who drove the Women's Union to political power and influence.

As was mentioned above, a huge number of women turned up political rallies and campaigns for reforms. Several hundred thousands of women came to the meetings and fairs. Women only gatherings for the petition of reform legislation including the *Sex Equality Law* were also frequent. Many aged men abhorred the activities of women and tried to prohibit their daughters and wives to join the gatherings. Nevertheless many women responded to the call of the Women's Union, participated in elections as nominees and voters.

In November 1946 the first election ever was held in North Korea to establish the PPC. The election was to vote for the city/county people's committees. At that time many nationalists inclined to Western-democracy opposed the election, because the method of the election was to vote "yea" or "nay" to a single list of nominees presented by the National United Front. Despite the opposition, most people turned up to cast ballots. The turnout rate of the voters was 99.6

percent.[58] Of course, this incredible proportion of turn-outs might be the result of the existence of the Soviet military and the coercive social pressure by the communists, the fever of the Korean people for self-governing also played a crucial role. Most women as well as men participated in the election.

Women participated in the election not only as the voters, but also as nominees. By the 1946 election, 3,459 members were elected to the city/county people's committees, among which 453 (13.1 percent) were women. In February 1947, another election for district people's committees was held. By this election, 53,314 members of district people's committees were elected, among which 10,035 (19 percent) were women. The National People's Congress was elected by the joint convention of the members of city/county people's committees on February17, 1947. The number of the members of the National People's Congress was 237, among which 34 were women (15 percent).[59]

The proportion of women among the elected may seem low. However, these double-digit numbers were surprising to many Korean people at the time. In comparison, the proportion of women in the first National Assembly in South Korea at the first election was 0.5 percent, electing only one woman out of 198 representatives.

The National People's Congress then selected the NKPC as the highest administrative body of North Korea. Among the 22 members of the NKPC, one woman, Ho Jong-Sook, was appointed to the Secretary of Propaganda. In the course of these elections, people began to take the political representation of women for granted.

---

58 *Choson Chungang Yongam* 1949: 83.

59 *Choson Chungang Yongam* 1949: 83–86.

The advancement of women into politics continued in 1949 when the first election for the DPRK was held. In 1949 election, a great number of women were again elected as representatives: at the Supreme People's Assembly, 69 women were elected out of 572 total representatives, making up 12 percent. At the city/county people's assemblies, 2,146 women out of 13,354 representatives were elected, making up 16 percent of proportion. At the district level women consisted of 15 percent of the representatives, numbering 8,494.[60]

Many women were also appointed to the positions of public administration and law-enforcement. During 1946 to 1949, the number of women working for public administration numbered 1,048; and the number of women serving in prosecutors' offices and courts was 1,697.[61]

Women were also active in social reforms. A large crowd of women turned out to political rallies and social campaigns. Several hundred thousand of women were reported to join the campaigns for land reform. The appearance of women in public places itself was a new phenomenon. Despite some outright criticism of women's activities, women continued to join the campaigns, making the presence of women all in the day's work.

Women's participation in illiteracy eradication campaign was notable. At the time of the Independence, there were 2.3 million illiterate people among which 65 percent were women. In fact, 90 percent of adult women were illiterate.[62] Many literate women jointly organized many evening-classes, special-classes and adults-school for women. Under the slogan of "Women, Let's

---

60 *Choson Chungang Yongam* 1953: 336-337

61 Kyung-Hye Lee: 74.

62 Kyung-Hye Lee: 33.

Overcome Illiteracy to Raise our Political Awareness and to Improve our Lives," women carried out a variety of campaigns such as performances, discussion meetings, radio broadcasting and publications in order to persuade women to come to the classes. In some areas, women formed a "train-campaign team" to explain the program to rail travelers. Many women also provided temporary nurseries for mothers with young children during their studies. North Korea boasted that it eradicated 98 percent of illiteracy by the end of 1948: it educated 320,000 people in 1946, 840,000 in 1947, and 1,140,620 in 1948.[63] Although the real success rate of illiteracy eradication could not be verified, the number of people who took the literacy class was genuine. The nationalists' advocacy for education again played a crucial role in this successful campaign. The literacy rate of women increased dramatically, recording another achievement of women.

Participation in the Workforce

Women's labor in industry was a new phenomenon that appeared during the 20th century in Korea. Korea remained an overwhelmingly agricultural society when it regained its Independence. Data from 1943 reveals among its 25 million inhabitants, only 550,000 worked in manufacturing or industry, 180,000 in mines, and all others in agriculture.[64] Women made up less than 10 percent of the small number of workers. In 1946 women comprised 8 percent of member-

---

63 *Choson Chungang Yungam* 1949: 135.

64 Hochin Choi : 291.

ship in the National Trade Union of North Korea, numbering only 21,761.[65]

As Kim Il Sung emphasized the importance of women's participation in the productive labor, the government tried to pull women into industries from its first and second one-year economic plans in 1947 and 1948. During the one-year economic plan period, major economic policy goals were: 1) to consolidate factories and enterprises in workable conditions; 2) to promote the production of necessary goods; and 3) to encourage agricultural production.[66]

Among the three economic goals, women were foremost encouraged to participate in agriculture. Since women's employment in the industry required skills and literacy, it took a considerable time and efforts to make women the working class. Considering women's conditions, Kim Il Sung urged the Women's Union to mobilize women in the countryside into the agricultural production.

An important question arising in building up the country at present is consolidation of the success achieved in the agrarian reform. First of all we should boost agricultural production and in this way demonstrate the superiority of the new system of landownership which is free from landlords and under which the tillers are the owners of lands. For this purpose, the women in the countryside who account for half the rural population must participate in farming more zealously than anyone else. This is important step not only to put the women on a par with men economically, but also to improve their position politically.[67]

---

65 Sung-Bo Kim, *Sajingwa Grimuro Bonun Bukhan Hyundaisa* 사진과 그림으로 보는 북한현대사 (Seoul: Yuksa Yunguhoe, 2004): 54-60.

66 Eui-Gak Hwang, *The Korean Economies: A Comparison of North and South* (Oxford: Clarendon Press, 1993): 35.

67 Kim Il Sung, *Works* 2: 191.

Production of textile materials had been regarded as women's job. Kim Il Sung also urged women to increase the production of silk and cotton. In response, many women joined in sericulture and production of cotton cloth. In Pyongnam Province alone, 7,000 women attended to lectures for basic sericulture techniques and jointly operated 713 silk cocoon farms. As a result Pyongnam Province achieved cocoon production higher than its target by 108 percent. In the case of cotton production, women were attributed to produce 832,639 rolls of cotton cloth during the winter of 1949.[68]

An increased number of women were employed in industries. However, the number of women workers in the industry remained negligible because of women's lack of skills. In 1947, the number of women workers in the industry remained to 30,000.[69] Therefore North Korea tried to train women for the requirement of industry. North Korea claimed that it had doubled the number of women with skills in four years, from 1946 to 1949. Despite the North Korean authorities' efforts, it is obvious that the number of women workers did not increase very much until the Korean War. The number of female workers in industry remained less than 50,000, with the number of skilled workers even smaller.

---

68 Kyung-Hye Lee: 79.

69 Kyung-Hye Lee: 81.

Table 2.2) The Increase of Workers and skilled Workers

Year	Increase Rate of Female Workers	Increase Rate of Female Skilled Workers
1946	100.0%	100.0%
1947	117.8%	100.1%
1948	161.3%	147.9%
1949	179.1%	198.9%

Source: Kyung-Hye Lee, *Nyusung Moonje Haaegyul Kyunghum* [녀성문제해결경험], (Pyongyang: Sahoegwa-hakwon Choolpan-sa, 1990): 86.

Even when women hoped to join the workforce, they faced many barriers, such as the responsibility of household work and child-caring, and the negative social perception to women's activities outside of the home. Therefore Kim Il Sung appealed women to participate in "voluntary work for nation-building." "Voluntary labor" meant unpaid work, monetarily or materially. In fact, the request of "voluntary labor" was demanding people to sacrifice their time and efforts for the sake of the public interest. Kim urged the Women's Union to "enlist the women in the residential quarters and housewives in the national effort."[70]

As a result, a great number of housewives and young women at home were called out to voluntary labor. The most notable case was the repair work of the Botong River of Pyongyang in May 1946. North Korea claimed that Kim Jong-Suk, Kim Il Sung's first wife, guided and led housewives to complete the repair work within 55 days, while the Japanese colonial authority had not fin-

---

70 Kim Il Sung, *Works* 2: 194.

ished for ten years.[71] Regardless of whether Kim Jong-Suk indeed led the repair work, it was true that most of the works were done by housewives. A huge number of housewives participated in the repair work. Since then "voluntary labor" of housewives in North Korea became a norm, depriving women of free hours at home.

The One-Year plan was successful: the value of total industrial output grew by 54 percent in 1947 and 64 percent in 1948, of which producer goods rose by 76 percent and78 percent, while consumer goods increased by 30 percent and 50 percent in respective years. The output of grains was 1,898,000 tons in 1946, 2,069,000 tons in 1947, and 2,668,000 tons in 1948, recording annual average growth rate of 11.9 percent during the One-Year plans. Many women participated in this process, and more than 50 women were decorated with the title of heroine of labor.[72]

These slow but steady increase of women's employment faced a dramatic turn with the break-out of the Korean War. Women were massively mobilized into the industry and agriculture. Almost all the agricultural production was carried out by women. Many industries were run by women alone. Mobilization of women during the War was not a matter of principle, but the matter of survival for the warring regime.

---

71 Kyung-Hye Lee: 85.

72 The title of heroes or heroines of labor originated from the Soviet Union and widely used in the socialist regimes. As a psychological incentive for labor the Soviet government decorated those workers who had shown extraordinary performances at work with the title of hero or heroin of labor (*Stakhanovite*). Kyung-Hye Lee: 81.

Supporting the War Efforts[73]

As in other modern wars, the Korean War mobilized women into every sphere of the war efforts. Women participated in the war efforts in three ways: a huge number of women joined the workforce "instead of their husbands and sons in the battlefield,"[74] mostly in agriculture[75]; some women volunteered the battlefields as nurses or combatants; and others were engaged in assistance works such as providing food and shelters to stationing military units, presenting comforts bags and letters for soldiers, and taking care of war-orphans.

First of all, women had to fill the void left by men on the home front. Women worked in factories, farms and mines. Many women took charge of her husband's lathe or her brother's drilling machine. In textile industry, women waged a campaign to take care of four or five machines at one time under the banner of "multiple machine operation movement."[76]

During the War North Korea lost 52 heavy industries and plants including the Hungnam Fertilizer Plant, Hwanghae Iron and Chongjin Steel Manufacture. Women maintained these plants by running the machines and repairing of those heavy industries. In the Whanghae Iron, women organized the Committee for

---

73 The impacts of the Korean War were huge, complicated and diverse. It shaped the concept of national security, the people's psychology and culture, and the economic development strategy. However, detailing the impact of the Korean War is beyond this book. Therefore this section focuses on the impact of the war to women in North Korea.

74 Kyung-Hye Lee: 88.

75 Young-Ja Park, *Bukhanui Gundaehwa Gwajonggwa Yusungui Yukhal* (1945-1980s) 북한의 근대화 과정과 여성의 역할 (1945-1980년대): 공장과 가정의 정치사회와 여성노동을 중심으로 (Seoul: Ph.D Thesis, Sunggyungwan University, 2004): 39.

76 Tae-Ho Park, *Chosun Inminui Jonguiui Chokguk Haebangjonjang-Sa 3* 조선인민의 정의의 조국해방전쟁사 3 (Pyongyang: Social Science Publishing House, 1983): 187-188.

the Defense of the Plant and Equipments and took charge of the protection of the plant and production of iron instead of men.[77] In the North Hamkyung Province alone, 2,300 women were employed in the steel, iron and textile industries within ten days of the outbreak of the war.[78]

Since most women lacked proper training, the enterprises and the authority organized many forms of educational and training program in conjunction with production. In reality, these training programs were simply assigning several unskilled workers under the direction of a skilled worker. The proportion of women among industrial workers reached up to 27 percent during the war. The proportion had been almost doubled in two years since the war broke out. However, the number remained small.

Table 2.3) Increase of the Proportion of Female Workers in Industry

Year	Proportion of Female Workers (%)
1948	11.0 %
1949	14.8 %
1950. June	15.9 %
1952. June	27.0 %

Source: Sanghwa Kim, "*Chosun Sanupui Baljon*," *Inmin Kyungjeui Baljon* [인민경제의 발전], (Pyongyang: Gwahakwon, 1954): 153

---

77 Jong-Ho Huh, *Chosun Inminui Jonguiui Chokguk Haebangjonjang-Sa 1* 조선인민의 정의의 조국해방전쟁사 1 (Pyongyang: Social Science Publishing House, 1983): 248-250.

78 Jong-Ho Huh: 251.

The largest number of women was mobilized into agriculture. As Kim Il Sung admitted, there remained only the elderly and women in rural areas after the break-out of the War. Women were named as the "masters" of rural community. Production of rice was the basic task of women in rural areas.

> Now there are only the elderly and women in rural communities since able men are mostly at the battle field. Therefore the masters of rural communities are women, and women should work harder.[79]

At that time, many works required physical strength, because the level of mechanization in agriculture was very low. Women had to shoulder manually all the hard labor such as ox-plowing, rice-transplantation and harvesting, grain thrashing and transporting. Since controlling a plow-ox required physical strength and technique, ox-plowing had been regarded as men's work. During the War, however, women had to do the ox-plowing as well. The Women's Union even organized a movement called for the "Women's Corps for Ox-Plowing." This movement appealed women to "revenge the enemy by increasing agricultural production on behalf of husbands, sons and brothers in the battlefield."[80] Many women learned to control oxen, and became the ox-plower. In Ryongang County, many housewives attended the lesson how to control oxen, which lasted for three years.[81] Unmarried young girls were not exempted from

---

79 Kim Il Sung, *Chojakchip 7* 저작집 7 (Pyongyang: Sahoe-gwahak chulpan-sa, 1980): 211. Author's translation.

80 Ryuksa Yunguso, *Choguk Haebangjonjang Siki Balhyundoen Hoobang Inmindeului Hyukmyungjok Saeng-hwalgipoong* 조국해방전쟁시기 발현된 후방인민들의 혁명적 생활기풍 (Pyongyang: Social Science Publishing House, 1976): 69-70.

81 *Minju Choson*, 1953.5.28 (3)

the task. A girl was praised and named as a "maiden Ox-Plower" by a local new paper.[82] As a result, while 3,394 women engaged in ox-plowing in 1951, the number of these women was almost tripled in 1952, to 9,916 in North Ham-kyung Province alone.[83]

The pruning of fruit trees had been also regarded as men's job. However, women also took the heavy shears for the production of fruits during the war. In many state-run fruit farms, women organized pruning classes for themselves and trimmed the branches properly, producing fruits at right time.[84]

Many women also "volunteered" to support the war effort. Most women joined together to send comfort bags to soldiers at the battlefield. The comfort bags included food, necessities and letters. Women in a county of Hwanghae Province sent 40 kg of rice to the army.[85] Women in other county sent a large lump of pork to the army annually.[86] Some women collected wild edible greens and sent them. Other women presented crafted cushions, socks, and pairs of gloves. Some women volunteered to take care of the war-orphans. The news-papers often ran articles about women who adopted several orphans during the war.[87]

In some cases, women actually joined the army. Within 20 days after the outbreak of the War, several tens of female students from Kim Il Sung Univer-sity, Pyongyang Technical College, Pyongyang Medical College volunteered to

---

82 *Hwanghae Ilbo*, 1953.1.23 (3).

83 Kyung-Hye Lee: 88.

84 *Rodong Shinmoon*, 1953.3.14 (3).

85 *Hwanghae Ilbo*, 1953.1.23 (1).

86 *Rodong Shinmoon*, 1953.5.28 (3).

87 *Minju Choson*, 1953.6.1 (3); *Rodong Shinmoon*, 1953.2.25 (3).

the army. Some of them became military nurses, others served as technicians at the battlefields.[88] In a word, women were omnipresent during the war, shouldering the responsibility of material production and supporting the army.

The Korean War destroyed almost everything on the Korean peninsula. According to figures published in the Soviet Union, 11.1% of the total population of North Korea perished, which indicates that 1,130,000 people were killed. In total about 2,500,000 people were killed. More than 80% of the industrial and public facilities and transportation works, three-quarters of the government offices, and one-half of the houses were demolished. With this devastation, traditional values and social customs were also destroyed. The persistent feudal marital customs also almost disappeared after the war.

During the turbulent times from Liberation to the Korean War, North Korea went through rapid and radical reforms. People were lined up by new identities. Lands were confiscated and allocated to men and women most of whom had never owned land. People became the "voters" and cast ballots for government. People were mobilized into many political and social campaigns. Many new laws were formulated and came into force instantly.

During this inception period, Kim Il Sung and North Korean communists made conscious efforts to liberate women from the old family system. They included women in almost all the legislations and reform measures. They allocated land to women as well as men. It was supposed to be the first step for economic independence. They paid attention to women when they formulated laws. The *Sex Equality Law* of 1946 provided women with equal rights with men in all spheres of state, economic, cultural, social and political life. The Labor Law

---

88 *Haebang Ilbo*, 1950.7.11 (1)

provided women with equal right to employment, including the principle of "equal pay for equal work." The *Labor Law* promised women to provide necessary conditions for employment. Cabinet resolutions also prepared to supply nurseries and kindergartens for working mothers.

Many women responded passionately to the communists' calls. Many women joined the Women's Union, participated in elections and political rallies, and found jobs outside of the home. The Women's Union grew rapidly in its membership and influence. For North Korean women it was the experience of upside-down and turbulence. It was the hour of revolution. However, the hour of revolution lasted only for five years. With the outbreak of the Korean War, revolution began to be postponed, re-interpreted, and distorted for war efforts. At the end of war, women had to rebuild the nation all over again, almost re-starting from scratch.

Chapter III

Reinstating
the Patriarchal Order
(1953~1989)

3.1 Establishment of the *Juche* Thought System

Formation of the *Juche* Thought System

The Korean War devastated the Korean society and economy. However, the devastation also provided an opportunity for the government to transform the nation into a communist society: most of the possible dissidents fled to the South; and the old social forces sustained heavy losses to their material bases. It was time to tighten the control over the people and centralize the economy.

Just weeks after the conclusion of the Armistice, Kim Il Sung convened the 6th Plenum of the Central Committee of the WPK on August 5, 1953. In this meeting, Kim delivered the report *"Everything for the Post War Rehabilitation and Development of the People's Economy."*[1] He reckoned that it was impossible to rehabilitate and construct every branch of the national economy simultaneously. Therefore he insisted that North Korea should start with building the basic industry. He believed that solid foundation of basic (heavy) industry would bring better opportunity for a balanced industrialization. His development plan was, in a word, to focus on heavy industry at the expense of light industry.

There was a conflict over the development strategy among the party leaders. This power struggle was a result of the profound ideological difference, similar to the "red vs. expert" conflicts that occurred in China and Russia. While Kim Il Sung put high priority on heavy industry and pursued a fast development and ideologically controlled economic policy, others advocated more realistic

---

1 Kim Il Sung, *Chojakchip* 8저작집 8: 1953.8-1954.6 (Pyongyang: Chosun Rodongdang Choolpan-Sa, 1980): 11-64.

approach that gave priority to restoration of agriculture and light industry. While Kim Il Sung envisaged rather autarkic, self-sustainable development, other light industrialist were advocating the international division of labor. It was political struggle over development and diplomatic strategies.[2]

During the conflict over economic strategy and ideology, Kim Il Sung intensified his attack on the gradualists who were predominantly Soviet Koreans, and stressed the virtues of self-reliance and Korean self-identity. The debates over the development strategy reveal that Kim Il Sung's plan was from the beginning self-sustaining and autarkic in nature. [3]

Kim Il Sung also planned to carry out socialist transformation and rehabilitation at the same time. In his address *"Everything for the National Unification and Independence and Socialist Construction in the North"*[4] in April 1954, Kim Il Sung declared to collectivize private farms and industries. In accordance with the strategy of Kim Il Sung, North Korea launched its Three Year Economic Plan in 1954, aiming to rehabilitate production facilities and capacities and to recover the total production to the pre-war level.

At the same time, Kim Il Sung introduced a new Citizen's registration system as a part of socialist transformation. The DPRK Cabinet Resolution No.28, *Resolution on the Registration of the Citizen's Identity* [내각결정 28호, 공민의 신분등록에 관한 규정] of March 5, 1955 was to re-shape the society and the

---

2 There had been many complicate events surrounding the development strategy and ideology among North Korean leadership. Even the leaders of China and Soviet Russia were engaged in the conflict. However, the details of the conflict are beyond the concern of this book. See, Balazs Szalontai, *Kim Il Sung in the Khrushchev Era: Soviet-DPRK Relations and the Roots of North Korean Despotism, 1953-1964* (Washington: Woodrow Wilson Center Press, 2006).

3 Adrian Buzo, *The Making of Modern Korea* (New York: Routledge, 2002):93-97.

4 Kim Il Sung, *Chojakchip* 9저작집 9: 1954.7-1955.12 (Pyongyang: Chosun Rodongdang Choolpan-Sa, 1980): 228-244.

public registration system by strengthening the security screen and by detailing the procedures of registration. This official registrations system was to replace the family registry. Since the traditional family registry had been the backbone of the old family system, its abrogation was the final blow to the old order. The family registry system, which still exists in South Korea, completely disappeared in North Korea.

Kim Il Sung waged the so-called "anti-sectarianists struggle" within the WPK in 1955, emphasizing the importance of the "*Juche* [주체: self-reliance] in ideology." In his concluding speech at the April Plenum of the Central Committee of the WPK, Kim criticized "those who flirted and surrendered to foreign forces" by names and demanded to eliminate the factional elements of the party and strengthen class education.[5] In the course of the debate over establishing the *Juche*, Kim managed to purge Hun-Young Park and Seung-Yup Lee who had represented domestic communists from colonial period, labeling them as "the spies for the US imperialists." He also purged other rivals including Gai Huh and Nyung-Ha Joo who were regarded as pro-Soviet Union, naming them also as sectarianists. At the Third Party Congress in April 1956, the WPK concluded the "anti-sectarianists struggle" and approved the leadership of Kim Il Sung.[6] At the same time, Kim Il Sung began to carry out intensive economic plan in order to establish the *Juche* [자립: self-sustenance] in economy. In August 1956, Kim Il Sung's position of post-war strategy became the state policy.

During the Three Year Economic Plan period, North Korea moved fast for

---

5 Kim Il Sung, *Selected Works*, Vol. 1 (Pyongyang: Foreign Languages Publishing House, 1971): 555–581. By insisting the *Juche* in ideology, he managed to purge both domestic sects and the pro-Sovet internationalist leaders who had preferred consumer goods production to heavy industry.

6 Report of the Central Committee to the 3rd Congress of the WPK, Kim Il Sung, *Chojakchip* 10:1956.1–1956.12: 175–305.

the centralization and collectivization of the economy. The collectivization of
the agricultural sector was completed in 1958, and later the trades and industries
were forged into cooperatives. By the end of 1958, the groups categorized as
private farmers, (private) craftsmen, industrialists and merchants disappeared.
Socialist transformation was, therefore, completed.

Table 3.1) Composition of Social Groups in North Korea (1958.12)

(in Percentage)

Category	1946	1953.12.1	1957.12.1	1958.12.1
Total	100.0	100.0	100.0	100.0
Workers	12.5	21.2	28.7	31.7
Office Employees	6.2	8.5	14.9	14.4
Members of Collective Farms	–	–	49.9	49.9
Private Farmers	74.1	66.4	3.2	–
Members of Cooperatives	–	0.5	2.2	3.2
Private Craftsmen	1.5	0.6	0.3	–
Industrialists	0.2	0.1	(0.01)	–
Merchants	3.3	1.2	0.4	–
Others	2.2	1.5	0.4	0.8

Source: *Choson Chungang Yongam* 1959 조선중앙년감 (Pyongyang: Choson Chungang Tongshin-Sa, 1959):
137.

The WPK held its fourth Party Congress in September 1961. This Congress again legitimized the "anti-sectionalists struggle" within the party and
confirmed the unchallengeable leadership of Kim Il Sung. The WPK also intro-

duced the first Seven Year People's Economic Plan, proclaiming "all-out mobilization for the construction of full-blown socialism."[7]

When Kim Il Sung visited Bandung in 1965 amidst the intensified Sino-Soviet dispute, he summarized the contents of the *Juche* as the self-reliance in ideology, independence in politics, self-sustenance in economy, and self-defense in national defense.[8] The *Juche* Thought was in effect to declare that North Korea would maintain diplomatic balance between the two disputant socialist nations as a sovereign state. By the pronouncement of the four contents of the *Juche* Thought, the basic formula of the *Juche* Thought was completed.

In October 5, 1966, the WPK held its second Conference of Representatives. Kim Il Sung delivered the address *"The Present Situation and the Tasks of Our Party"*[9] to the Conference and demanded to establish the *Juche* and solidarity within the party. He criticized the international dogmatism and revisionism, and pointed out the importance of strengthening the party as the staff of the revolution and mobilizing the mass around the party. In order to strengthen the party, he emphasized, the party should intensify political ideology education for the mass and defend the solidarity and integrity of the party.

In this address, Kim also spoke of the construction and development of socialism and communism. If socialism and communism were to be constructed successfully, both the two fortresses, the material and the ideological, should be occupied. Without occupying the ideological fortress, the revolutionary gains that had been won were in danger of being lost. For the occupation of the ideo-

---

7 *Choson Chungang Yungam* (DPRK Central Yearbook) 1962: 13–62.

8 Kim Il Sung Speech at the Ali Arham Social Science Institute in Indonesia (1965.4.14), *Choson Chungang Yungam* (DPRK Central Yearbook) 1966–67: 19–35.

9 *Choson Chungang Yungam* (DPRK Central Yearbook) 1966–67: 376–448.

logical fortress, Kim called for the *"revolutionization and working-classiza-tion*[10] *of the whole society."* His point was to intensify ideology education and establish the Unique System in the whole society. It was the precursor of the personality cult. In response to his call, the Conference adopted a decision that demanded to intensify ideology education.

In May 1967 the 15th Plenum of the Central Committee of the 4th WPK was convened in order to discuss the establishment of the Unique System. The Unique System refers to "the only" system of Kim Il Sung's *Juche* Thought. It states that the party and the society should follow the ideals of Kim Il Sung alone, without any reference to other thought. In the course of the discussion, a number of high ranking party members who opposed to the increased person-ality cult of Kim Il Sung including Geum-Chul Park and Hyo-Sun Lee were at-tacked and purged from the party. The contents of the discussions in the Plenum were never open to the public. However, Kim Il Sung mentioned that "the party should firmly establish the Unique Thought System in the party in accordance with the Decision of the 15th Plenum of the 4th WPK" in his speech on June 20, 1967.[11] Kim Jong Il reportedly led this attack, paving his way to power. Since this Plenum the personality cult of the Kims was carried out in full-scale under the name of establishing the Unique System.

Official publications of North Korea undoubtedly display the characteris-tics of the Unique System. Books and documents published after 1967 contain

---

10 The expression *"working-classization"* is, strictly speaking, not an English word. In Korean, however, it is easily understood. It means making the people the working class. The English word came from North Korean official publications. I tried to follow North Korean terminology as much as possible.

11 Kim Il Sung, "Dang-Daepyojahoe Gyuljong-ul Chuljohee Gwanchulhagi Wihayo (당대표자회 결정을 철저히 관철하기 위하여: Fully Accomplishing the Decision at the Conference of Representatives)," Kim Il Sung, Chojakchip 21: 1967.1-1967.12 (Pyongyang: Chosun Rodongdang Chulpan-Sa, 1983): 315-350.

a vast volume of texts about the extraordinary achievements and revolutionary personalities of the Kim family. The DPRK Central Yearbook 1968 began
with "Chronicle of the Revolutionary Activities of Kim Il Sung," "Invincible
Anti-Japanese Revolutionary, Kim Hung-Jik," and "Let's Follow the Model of
Lady Kang-Ban-Suck."[12]

The fifth Party Congress of the WPK in November 1970 changed the
Party Covenant, and specified the *Juche* Thought of Kim Il Sung as the guiding principle of the Party. That change was a substantial divergence from the
original Marxist-Leninist principles. The Congress also proposed the *"Three
Revolutionary Tasks* [3대 혁명과제]" in order to occupy the two fortresses of
revolution. The *Three Revolutionary Tasks* refers to revolutionizing the thought,
techniques, and culture of the people. Revolutionizing thought requires people
to study, memorize, and follow without questioning Kim's *Juche* Thoughts.
Revolutionizing techniques requires people to research, innovate, and improvise
at work with whatever is provided at the time. Revolutionizing culture requires
people to mold "socialist personality" which can be summed up as *"One for all,
all for one."*

In accordance with the new Party Covenant, the *Socialist Constitution* of
1972[13] was promulgated. This Constitution announced that North Korea inher-

12 *Choson Chungang Yungam* (DPRK Central Yearbook) 1968: 1-69 (Prior to the main contents).

13 *Choson Chungang Yungam* (DPRK Central Yearbook) 1973: 1-8 (Prior to the Table of Contents)
⟨ Excerpts from Socialist Constitution (1972) ⟩
Article 3. The Democratic People's Republic of Korea is a revolutionary State power which has inherited
the brilliant history of the glorious revolutionary struggle against the imperialist aggressors and for the
liberation of the homeland and the freedom and well-being of the people.
Article 4. The Democratic People's Republic of Korea is guided in its activity by the *Juche* idea of the
Workers' Party of Korea which is a creative application of Marxism-Leninism to country's reality.
Article 49. In the Democratic People's Republic of Korea the rights and duties of citizens are based on the
collectivist principle of "One for all and all for one."

ited the brilliant traditions that were created during the glorious revolutionary struggle (Article 3) and was to be guided by the *Juche* idea (Article 4). Kim Il Sung's life became the basic history of the state. The Socialist Constitution also declared that the rights and duties of citizens are based on the collectivist principle of *"One for all and all for one"* (Article 49). The Constitution created office of the President and the Central People's Committee (CPC) headed by the President. This structural change was designed to strengthen the CPC's and the President's control over the government at the expense of the Supreme People's Assembly. While announcing the completion of socialist transformation, the *Socialist Constitution* ended in creation of a dictatorship.

The Rise of the Dear Leader

With the establishment of dictatorship, a new attempt to preserve and pass the system to next generation began. For a while the throne seemed to be des-

---

Article 51. Citizens all enjoy equal rights in the political, economic and cultural and all other spheres of State and public activity.

Article 52. All citizens who have reached the age of 17 have the right to elect and be elected, irrespective of sex, race, occupation, length of residence, property status and education, party affiliation, political views and religion.

The Citizens serving in the army also have the right to elect and be elected.

Those who are deprived of the right to vote by the court, and mentally-ill persons are denied the right to elect and be elected.

Article 62. Women hold equal social status and rights with men.

The State affords special protection to mothers and children through maternity leave, shortened working hours for mothers of large families, expanded maternity hospitals, nurseries and kindergartens and other measures.

The State frees women from the heavy burdens of household chores and provides every condition for them to participate in public life.

Article 63. Marriage and the family are protected by the State. The State pays great attention to consolidating the family, the cell of society.

tined for a brother of Kim Il Sung. However, during the 1970s, the throne was decided to be inherited by his eldest son, Kim Jong Il.

Kim Jong Il began his party career as an advisor to the party's Organization and Supervision Department immediately after his college graduation in 1964. Since the party's Organization and Supervision Department dealt with inspection and supervision, which in effect meant surveillance, of the party leadership, Kim Jong Il obtained an effective position for purging possible rivals. He managed to brand Geum-Chul Park and Hyo-Sun Lee as "bourgeois revisionists" and purge them in 1967. He became the Deputy Secretary for the party's Propaganda Department. Under his leadership "revolutionary operas" including the famous Blood Sea, the Destiny of a Vigilant, and the Flower Selling Maiden were produced and performed worldwide. He paid much attention to propaganda through literature and popular arts. As a result, big screen movies and giant stage performances blossomed during the 1970s.

In 1974 Kim Jong Il was appointed secretary of both the Organization and Supervision Department and the Propaganda Department, which were the core organs of the communist parties. The Central Committee of the WPK in February 1974 designated Kim Jong Il as heir to Kim Il Sung and vigorously extended its campaign for the succession. Since then he began to be referred to as *"the Party Center* [당중앙]" in the North Korean media without name, and began to control the daily work instead of his father. In the sixth Party Congress in 1980 Kim Jong Il was elected member of the Politburo, Party Secretary, and member of the Party Military Committee, finalizing his power succession. North Korea's official yearbook, *DPRK Central Yearbook* [조선중앙년감], has printed the names of both Kim Il Sung and Kim Jong Il in gothic, in order to make the names conspicuous, since its 1981 edition that covered the 6th WPK Congress.

Before 1981, only Kim Il Sung's name had been printed in gothic in the main contents. *DPRK Central Yearbook* 1982 was the first to include the "working visit" of Kim Jong Il to the provinces; and the DPRK Central Yearbook 1983 was the first to contain the separate section of the Kim Jong Il's writings. His first writing in the Yearbook was "On the *Juche* Idea [주체사상에 대하여]."[14] His status became almost equal to Kim Il Sung. Kim Jong Il also began to be called the Dear Leader.

Kim Jong Il strengthened his grip on power through ideological and cultural indoctrination. He proclaimed that *Juche* Thought is the only, the "Unique" guiding principle of the party and the whole society, formulated "*Kim Il Sung-ism*" [김일성주의], and proposed the "*Ten Principles of Establishing the Unique Thought system*" [유일사상체계 확립을 위한 10대 원칙]." All these were designed to enforce loyalty from the North Korean people to the Kim family "generation after generation."

Under Kim's leadership all North Korean media including papers and television channels launched a series of political education programs. These programs include "*The Course on the Principles of Juche Thought*," "*The Course on the Theory of Juche Thought*" and "*Learning Juche Thought*." These programs still air today in every form of media in many different guises and under different titles.

In 1986 Kim again introduced the "*Theory of Socio-Political Life* [사회 정치적 생명체론]."[15] This theory takes a holistic view of political organization,

---

14 *Choson Chungang Yungam* (DPRK Central Yearbook) 1983: 124–159.

15 Kim Jong Il, "*Juche*-Sasang Gyoyang-eso Chegidoenun Myutgaji Moonje-e Daehayo (주체사상교양에서 제기되는 몇가지 문제에 대하여: On several Issues regarding the Educuation of the *Juche* Thoughts)," Sunchip 8 김정일선집 (Pyongyang: Chosun Rodondang Choolpan-Sa, 1998): 432–471.

regarding a political entity as an organism. According to this theory the political leader is the brain, and the masses are the body of the organism. Without a brain, the body is as good as dead. Without a uniquely qualified leader, the state or the nation disappears in history. History demands such leaders, and the Kim's were the leaders.

The Legal System

In accordance with the *Socialist Constitution*, many laws have to be written. However, the contents of amended laws were as the same as the old ones. In most amendments, adding the *Juche* Thought and the collectivist ideas was the most conspicuous change.

The *Socialist Labor Law* of 1978[16] repeated the phrase in the *Socialist*

---

16 *Choson Chungang Yungam* (DPRK Central Yearbook) 1979: 127-136.

〈 Excerpts from the Socialist Labor Law (1978)〉

Article 3. Under socialism labor is carried out collectively by the working people for the common aims and interests.

The working people in the Democratic People's Republic of Korea work jointly, aiding and helping each other on the collectivist principle of "One for all and all for one."

Article 4. Under socialism the citizen is bound in duty to participate in labor. All able-bodied citizens in the Democratic People's Republic of Korea take part in social labor according to their abilities.

Article 5. Under socialism all working people have the right to work.

In the Democratic People's Republic of Korea unemployment has been abolished for good and all. All working people choose their occupations according to their wishes and talents and are provided with secure jobs and working conditions by the State.

Article 16. The working day is eight hours. According to the difficulty and special conditions of labor, the State may set the working day at seven or six hours.

The working day of a woman worker with three or more children is six hours.

Article 30. State institutions, enterprises and social cooperative organizations should allocate manpower correctly in accordance with sex, age, physical conditions, whishes, technical and skill levels so that the working people may give full scope to their creative wisdom and abilities.

Article 31. The State shall provide all conditions for women to participate actively in social labor.

The local government bodies and the relevant State organs, enterprises and social cooperative organizations

Constitution, claiming that it was based on the principle of collectivism, the principle of "*One for all and all for one*." All the workers have the duty and right to work. Except the collectivist principle, other clauses of the 1946 *Labor Law for Workers and Office Employees* remained almost the same. The principles of the eight hour working day and equal pay for equal work remained, with some changes in language. The protection of women was reiterated with special provision of shorter working hours for mothers.

The *Socialist Labor Law* provided maternity leave for mothers for 77 days. Since 1986 onwards, further, the duration of maternity leave was reported to be extended to 150 days, 60 days before and 90 days after the birth of the child.[17] Although there is no legal document to confirm the extension of maternity leave to five months, many North Korean refugees testified that the extension of maternity leave was instituted by Kim Jong Il.[18]

---

should build up nurseries, kindergartens, children's wards, public service facilities for the convenience of working women, and organize home industry work-teams and home cooperatives so that women who do not go to work may join them if they wish.

Article 37. Distribution by the quantity and quality of work done is an economic law of socialism; and distribution by accomplished work is an effective means of raising the working people's enthusiasm for production and technical and skill levels and stimulating the development of the productive forces.

The State thoroughly carries out the socialist principle of distribution according to the quantity and quality of work done while steadily elevating the working people's political and ideological consciousness.

Irrespective of their sexes, ages and nationalities the working people receive equal remuneration for equal work.

Article 59. The State pays special attention to the labor protection of working women.

State institutions, enterprises and social cooperative organizations should provide adequate labor protection arrangements and sanitary facilities for working women.

It is not allowed to assign arduous and unhealthy labor to women or to assign pregnant or suckling women to night work.

Article 66. In addition to the regular and additional holidays, the working women shall have an maternity leave, 35 days before and 42 days after the childbirth, irrespective of the length of their services.

17 Kyung-Hye Lee: 147.

18 Testimonies from Hyung-Soon Kang and Bong-Rye Choi. Gookto Tongilwon Tongilwon (NUB), *Bukhan Juminsaenghwal Siltae Chosa* 북한 주민생활 실태조사 (Seoul: Gookto Tongilwon, 1989): 45.

In the fifth Congress of the WPK in November 1970, Kim Il Sung proposed that public-care and public-rearing of children should be one of the major tasks for cultural revolution in communist policy. In line with Kim's proposal the nursing and upbringing of children laws were gathered into a single code in 1976. The *Law on the Nursing and Upbringing of Children* [아동보육교양법][19] was adopted at the sixth session of the Fifth Supreme People's Assembly on April 29, 1976.

The *Law on the Nursing and Upbringing of Children*, which consisted of five chapters and 58 articles, declared children to be the future, the reserves for communist builders, and successor to the revolution (Article 1). The Law also made it clear that it was guided solely by the *Juche* idea.

The Law promised that all children in public nurseries and kindergartens would be raised free of charge (Chapter 2). Chapter 2 of the law (from Article 11 to Article 21) promised the raising of children at state and public expense. Article 12 stipulated that the state and social and cooperative organizations responsible to provide everything necessary for children. Also, the state and the social and cooperative organizations were responsible for providing "*everything necessary*" for the nursing and upbringing of children in accordance with the principle: of "T*he best things* to the children." However, this clause does not mean the provision of "*everything necessary*" for completely free of charge. The children were supplied with food from the birth at the expenses borne by the state, social, and cooperative organizations. Other necessities like children's clothes, shoes, and other goods were provided at low prices.[20]

---

19 *Choson Chungang Yungam* (DPRK Central Yearbook) 1977: 214–215. See Appendix 3.

20 Article 17 of the Nursing and Upbringing of the Children.

When the economy declined severely, even the children's foods stopped to be provided. Beginning in the late 1980s, nurseries and kindergartens began to demand the parents to supply their own snacks and toys for the children. In some areas, the cost of the "snacks" was almost a quarter of the monthly wage for a parent.[21]

The essence of the *Law on the Nursing and Upbringing of Children* was also the ideological education of the children from very young age. The *Law on the Nursing and Upbringing of Children* announced that it had inherited the "brilliant revolutionary traditions created in the glorious anti-Japanese revolutionary struggle for the liberation of the country and the liberty and happiness of the people" (Article 4). Also the law was to be guided solely by *Juche* idea (Article 5). The law was to contribute "to training all of the children to be new revolutionary men of the *Juche* type" (Article 6). Nursing and upbringing of the children were, in the end, to ensure the future generations to be loyal to *Juche* idea.

Despite the new Constitution, no special progress in laws on women's status was made. Although the *Socialist Constitution* provided for the guarantee of gender equality and protection of women (Article 62) as well as the guarantee of general equality (Article 51), the content was the same. Instead, the *Socialist Constitution* promised to pay great attention to consolidating the family, the cell of society (Article 63). The family, not an individual, was declared to the cell of society. The responsibility to consolidating the family needed to be met by the family members, particularly by women.

The Constitution was based on the assumption that household chores were

---

21 Gookto Tongilwon (NUB), *Gwisoonja Jeungunul tonghaebon Bukhancheje Byunhwa Siltae*귀순자 증언을 통해 본 북한 체제변화 실태 (Seoul: National Unification Board, , 1991): 184.

to be done by women. Although the Constitution obliged the state to free wom-
en from the burdens of household chores and to guarantee all the conditions for
women to advance into the society (Article 62), it failed to make the household
work the joint responsibility of the couple. The state searched for the way of re-
lieving the burdens of women, only because women needed to enter the society.
The idea of shared responsibility of the couple over the burdens of household
chores was never conceived. All the provisions were similar in the contents to
the previous Constitution. Therefore, an enactment of a new law or an amendment of existing law for women was not needed. Not until 1990, a new law regarding women had been formulated. While the period from 1945 to 1953 was a
short but revolutionary era, the following period was a long and retroactive one.

Economic Decline

North Korea launched its first Five-Year plan (1957-1961) in 1957, and
succeeded in reaching the target value of industrial output within two and a half
years. During this period, the total value of industrial output rose more than 3.5
times, and the average growth rate of industrial output was 36.6 percent.[22] With
this economic success in background, Kim Il Sung strengthened his grip on
power.

However, the next economic plan was a total failure. North Korea
launched its first Seven-Year plan (1961-1967) in 1961, instead of 1962 as previously planned because the first Five-Year plan was completed before the target

22 *Choson Chungang Yungam* (DPRK Central Yearbook) 1962 조선중앙년감 (Pyongyang: Chosun Choongang
Tongshin-Sa, 1962): 18.

year. North Korea focused on an inward-oriented industrialization policy with the emphasis on heavy industry. Kim Il Sung believed that the route to an advanced, affluent communist economy was to be accomplished through heavy industry.[23] As a result, the first Seven-Year plan unrealistically emphasized heavy industry, causing the targets for the agricultural sector to remain unrealized by the end of the target year, 1967. Therefore, North Korea had to set additional three years in order to achieve their goal. The first Seven Year plan ended in 1970.

Facing failure in its first Seven-Year plan, North Korea tried to open its economy by importing techniques and industrial plants from the West in the early 1970s. However, the first tide of the 1973 world oil crisis left North Korea heavily indebted. Although the first Six Year Economic Development plan (1971-1976) achieved barely what it aimed for, North Korea spent a year (1977) to prepare for next plan. Despite this buffer year, the second Seven Year plan (1978-1984) was a clear failure. North Korea had to set another adjustment period for two years, from 1985 to 1986.

Even with this decline, the North Korean economy did not become desperate until the 1990s. During the 1970s and 1980s North Korea exerted itself in building many monumental structures in order to boast its socialist society, including the Tower of the *Juche* Thought, the Arch of Triumph, the Great People's Library, and the Lock Canal of the Daedong-River. However, since North Korea's economic strategy focused on the development of heavy industry, people suffered from the shortage of consumer goods.

The collapse of the East European communist countries and the Soviet

---

23 Eui-Gak Hwang, *The Korean Economies: A Comparison of North and South* (Oxford: Clarendon Press, 1993): 41-44.

Union by the end of the 1980s and early 1990s deprived North Korea of markets and investors. The world began to expect North Korea to collapse. Unexpectedly, North Korea held the Thirteenth World Festival for Young Students in July 1989. The festival seemed a great success to outsiders. Many young students from around the world, including a South Korean student, visited Pyongyang. It was one of the biggest openings for North Korea in decades. Visitors to Pyongyang praised the natural beauty of the city. The South Korean government was humiliated and ridiculed because it unsuccessfully attempted to prevent the student from going to the North. North Korea showed off its stability and its will to unification.

However, the festival was a serious failure in an economic sense. Since most of the visitors came from poor countries, mainly from former communist societies, the large cost was left to North Korea. Many refugees from North Korea claimed that the *"Arduous March,"* which officially refers to the years from 1995 to1998 and depicts the struggle for survival of the North Korean people, actually began in 1989, with the festival.

3.2 Boasting of the Emancipation of Women

The Increase of Kindergartens and Nurseries

Kim Il Sung has always demanded women to participate work outside of the home as a prerequisite for emancipation. This ideological imperative was compounded by the labor shortage after the Korean War. In the aforementioned address, *"Everything for the Post-War Rehabilitation and Development of the People's Economy"* of 1953, Kim demanded that the party should supplement and expand the labor force by massively mobilizing women.

In order to mobilize women in the labor force, the North Korean leadership resumed its effort to increase public child-care facilities as soon as the Korean War ended. In a field visit to the Chongdong Mine in 1957, Kim Il Sung instructed that building offices was not urgent, but providing nurseries was to be the priority.[24] In line with his instruction, the government made a great effort to provide nurseries and kindergartens.

The Cabinet Resolution No.84, *On Mobilizing More Women to the Economic Activities* [인민경제 각 부문에 여성들을 더욱 광범히 인입할데 대하여] of 1957[25] obliged the state and enterprises to set up and run nurseries and kindergartens without charge to parents. As a response, The Cabinet Resolution No. 46 of 1964[26] decided that every city and county government had to build three or four kindergartens and four or five nurseries in their jurisdiction. This Resolution also set up a higher criterion for qualifications of nursery governesses and kindergarten teacher: nursery governesses had to graduate from at least middle school, and kindergarten teachers from technical colleges. This Resolution obliged the local authorities to give a preferential treatment to the child-care facilities in the provision of foods and necessities.

In addition to the increased child-care facilities, mothers with many young

---

24 Kyung-Hye Lee, *Nyusung Moonje Haekyul Kyunghum*녀성문제해결경험 (Pyongyang: Sahoegwahak Choolpan-Sa, 1990): 123.

25 Gookto Tongilwon, *Bukgoe Pupryungchip 2* (Seoul: Gookto Tongilwon, 1971): 554.

26 Cabinet Resolution No. 46 "On Reforming and Strengthening the Operation of Nurseries and Kindergartens (1964.7.1): *Choson Chungang Yungam* (DPRK Central Yearbook) 1965:189.

children were allowed to have more time off for the sake of household works. The Cabinet Resolution No.23 of 1966 reduced the working day for mothers with three of more children under the age of thirteen. [27] While normal working hours were eight hours a day and six days a week, these mothers with many children only needed to work six hours a day and six days a week. If the nature of the work place did not allow for shorter work hours, working mothers could work eight hours a day and five days a week, allowing extra one day-off a week.

In 1968, the Cabinet Resolution No.56 demanded the state and the society to increase the production of children's food by setting up special work-teams in food factories and by building at least three to four special children's food facto-ries in each city or county.[28] In addition, the Cabinet Resolution No. 63 in 1969 diversified child-care facilities such as monthly, weekly and daily facilities. The Cabinet Resolution 63 also obliged the authorities to provide fresh-cooked hot meals for the children, and urged to set up special provision centers for the child-care facilities.[29] As a result, 70 percent of nursery-aged children were able to be accommodated in nurseries in 1970.[30]

Despite the negligible numbers of facilities at the initial stage and the setbacks after the Korean War, the North Korean government succeeded in in-creasing nurseries and kindergartens to accommodate almost all the target age children by the 1970s. In 1990, North Korea proclaimed again that the children

---

27 Cabiner Resolution No.23, "Regulations on the Working Hours of Working Mothers," 1966.9.27 decided; 1966.11.1 came into force. *Choson Chungang Yungam* (DPRK Central Yearbook) 1966/67: 165.

28 Jae-Han Kim, *Orini Boyuk-gyoyang Kyunghum* 어린이 보육교양 경험 (Pyongynag: Sahoe Gwahak Chulpan-Sa, 1986): 45; *Choson Chungang Yungam* (DPRK Central Yearbook)1969: 263-265.

29 Kyung-Hye Lee: 125.

30 Kyung-Hye Lee: 126.

were fully taken care of by the state and the society at a variety of facilities such as nurseries, kindergartens, special schools for the talented, and children's parks.[31] One of the most important conditions for employment of women, therefore, was fulfilled.

Table 3.2) The Increase of Kindergartens and Nurseries

Year	No. of Facilities	No. of Children
1946	64	3,918
1949	128	9,276
1953	82	3,213
1956	397	18,553
1960	12,094	689,974
1966 [1]	38,469	1,667,000
1970 [2]	8,600 (n)+6,800(k)	1,200,000 (n)+ 950,000(k)
1975 [3]	60,000	3,500,000
1990 [4]	60,000	1,660,000

Source: 1) Tae-Young Lee, *Bukhan Yusong* 북한여성(Seoul: Shilcheon Moonhack, 1988): 225.
  2) *Choson Chungang Yungam* (DPRK Central Yearbook) 1971: 255.
  3) *Choson Chungang Yungam* (DPRK Central Yearbook) 1976: 335.
  4) Speech of the DPRK head of Delegation to the 85th IPU Congress, cited by Central Radio and Pyongyang Radio Broadcasting, May 1, 1990.
  ** n= nurseries; k=kindergartens

---

31 Speech by Yun-Koo Yo, the head of the DPRK Delegation to the 85th IPU Congress. Cited by Central Radio and Pyongyang Radio Broadcasting, May 1, 1990.

Working-Classization of Women

Despite the constant demand for women to participate in the labor, there occurred a phenomenon that women retreated to home after the Armistice in 1953. The proportion of women in the industry fell by 3 percent during 1953 and 1956. The North Korean government needed to invent new measures to encourage women to work.

The first measure was the categorization of the labor forces. The Cabinet Resolution No.18 in February 1956[32] demanded the state to record all the possible labor forces and utilize the forces most effectively. This Resolution instructed the labor authorities to "investigate the labor-capable population, overhaul the labor management system and strengthen the guidance and inspection of the effective usage of labor." The investigation of the labor population included women with age, marital status and physical conditions. It became the basic document for employment of women.

The second measure was the segregation of the labor along line with the sex. Kim Il Sung mentioned several times women's physical weaknesses and the need to pay special attention to working conditions for women.[33] His demand for "special attention" for women, however, unwittingly led North Korea to segregate labor along line with sex. Women were concentrated in light industry and agriculture. The working-classization in principle required women to be engaged in the productive labor. However, women's jobs were in general centered

32 Young-Ja Park, *Bukhanui Geundaehwa Gwajong-gwa Yusungui Yukhal, 1945-1980 Nyundae* 북한의 근대화 과정과 여성의 역할 , 1945-1980년대: 공장과 가정의 정치사회와 여성노동을 중심으로 (Seoul: Ph. D Thesis, Sunggyungwan University, 2004): 46.

33 Kim, Il-Sung, "On the Revolutionization and Working-Classization of Women"; "On the Future Tasks of the Women's Union"; "On Present Internal and International Situation and the Tasks of Women" etc.

on the traditional caring works.

The Cabinet Resolution No.84, *On Mobilizing More Women to the Eco-nomic Activities*, obliged the state and the society to increase the employment of women in industries, presenting target labor participation rates of women for each industrial section: in education and health care, women should comprise more than 60 percent of workers and in other light industries more than 30 per-cent by the end of 1961.[34]

The segregation of labor by the sex was intensified with its Seven-Year Economic Plan. When North Korea launched it first Seven-Year plan in 1961, which was actually the first intensive economic development plan of its kind, it put disproportional emphasis on heavy industry. Emphasis on heavy industry called for a thorough reassignment of the labor force. North Korea launched the operation for the replacement of labor between men and women in 1962. The Cabinet Resolution No.3 of 1962 and the Cabinet Resolution No.70 of 1967 de-manded labor authorities to "firmly grasp the situation of labor capability among women who were housewives or dependant" and employ them in place of men who were to be reassigned to mines, forestry, and fisheries. This operation co-erced many housewives to be employed in light industry, replacing men for the sake of heavy industry. In 1962 alone, about 40,000 men moved from light to heavy industry.[35]

The concentration of women on the light industry was once again em-phasized by Kim Il Sung in his address in 1971. At the fourth Congress of the Democratic Women's Union, Kim Il Sung gave the speech "*On the Revolution-*

---

34 Gookto Tongilwon, *Bukgoe Pupryungchip 2* 북괴법령집 2 (Seoul: Gookto Tongilwon, 1971): 554.

35 Young-Ja Park: 54.

ization and Working Classization of Women,"[36] summarizing the most important tasks for women as the revolutionization and working-classization. In this address, Kim predicted that all distinctions in labor such as those between heavy and light industry, and between industry and agriculture would finally disappear in a communist society where the productive forces would be highly developed. Until then, however, North Korea should "replace men's work force in light labor with women's so as to let the women do easy work and men hard jobs."[37]

The Cabinet Resolution No. 84 and the 1971 speech were resonating of Kim Il Sung's concept of women's work. Caring or nurturing job or "easy work" was women's work. By concentrating women on the "women's work," North Korea was able to employ men in heavy industry.

The third measure was the creation of the "local industries." North Korea realized that urging married women to commute to distant factories and offices was ineffective and unrealistic. Since women were regarded as the only ones responsible for housework, putting women away from home was also deemed undesirable. Therefore, it became important to create works in the vicinity of the houses of married women. Kim Il Sung initiated the *"Guideline for a Dramatic Increase in the People's Consumer Goods by Developing Local Industries"* at the Plenum of the Central Committee of the WPK in June 1958.[38] This guideline demanded every county to establish at least one local industry and employ housewives. Thus establishing factories close to homes contributed to increasing both the employment of women and the production of consumer goods.

---

36 Kim Il Sung, *On the Revolutionization and Working-Classization of Women* (Pyongyang: Foreign languages Publishing House, 1974).

37 *On the Revolutionization and Working-Classization of Women*:16.

38 Kyung-Hye Lee: 91.

These "local industries" did not have to be large factories or plants. In Gaechon County, Pyongnam Province, five weaving machines in a house constituted a factory that employed several housewives and produced cloth. Women in Changsung County, Pyongbook Province operated several spinning machines in a house.[39] By operating these domestic industries, North Korea claimed that more than a thousand "local industries" were established within a month, and two thousands within a year.[40]

North Korea twice held the National Conference for Workers in the Local Industries in 1970 and 1980, encouraging people to continue to operate and strengthen local industries. By the end of 1980, local industries doubled compared to 1969, recording on average 18 industries in each county.[41]

The fourth measure to increase the participation of women in the labor was to pull women into agriculture. As North Korea resolved its labor shortage by moving the labor force from rural areas to industrial centers during its industrialization period,[42] women had to fill in the agriculture labor force. Women composed almost 80 percent of collective farmers and 70 percent of light industry workers in the early 1970s.[43] In North Korea, farmers are always depicted as women with a roll of silk cloth or a sickle, while workers are depicted as men with hammer,[44] reflecting the overwhelming proportion of women in agriculture.

---

39 Kyung-Hye Lee: 91.

40 Kyung-Hye Lee: 92.

41 Kyung-Hye Lee: 93.

42 Chang-Geun Lee, *Rodong Haejong-saop Kyunghum*로동행정사업경험 (Pyongyang: Sahoegwahak Choolpan-Sa, 1989): 80-81.

43 Yusung Gaebalwon: 63.

44 Kyung-Hye Lee: 98.

The last measure was institutional coercion. The public distribution and the mandatory work assignment obliged women to be employed. The public distribution system provided all people, in normal times, with food and basic necessities on very low state-set prices that was almost negligible. It provides employed adults with 600 grams of grain, but housewives with only 300 grams of grain. Under the constant shortage of food and consumer goods, being a housewife with half a food distribution is a luxury not affordable for ordinary people. Also it is practically impossible for unmarried women to remain at home, because the authorities assign jobs as soon as people leave high school, except for those who go to college or enter the army. The old and the married were allowed to stay at home, with some disadvantage attached. Until North Korea suffered severe economic decline during the 1990s, the public distribution and the work assignment system had been the most powerful measure to encourage women to be employed.

All these measured resulted in the "working-classization" of most women. The proportion of women in the industry surged in 1958 by 10 percent. By the end of September 1960, the number of workers in the industry and offices increased by 640,000 from 1956. The number of female workers reached up to 500,000, which was almost tripled from 170,000 in 1956.[45] The proportion of women in the industry increased to from 33.3 percent in 1961 to 34.9 percent in 1962, and 36.2 percent in 1963.[46] The proportion of women in the labor force of all industries and collective farms was reported to be 48 percent in 1976 and 49

45 *Choson Chungang Yungam* (DPRK Central Yearbook) 1961: 116.

46 Yusung Gaebalwon (Research Institute on Women's Development), B*ukhan Yusungui Chiwi-e Gwanhan Yungoo*북한여성의 지위에 관한 연구: 여성관련 법 및 정책을 중심으로 (Seoul: Yusung Gaebalwon, 1992): 62

percent in 1991.[47]

Table 3.3) The Proportion of Women in the Industry

Year	Proportion of Women in the Industry (%)
1953	26.2 %
1956	19.9 %
1958	29.0 %
1960	32.3 %
1962	34.9 %
1964	37.3 %
1971	53.7 %

Source: for 1953, 1956, 1960 and 1964, *Choson Chungang Yungam* (DPRK Central Yearbook) 1965, p.481; for 1958, and 1971, Lee, Tae-Young, *Bukhan Yusong*,1988, p.190; for 1962, *Choson Chungang Yungam* (DPRK Central Yearbook) 1963, p.234.

In fact, according to some reports, women comprised of more than half of the labor force, because women had to fill the void left by young men who were in military service for ten years. According to the Central Statistical Bureau of the DPRK, its sex-ratio rapidly dropped since the 1970s, falling to 84.2, showing an extreme anomaly in sex ratios.[48] Nicholas Eberstadt named this phenomenon the "missing males" problem, suspecting that these males were in fact mo-

---

47 For 1976, *Rodong Shinmoon*로동신문 (July 30, 1976); for 1991, in the address by Yun-Gu Yo at the 85th IPU Congress (Pyongyang: May 1, 1991).

48 Nicholas Eberstadt and Judith Banister, *The Population of North Korea* (Berkeley : Institute of East Asian Studies, University of California, Center for Korean Studies, 1992): 32.

bilized into the army. Regardless of whether these missing males were indeed in the army, the reported sex ratio would demand a high level of female participation in the labor force. Figures on the population by occupation reported by the DPRK in 1986 also provide evidence that women made up more than half of the labor force. Working-classization of women was, therefore, completed, at least in statistics.

Table 3.4) Population by Occupation in 1986

(in 1,000)

Occupation	Total	Men	Women	Proportion of Women (%)
State Worker	6,830	2,990	3,840	56
Official	2,060	855	1,205	59
Farmer	3,141	1,305	1,836	59
Coop Worker	110	41	69	63
Total	12,141	5,190	6,950	57

Source: Eberstadt and Banister, *The Population of North Korea*, UC Berkeley, 1992, p.80; Proportion of women added.

In 1993 North Korea accepted the recommendation to hold a population census by the United Nations Population Fund (UNFPA), and reported the result to the outside world for the first time.[49] The census result also contained a strange anomaly. There was a difference of 0.7 million men between the population by region (province) and the population by age. The "missing males" prob-

---

49 The census was held in January 1994, based on the date of December 31st, 1993.

lem recurred, and the total population by age was smaller than the total population by region by 0.7 million, particularly in the young men's group. The void of
these missing males certainly needed to be filled by women. The real proportion
of women in the work place, therefore, might be higher than originally reported.

Table 3.5) Population by Age and Province in 1993

Population	Total	Male	Female	Sex Ratio
By Province	21,213,378	10,329,699	10,883,679	51.30
By Age	20,522,351	9,677,663	10,844,688	52.84
Age 20-25	1,862,989	765,478	1,097,510	58.91

Source: DPRK, Population Census, 1995. Sex ratio added.

Improving Skills among the Women Workers

When North Korea recruited many women into the industry within a remarkably short period of time, most female workers had no experience or lacked
the relevant skills for their jobs. The authorities had to improve the skills and
discipline of the newly recruited workers very fast. In order to improve skills
and discipline, North Korea relied on the method of settling each worker in one
specific section of a production line and minimizing the mobility of workers.[50]

Since North Korea assumed that women should take care of the children

---

50 Young-Ja Park: 58.

and housework, settling female workers necessitated an increase of child-care and housework saving facilities in each factory, and recognition of the value of long service in one sector. The government focused first on building, or improvising, nurseries in factories where women were employed on a large scale, and urged the factories to establish ready-made food markets, cleaners, and other convenience stores. The government also provided preferential treatment for longer service: teachers of elementary and middle schools, 70 percent of whom were women, received the honor of high achievement, even without special achievement at all, after they remained at that job for more than 30 years; medical nurses, almost all of whom were women, received a bonus in their salary after 20 years of service.[51]

North Korea then emphasized on-the-job training. The government directed the factories to run skills-training classes in 1958, and demanded that workers enhance their level of skills by at least one grade for all workers in 1959.[52] These directives were issued in order to enhance skills of new workers by mobilizing skilled workers into training. Since these directives lacked enforcement mechanisms other than ideological duty, however, the training was not successful. The government once again issued the *"Regulation on Skills Training on-the-Job"* in 1959. This regulation provided punishment clauses that stipulated those who neglected training the new workers were eligible to be fined by up to 25 percent of their wages.[53] The government also instructed that the education on party policies, Kim Il Sung's works, factory labor discipline, labor protective regulations,

51 Kyung-Hye Lee: 174.

52 Young-Ja Park: 60.

53 Jong-Ok Lee, "For the Implementation of the Regulation on Skills Training on-the-Job", *Rodong* 로동 (1959, no.4): 25-27.

and the rights and duties of the workers should be accompanied by skills training.

In November 1959, the government issued Cabinet Resolution No.67 that suggested targets for the State Planning Committee and the people's committee of all levels in order to enhance labor discipline among the workers. Cabinet Resolution No.9 of 1961 provided the national standard for labor conditions including the work hours, managerial responsibilities, the rights and duties of the workers, the procedure of employment and dismissal, and punishment within the industry. These Cabinet Resolutions developed into the Regulation of the DPRK Ministry of Labor in 1965. As the result of all the efforts, North Korea claimed that it succeeded in increasing the proportion of women among "skilled workers and experts." In 1993 the proportion of women in this group reached 42%.

Table 3.6) Increase of Female Skilled Workers and Experts

(in 1,000)

Year	Total	Male	Female	Proportion of Female (%)
1963	284	241	43	15
1989	1,350	850	500	37
1993	1,790	1,030	760	42

Source: Miryang Youn, "The Social Status and Roles of Women," Sejong Institute ed., *Bukhanui Sahoe Munhwa* 북한의 사회문화(Seoul: Hanul, 2006): 475.

North Korea came to proclaim that it accomplished the emancipation of women with the full provision of child-care facilities and other labor saving institutions for mothers, the improvement of skills and qualifications among women, and with full employment of women.[54] However, in reality, North Korea succeeded in only mobilization of women in the labor force. The segregation of the labor along line with the sex was enforced by the state. Women were concentrated in the "womanly" work. The women's jobs were in general less rewording than men's. In the society as well, women were supposed to be polite and submissive to men. Women were under-represented in the politics and the top jobs. Women in North Korea were not emancipated at all.

3.3 Working-Classization in Traditional Gender Relations

A Working-Class Performing Unproductive Works

The failure in the emancipation of women was not unique in North Korea. The inequality between the sexes had been in existence since the prehistoric era. Although modern democracies began to promise equality of all spheres, the concept of feminine womanhood and masculine men remained strong in most societies. Legal guarantee and the economic employment of women fell short of changing the gender relations in the society. The persistent gender inequality

---

54 Speech by Yun-Koo Yo; and the book by Kyung-Hye Lee etc.

was an omnipresent phenomenon of the world. However, there were some idiosyncrasies in the case of North Korea.

The first idiosyncrasy of North Korea came from Kim Il Sung's idea on women's work. Kim Il Sung held the absolute power of final decision, and could have succeeded in changing gender relations in North Korea. However, his idea on women's work itself was woven by the traditional concept of womanhood. He cherished the traditional concept of womanhood and women's work. In one of his many hagiographies, he demanded women to be feminine in the way that "Korean women had long kept throughout the history." Kim Il-Sung was reportedly emphasizing the importance of keeping the traditional virtue of Korean women. He demanded female members to keep their appearance clean and tidy despite the harsh environment during the guerrilla warfare.

In the summer of 1936, the Great Leader was commanding the Korean People's Revolutionary Army (in the war against the Japanese) in a small village in Musong area. One day, female members of the guerrilla army were taking a time for rest with the Great Leader. The Great Leader explained the miserable life of Korean women who were disdained and abused at that time. He praised the female members of their great performance in the struggles. He continued to give a priceless lesson for the female members.

"Of course it is very important for women to fight for their emancipation and their rights. One of our goals in waging war is also to achieve emancipation. However, women should not focus on their emancipation and rights only. Women should not forget the beautiful and noble virtues of Korean women that Korean women had long kept throughout the history. ... Women should be feminine. Your courteous and humble behavior will enhance your dignity, and thus make you respected and trusted. In this sense, our female members should set a good example for the local people."

He continued to explain the beauty of the virtuous nature of Korean women in the history of the Courteous Nation in the East [동방예의지국]. ....

The Great Leader always paid special attention to the life of female members. He said that female guerilla members were so conspicuous among the people that women should always bring with them an extra skirt (to keep their appearance tidy).

This anecdote reveals his idea on femininity. Women should remember, and hence emulate, the traditional virtues of Korean women. Women should be courteous, humble, and tidy in their appearances, wearing always clean "skirt." This idea led him to the concept of "unproductive" women's work.

Kim Il Sung often urged the party to employ women specifically "in office works such as merchant, postal services, health, cultural and educational occupations." He analyzed that women were physically weaker than men; therefore the authorities should "replace men's work force in light labor with women's so as to let the women do easy work and men hard jobs."[55] In other occasion, he suggested that women should do office jobs "so that men were free to do the production."[56]

In fact, his idea of the working class was not clear and consistent. While he demanded women to participate in "productive labor," he also urged the party and society to employ women in care-taking jobs in order to allow men to do the "production." While believed that household chores should be done by women, housework and caring for other people were regarded as "non-production" as well. All these addresses prove that he regarded most of women's work as supplementary to men's work and unproductive. Women's works were only

55 *On the Revolutionization and Working-Classization of Women*:16.

56 *Choson Chungang Yungam* (DPRK Central Yearbook) 1954–55: 4.

to free men to do the production.

His idea of non-productive women's work was also reflected in the North Korean labor system. North Korea divided the category of labor as industry, agriculture, construction, maintenance, mining, architecture, transportation, communications, machinery, merchandizing, service, purchase, food distribution, civil engineering, education, culture, health, and science. It also categorizes labor as "productive" and "non-productive" labor. Productive labor was comprised of industry, agriculture, construction, transportation, mining, fishery, architecture, and machinery, while non-productive labor was comprised of merchandizing, services, food distribution, civil-engineering, education, culture, health, and science.[57] Except for agriculture and light industry, most of the women's work was regarded as "non-productive."

Working-classization of women in North Korea, therefore, meant that mobilization of women into the supplementary and unproductive works. Kim Il Sung' ideas of women's work and the working-classization of women ended in creating a working class performing unproductive work. The full employment of women in this labor structure was to support and sustain the traditional gender relations.

Power Succession and Women

The second idiosyncrasy of North Korea emerged from the political power succession. The dynastic power succession from father to son in a proclaimed

---

57 Chang-Guen Lee, *Woori Dang-e uihan Rodong Haejongrironui Shimhwa Baljon*우리당에 의한 로동행정 리론의 심화발전 (Pyongyang: Sahoegwahak Choolpan-Sa, 1992): 77.

socialist country required a convincing logic for legitimacy. North Korea resorted to reinstating the traditional concept of succession.

When Kim Il Sung consolidated his power within the party and called for
the *"revolutionization and working-classization of the whole society"* in 1966,
he launched a campaign for personality cult of the whole Kim family. The revolutionization required to intensify ideology education and establish the Unique
System in the whole society. The ideology education came to be, in reality, the
personality cult of Kim Il Sung and the Kim family. All the members of the Kim
family were all praised as heroes of Korean people. Kim Il-Sung's grandfather,
Kim Bo-Hyun, was depicted as the leader of the anti-foreign invasion struggle
that destroyed the *USS Sherman*. Kim's father, Kim Hyung-Jick was described
as an independent activist and teacher, and his uncles and brothers as having all
fought against Japanese colonialism.

One of the most important figures of the Kim family was Kim's mother,
Kang Ban-Sok. As soon as the book titled *Let's Follow the Model of Lady Kang
Ban-Suck* [강반석 녀사를 따라배우자][58] was published in 1967, women were
mobilized into classes and lectures to learn about Kang. The Women's Union
launched intensive education campaigns for its members. It organized study
groups in every town and county. Its monthly magazine, *the Korean Women*,
published many serials examining and understanding the life of Kang.

Kang Ban-Sok was born into a family with progressive and revolutionary
traditions – a different kind of noble blood. She cherished the qualities of indus-
triousness and caring. She supported her husband's revolutionary struggle and
carried the burden of all household chores and the hard labor required to support

---

58 *Let's Follow the Model of Lady Kang Ban-Suck* 강반석 녀사를 따라배우자 (Tokyo: Chosun Chungnyun, 1967).

resistance members. She never complained to her parents-in-laws and never uttered bad words towards others. Kang allegedly cooked more than ten times a day for the family and for the resistance. Even when she fell ill, she sewed overnight for the young resistance members. North Korea officially claimed that she had established a women's organization for independence, *Anti-Japanese Women's Association* [반일부녀회] in 1920, which became the embryo organization of the Democratic Women's Union of Korea.

She also taught Kim Il Sung to be the true leader of Korean people. When the baby Kim Il-Sung began to learn how to speak, Kang Ban-Sok taught her son first of all how to call his grandparents and parents properly, educating him to say not "mom" or "dad", but "grand father" or "father." After Kim Il-Sung learned many words, Kang-Ban-Sok made a song that was intended to cultivate a great vision in the young mind.

The sky is high and infinite,
The earth is vast and boundless.
You will be in the future
Higher and Vaster than the sky and earth.[59]

All these "virtues" of Kang are resonant of those of traditional noblewomen: obedient to husbands and parents-in-laws; refraining from talking; industrious in work; and intelligent enough to teach children. Traditional womanhood was thus to be reinstated.

The Great Mother Lady Kang Ban-Sok never answered back or excused herself to

---

59 *Let's Follow the Model of Lady Kang Bansuck* 강반석 녀사를 따라배우자 (Tokyo: Chosun Chungnyun, 1967).

the parents-in-laws. She took the blame even when her brothers-in-law or sisters-in-law made mistakes, and said that was her fault. "I made a mistake. Please forgive me. I am going to undo the wrongs in the future." Covering up her mistakes was out of question.[60]

(When guerrilla warriors abruptly visited her during the 1930s) Whenever they came, the Great Mother warmly welcomed them despite her illness. Although she had to rely on a bowl of porridge made out of wild greens a day, or skipped meals, she always kept aside a small amount of rice for the young warriors. Whenever the warriors came, she treated them with bowls of hot rice. At nights, she mended their worn-out clothes and (hand-made) shoes by knitting and needling.... If young warriors presented her with medicine, she never used it for herself. She used it for warriors instead....

The Great Mother with her whole heart prepared the uniform for her son in order to protect him from the enemy bullets, piercing cold, and from rain and snow during the days when the Great General (Kim Il Sung) was leading the military to anti-Japanese armed struggle.[61]

The idolization of Kang was, however, soon replaced by the cult of Kim Jong-Suk, Kim Jong Il's mother. After Kim Jong Il was appointed secretary of both the Organization Department and the Supervision and Propaganda Department, a statue and a museum of Kim Jong-Suk were constructed in her birth place in October 1974. Since then, Kim Jong-Suk and Kang Ban-Sok have been called the Great Mothers. Both were called as the mother of the revolution. However, as Kim Jong Il came to exercise as much power as his father did, the

---

60 *Kang Ban-Sok Nyusarul Ddara Baewooja*: 24.

61 "Remembering the days of Building the Anti-Japanese Military Coalition," *Chosun Nyusung* (조선녀성: Korean Women), April-May 1981 (Pyongyang: Chosun Minjoo Nysung Dongmaeng, 1981): 32.

eulogy of Kim Jong-Suk overshadowed that of Kang.

In 1978 two books, *Hyukmyungui Omoni* [혁명의 어머니: The Mother of the Revolution]"[62] and *Boolyo-boolgoolui Hyukmyung Toosa Kim Jong-Suk Dongjirul Hoesanghayu* [불요불굴의 혁명투사 김정숙 동지를 회상하여: Memoir of the Invincible Revolutionary Warrior, Comrade Kim Jong-Suk]"[63] were published. The first book claimed that Kim Jong-Suk had first been revered and praised in a book published in South Korea, and that it was a reprinted version of former one. Since then, Kim Jong-Suk was begun referred to as *"the Royal Guard* [친위전사]," emphasizing her role as the most loyal bodyguard to Kim Il Sung. When Kim Jong Il became the official heir in 1980, the names of her birthplace, a teacher's college, and a women's high school in the region were changed to bear her name.[64] *Chuson Yusung* (Korean Women), the official magazine of the Women's Union, continues to run many serials related to Kim in the 2000s under the title of "Following the Heroin in the Anti-Japanese Struggle, Comrade Kim Jong-Suk" and so on.

Kim Jong-Suk has also been described as being as obedient and loyal to her husband as Kang was. A few differences are found, however, due to an absence of parents-in-laws for Kim, since she met Kim Il Sung after his parents passed away, and due to the fact that she was a warrior during the armed struggle. Kim was reported to have been indeed an excellent shooter and agile warrior. She was allegedly so loyal and obedient to her husband that she tip-

---

62 See, *Hyukmyongui Omoni*혁명의 어머니 (Pyongyang: Inmoon Gwahak-Sa, 1978).

63 Chosun Rodongdang Ryuksa Yungooso, *Boolyo-boolgoolui Hyukmyung Toosa Kim Jong-Suk Dongjirul Hoesanghayu* 불요불굴의 혁명투사 김정숙 동지를 회상하여 (Pyongyang: Geumsung-Chungnyun Choolpan-Sa, 1978).

64 Decision of the Central People's Committee (1987.8.17), *Choson Chungang Yungam* (DPRK Central Year-book) 1982: 83-84.

toed when she walked past where Kim Il Sung was working, and chopped fire-wood silently in order to not disturb her husband's rest.[65] In a famous movie, "The Royal Guard," she was depicted to provide her husband with a pair of foot warmers made of her own hair.[66] Several times during the independence struggle Kim saved the life of her husband with her bravery and her absolute loyalty to Kim Il Sung. In the famous group sculpture called *the Water of the Mother-land*, Kim Jong-Suk is poised as kneeling and offering to her husband a cup of water with both hands. This posture is the most succinct symbol of Kim Jong-Suk, *the Royal Guard*, who is so loyal and obedient to her husband.

She was also presented as a great teacher. She provided full explanations to her son's inquiries; she was strict with regard to disciplines but very gener-ous in love and care; she never used a bad word in any circumstances; and she taught him not only reading and arithmetic, but also history and culture. Given the fact that she did not receive any formal education, her alleged erudition was apparently unconvincing.

One snowy afternoon, Kang Kil-Bok carelessly put the broom and dustpan into a barn after sweeping the snow. The Great General was about to go out to office, and saw this. The Great General looked into the barn and said: "Brooms and dustpan should be cleaned completely after use." Then he tried to reach the broom and dustpan. At that moment, Lady Kim Jong-Suk in no time came to the Great Gener-al, and picked the broom and dustpan. She said in a humble attitude: "It's my fault. I will do it again." She cleaned them and put them away with utter caution.... She always answered "yes, Sir" to her husband. When some women asked her why she was so polite to her husband even after having children together, she said that: "At

---

65 "Choongsungui Ssiasul Ppoorisimyo (Planting the Seeds of Loyanty)," *Chosun Nyusung*, July 1982, 1982): 16.

66 Film "Chinwi Jonsa"(The Royal Guard: 1984); "Chinwi Jonsaui Soonggohan Googam (The Sublime Model of the Royal Guard)," *Chosun Nyusung*, April 1984: 15–16.

any time and in any place, I always respect him as the Commander-in-Chief and the Great Leader of our nation."[67]

The Mother of Revolution, Lady Kim Jong-Suk devoted herself to make her son the communist revolutionary with intelligence, virtue, physical strength and many-sided learning. The young son was really intelligent and well-talented. In particular, he was gifted in arts. The revered Lady respected all the talents of her son, and paid meticulous attention to education in order to fully cultivate all of his talents.... She taught her son how to read and write at a very early age. She also educated him with history, nature, geology and other knowledge. Moreover, she taught him songs, dances, games, as well as painting and handicrafts. In the evening, she told him stories. Those stories were not simple pastime things. Those stories had morality and instruction. She told him stories with the intention of education.[68]

Kim Jong-Suk also tried to be seen as virtuous in traditional terms. Although she was a guerilla warrior, Kim Jong-Suk regarded household work as women's "duty as women."[69] She demanded women to take the whole burden of housework by themselves. She also urged women to be feminine and pretty. At the congratulatory gathering for the promulgation of the *Sex Equality Law* in 1946, she warned women not to misunderstand the law.

"We should not forget our duty and virtue as women. We should be strong and adamant in revolution, but feminine and polite in daily life. Our language and attitude should be polite and fine."
The Lady instructed us that women should have good etiquette, be harmonious

67 "Hyukmyungui Omoni Kim Jong-Suk Nyusarul Mosigo (My Memory on the Mother of Revolution, Lady Kim Jong-Suk)," *Chosun Nyusung*, February 1982: 29–36.

68 "Chinhee Gyosaga Doesiyo (Assuming the Role of the Teacher)," *Chosun Nyusung*, December 1981: 25.

69 Kim Jong-Suk's alleged comment from "Gwijoonghan Jichim (Priceless Instructions)," *Chosun Nysung*, July 1982: 15

with neighbors, serve the husbands and in-laws well and dress properly as well as tightly manage the properties of the nation and the collective.[70]

The descriptions of the Great Mothers were so saintly that it is almost impossible for a human being to behave like them. They were depicted as altruistic, devoted, sacrificial, intelligent, enduring and perseverant. Any religion would canonize them. However unrealistic they might be, these descriptions were indicating the ideal women of the North Korean leadership. The panegyrics of the Great Mothers painted them as invincible warriors in the struggle against the enemy, loyal and virtuous wives to their husbands, and devoted and wise mothers to their sons. It was perfectly resonating of the Confucian virtues of noble women of the *Chosun* Dynasty. A woman's virtues were chastity, submissiveness, patience, quietness, compliance and equanimity without jealousy. The dynastic power succession to Kim Jong Il, therefore, resulted in fully reinstating the traditional patriarchal order in gender relations in the society.

3.4 Patriarchal Order in the Family

Subjugation of Wives

During the early stage of the regime, the government and the party attempted to reduce the influence of familial relationships and to dissolve the traditional patriarchal family. However, as the communists consolidated power, the

---

70 "Gwijoonghan Jichim (Priceless Instructions)," *Chosun Nyusung*, July 1982: 15

family was re-evaluated as the cell of the society. Re-evaluation of the family ended in reinstating the traditional women's role as wise mothers and good - i.e., submissive - wives. The personality cult of the Great Mothers also contributed to a great extent to the expectation that women needed to be wise mothers and submissive and obedient wives.

Even though the government emphasized the importance of women's labor outside the home and tried to enhance the role of women in society, the women's situation within the family remained unchanged. Men were regarded as the head, the main breadwinner, and the protector of the family. Women were considered to be secondary supporters for the family and subjugated to men. The authorities were eager to educate women to be submissive to husbands and in-laws in order to make the family peaceful and happy.

The *Chollima*, the only public magazine of North Korea, and with more than 120 million circulations, taught women to refer to their husbands as "our master" or "our headship," not as "my husband," while men refer to their wives as "my wife" or "my housekeeper." Women should talk to their husbands "with deep respect" and "with carefully selected words" for them.[71] The Women's Union also instructed women to be docile and kind to in-laws and neighbors.

> In order to be suitable to simple, soft and docile characteristics of our women in Chosun, we should express ourselves in a womanly way so that we can show our refined and cultivated manner.
> Our women will face parents-in-laws, husbands, guests and neighbors everyday. Bright faces and docile and kind words of our women will greatly influence the

---

71 "Booboo Sai-e Choogo Banun Mal (Mutual Designations between Spouses)," *Chollima* 천리마, April-May 1981: 118-119; "*Sedaejoorul Boorusun Mal* (How to Refer to the Head of the Family)," *Chollima*, November 1988: 80.

harmony and mutual respect among the neighbors.[72]

Docility was one important requirement for married women. Stubborn wives were regarded to deserve being beaten by their husbands. Domestic violence was reported as a common practice. Many women refugees invariably testified that nine out of ten wives were subject to domestic violence by their husbands.[73] Domestic violence is not yet recognized as violence by the law. People regard domestic violence as a typical familial affair that should not be the concern of other people.

In North Korea, particularly in rural areas, many married couples live with their parents, mostly with the parents of their husbands. Taking care of the in-laws, therefore, has been one of the most difficult tasks of married women. In order to keep the family peaceful, it should be the daughter-in-law who is to be sacrificed.

We, the daughters-in-laws, should well understand, deeply respect and faithfully serve our mothers-in-laws so that the families would be harmonious. When the families are harmonious, we can do our job better. It may seem a trivial matter how we young women serve our mothers-in-laws. However, it is in fact a matter of the revolutionization of the family, and a matter of crucial importance. The family that is the cell of society should be revolutionized in order to revolutionize the whole society. Therefore, it becomes a huge matter.[74]

---

72 "Yusungui Onowa Kyoyang The Language of Women and Civility," *Chosun Nyusung, January* 1990: 36–37.

73 Miryang Youn, "Yusungui Chiwiwa Yukhal," *Bukhanui Sahoe Moonhwa* 북한의 사회문화 ed. by Bukhan Yun-goo Center, Sejong Institute (Seoul:, Hanul, 2006): 492–494.

74 "Chaguen Moonjega Anida," *Chosun Nyusung*, September 1981: 48.

Many novels and films, which followed the party policy and presented the desirable way how people should think and behave, depicted female characters as devoted workers and committed communists as well as docile wives to their husbands. A housewife of a university professor rushed to the campus with an umbrella as soon as a drop of rain fell; she also stayed awake all night making tea and snack while her husband was working overnight.[75] In a certain novel, a woman was always worried about whether her cooking pleased her husbands or not; although she was employed, she also tried hard to come home during lunch time in order to prepare a "hot meal" for her husband.[76]

Marriage, Divorce and Remarriage

In North Korea, marriage was, and largely still is, regarded almost mandatory. If a woman did not get married before her thirties, people suspected that she had some disturbing secret or unforgivable past. Only devoted labor heroines were excused to remain single. In fact, many labor heroines in novels and films were depicted as unmarried because they were so devoted to their work that they could not afford personal lives. Nevertheless, labor heroes were never depicted unmarried.

Until the end of the 1970s the government encouraged, and in a sense imposed, late marriage. Since the government regarded the household chores as women's work, making married women devote time to their job had limitations.

---

75 Bohaeng Kim, *Rodong Gajong*로동가정 (Pyongyang: Moonye Choolpan-Sa, 1979): 123.

76 Ohn-Jook Lee, "Yusunggwa Gajong Saenghwal," *Bukhan Yusungui Saenghwal Siltae*북한여성의 생활실태, ed. by Bong-Sook Sohn: 1991): 73-74.

Married men also had to take care of the family. Therefore the government urged people to work hard to build the socialist country, postponing marriage. While the marriage age by law was 17 for women and 18 for men, the average age for the first marriage was reported at 26~28 for women and 30~31 for men because of the late marriage policy.[77] However, because of the economic decline, the government relaxed its late marriage policy after the 1980s. Partly because of the relaxation of the late marriage policy, and partly because of the coming of age of the baby-boomers of the early 1960s, the number of marriages per 1,000 population surged during the 1980s.

Until the end of the 1980s, the most desired groom was a man with party membership. Members of the WPK were assigned to powerful jobs and exerted a great influence over every aspect of daily lives. They were given better and larger quantities than others in the public distribution system as well. The next was an engineer, a technician, or those who were engaged in foreign trade, because they had a specific means of living or access to foreign goods. By comparison, men picked wives mostly on the criterion of beauty. Both men and women had to take the family background of the other party into account. In many cases, a man or a woman was deserted by their fiancé on the grounds of a bad family background.

While there had been relatively high rate of divorces until the early 1950s, divorce rates reduced to half after divorce by consent was rescinded. The major causes of divorce were adultery, abuse by the husband and in-laws, chronic disease and "counter-revolutionary" behavior of a spouse. While the most common reason for filing divorce was adultery, the most certain cause for getting

---

77 See testimonies of the refugees in *Bukhan, Geu Choongkyukui Silsang* 북한 그 충격의 실상 (Seoul: Chosun Ilbo-Sa, A separate-volume Supplement for *Wolgan Chosun*, Jasnuary 1991).

divorce was counter-revolutionary behavior, or even suspicion, of a party. The term "counter-revolutionary" could be applied to a variety of attitudes, behavior, speech, performances and familial lineages. The descendants of landlords or nobles could be easily suspected to be counter-revolutionary. Treating the pictures of Kim Il Sung and Kim Jong Il badly was certainly counter-revolutionary, if not treasonous. If a relative of a spouse became involved in political crime, the WPK sometimes urged the other spouse to file divorce, because one having relatives who were charged with political crimes was also in danger of becoming counter-revolutionary.

When the court decided divorce, it also determined child custody. Many refugees reported that the court tended to rule in favor of mothers. If a mother insisted on keeping her child, the court sometimes ordered the father to pay for child allowance, but not always. Divorce itself was a stigma for both men and women, because divorce was considered to be the evidence of relaxed morality or of some defects.

Table 3.7) Marriage and Divorce

Year	The Numbers of		Marriage Per 1,000 Population	Divorce Rate	
	Marriage (A)	Divorce (B)		Per 1,000 Population	Per Marriage (B/A *100)
1953	30,564	3,453	3.9	0.4	11.5
1956	107,098	4,124	11.4	0.4	3.9
1965	107,493	3,021	8.7	0.2	2.8
1970	86,639	3,971	5.9	0.2	4.6
1975	84,819	3,714	5.3	0.2	4.4
1980	99,871	4,359	5.8	0.2	4.4
1985	142,753	4,526	7.6	0.2	3.2
1987	188,007	4,231	9.7	0.2	2.3

Source: Youn, Miryang, *Women in Two Nations and Four States*, LSE Ph.D. Thesis, 1997, p.237.
· Calculation based on the numbers of marriage, divorce and population.
· The numbers of marriages and divorces were reported by the Central Statistics Bureau (CSB) of the DPRK and cited by Eberstadt and Banister, 1992, p.64; the numbers of population were reported by the CSB and cited by Eberstadt and Banister, 1992, p.22.

Remarriage of women was less common than that of men. Even though the law and the communist party advocated the right of widows to remarry, remarriage of women was regarded as less-desirable, if not undesirable, by a majority of the population. Most female characters of films and novels tended to be depicted as unmarried and labor heroines after their only love had left them.[78] Widowed mothers also struggled to educate their children alone, never to get married again. However, men's remarriages were assumed to be natural. Wed-

---

78 See North Korean films "Doraji Kkot (Balloon Flowers:도라지꽃, 1987)" and "Yul-nebun-che Gyuool (The 14th Winter: 열 네번째 겨울, 1980)" etc.

ding ceremonies for a second, or third, marriage are very rare, though.

Praising Motherhood with Enforced Birth Control

North Korea praised motherhood, and for a while adopted pro-natal policies. Two months after Kim Il Sung consolidated his power at the Fourth Congress of the WPK in September 1961, he held the National Mothers' Conference [전국 어머니대회] in Pyongyang. The leaders of all levels of the Women's
Unions and selected exemplary mothers gathered together at this conference.
Kim Il Sung gave an address, *"Mothers' Task in the Up-bringing of the Children* [자녀교양에서의 어머니들의 임무]." In this speech, he emphasized that: first,
the methods of the up-bringing of the children should be a positive inspiration;
second, mothers themselves should be a communist for the up-bringing; third, it
was necessary to carry out a campaign that urged mothers to take good care of
the children and the houses, and to prevent illnesses among children; fourth, the
Women's Union should take more active role in education of the children.[79]

After this Conference, the Women's Union established "Mothers' School"
all over the country, and exerted itself to mold mothers as communists. The
communist mothers referred to working mothers who were actively engaged in
the labor out side of the home, and who at the same time bare the burden of the
up-bringing of the children and home making alone. In the first Plenum of the
Third Supreme People's Assembly, the head of the Women's Union proudly reported that women were shouldering triple burdens as wives, mothers and labor

---

79 Miryang Youn, *Bukhanui Yusung Chongchaek*북한의 여성정책: 136.

heroines.

> In the era of the WPK, we women are enjoying the life of worth and happiness in
> every aspect of the state life including politics, economy and culture, by the deep
> love and parental care of Great Leader Kim Il Sung....Today we women are, as
> prudent housewives and loving mothers as well as Chollima heroines that were
> reborn by the education of the Party, strenuously fighting for the happiness of our
> own and the prosperity of our nation in every front of the socialist revolution.[80]

While continuously emphasizing motherhood, the North Korean government enforced birth control during the 1970s when North Korea began to feel
the economic slowdown. At first the government relied on the voluntary cooperation of the married couple to limit the number of children to three. If a married
couple wanted to have a contraceptive, the health authority provided it free of
charge. The contraceptive method was basically uterine loops. Contraceptive
pills were not available. Since the uterine loops were made of metallic material
and manufactured primitively, there were many side-effects like back pain and
bleeding. Therefore most women avoided the loops.

By the late 1970s the government reinforced birth control. The government demanded the family to limit the number of children to two, and mobilized
the Women's Union to educate women for birth control. Kim Jong Il was reported to mention that: "No-child is not bad. One child is good. Two children are ac-
ceptable. But those who have three or more children have no sense of honor."[81]

80 Gookto Tongilwon, *Choigo Inmin-Hoeui Charyochip 2* 최고인민회의 자료집 2 (Seoul: Gookto Tongilwon):
1140-1142.

81 Testimony of Man-Chol Kim, Re-quoted from Ki-Won Chung, "Nambukhanui Ingoo Goojo Byunhwa,"
Bundan Ban-Segi Nambukhanui Sahoe-wa Moonhwa 분단 반세기 남북한의 사회와 문화, ed.by Geukdong
Moonje Yungooso (Institute of Far Eastern Studies), Kyungnam University (Seoul: IFES Press, 1996): 41.

His instruction urged the authorities to carry out more active campaign for birth control. Several refugees reported that birth control was almost compulsory in 1974 that the number of births that year was actually dropped significantly.[82]

North Korea reported to the Fourth Conference on Population of Asia-Pacific Region that the rate of contraceptive practice among the married women was 68 percent in urban areas, and 53 percent in rural areas.[83] However, after the famine during the mid-1990s claimed numerous lives and reduced the population of North Korea, the government changed its policy and encouraged people to have more children. Nevertheless, women tried to avoid pregnancy during economic crisis.

Daily Life of Married Women

As menial works were expected to be done by women, almost all the household tasks were expected to be done by wives. For most North Korean men, helping wives with shopping was regarded as degrading, even if there was no car or cart to move heavy goods like a 20 kg bag of rice. Helping wives in cooking or changing diapers for their own children were out of the question. They should be masculine and dominating. This resulted in a chronic lack of sleep and overwork for married women. Most married women with children could only afford around four or five hours of sleep. If they had to work overtime or if anyone of their household was sick, married women had to sacrifice

---

82 Testimony of Mr. Lee who was born in 1974. Interview by Sejong Institute (November 7, 2002).

83 Ki-Won Chung: 41

their sleep even more.

Table 3.8) Daily Time Table of Married Women

Time	Women's Task	Other Family
05:30~06:00	Wake-up and Preparing Breakfast	
06:00~06:30	Breakfast and Preparing for Work	Wake-up and Breakfast
06:30	Drop Children to Nursery or Kindergarten	
07:00	Arrive at Work Place	Arrive at Work Place
07:00~07:30	Study Meeting (Ideology Education)	
07:30~08:00	Work Instructions	
08:00~12:00	Work Hour Breast-Feeding for 30 minutes	
12:00~13:00	Lunch (**at Home with the Family**, in general)	
13:00~14:00	Group Recreation/Exercise	
14: 00~18:00	Work Hour Breast-Feeding for 30 minutes	14:00~16:00 Voluntary Labor (Elementary School Pupil)
18:00~19:00	Work Evaluation Meeting	
19:00~20:00	Pick-up the Children and Return Home	Men: Study Meeting
20:00~21:00	Preparing for Supper	Men: Return Home
21:00~24:00	Supper, Dish-Wash, House Cleaning and Hand-Laundering	Men: Supper and Sleep

* Extract Women's Schedule from "Basic Time Table of North Koreans," in Seo, Dong-Ik, 1995, Vol.2, p.89.

In the daily time table of married women, one peculiarity attracts attention. In general, married women came back home during lunch time, and served a hot meal to their family.[84] Several factors contributed to this peculiar phenomenon. First, restaurants and cafeterias for lunch were very rare in North Korea. Even where there was a restaurant, people had to produce two documents to have meal in the restaurant: the food ticket and a certificate of approval for dining out from the authorities. Without the two documents, people could not use the restaurants. Using restaurants was, therefore, out of the question for the ordinary workers. The responsibility to feed their family in this circumstance fell on women. Second, making lunch bag was more difficult than preparing meal at home because foodstuffs easy to carry were rare in North Korea. Third, coming back home during lunch time was not wasting long time since most people were employed or enrolled in school near their home. And Fourth, and most interesting, people took it for granted to have lunch at home irrespective of whether the wife was employed or not. Preparing meals was regarded as the duty of the wives, no matter what.

Although the labor laws reduced working hours for mothers with young children, all the household chores and caring of children consumed longer hours than the reduced work hours. In the case of unemployed women, they were expected to attend longer hours of political study, meetings of the Women's Union and voluntary labor.

---

84 Testimony of Bong-Rye Choi. Gookto Tongilwon, *Bukhan Juminsaenghwal Siltae Chosa* 북한 주민생활 실태 조사 (Seoul: Gookto Tongilwon, 1989): 15.

3.5 Male Superiority in the Society

In Education System: Molding "Feminine" Women

Since 1972, North Korea has provided eleven years of compulsory school-ing, for children ages five to sixteen. Compulsory schooling includes one year of kindergarten, four years of elementary school, and six years of secondary (middle and high) school attendance. After eleven years of schooling, students have to choose whether to advance to higher education, which depends on the class of the student's family, or to enter the labor force. For males, military service was an attractive alternative for decades, which also depended on the class of the family.

Kim Il Sung presented the *Theses on Socialist Education* in 1977, claim-ing to prescribe the fundamental principles of socialist pedagogy. He suggested that the fundamental principles of socialist pedagogy consisted in revolution-izing, working-classizing and communizing men and women. He emphasized the importance of ideology. In the same vein, he emphasized the importance of combining theory and practice and connecting education and production. In accordance with the Theses, the North Korea educational curriculum provided overwhelming class hours for *Juche* ideology and vocational preparation. In the elementary school, pupils learn basic reading, writing and arithmetic, and the life and philosophy of Kim Il Sung. In secondary school, students begin training in science and technology, in addition to the *Juche* Thoughts. North Korean uni-versities, with the only exception being Kim Il Sung University, are more like vocational institutes than scholarly ones. North Korea also encourages people to improve their technique and knowledge by attending factory or farm colleges. These factory or farm colleges provide a complementary system of study-while-working for adults.[85]

North Korea tended to segregate the courses along line with the sex. Male and female pupils were separated from the elementary school onwards; elementary schools also ran separate boys' and girls' classes; and secondary schools were all single-sex establishments until the 1990s, except for a few special schools for the privileged or gifted.[86] Official curricula for boys and girls were also different: in secondary school, girls' schools offered home economics, embroidery, sewing and knitting as compulsory courses whereas boys' schools offered basic electricity and mechanical training.

In school curriculum, "femininity" was emphasized for girls. Femininity in North Korea meant being polite, courteous, quiet, modest, compliant, and submissive. Therefore girls should be educated to be feminine from a very early age on. Girls were required to be more polite, more courteous and quieter than boys. Girls were not assumed to walk through where boys gathered around. Girls were not allowed to show their teeth or open their mouths wide while their laughing – i.e., women should hide their mouth while laughing.[87] The two most often heard teachings for girls were "women should be feminine" and "women should be modest and clean." Teachers even told them that girls should not stand against boys.[88] In most cases, school regulations demanded that girl students wear skirts,

---

85 However, the quality of these factory- and farm-colleges is so poor that South Korea does not recognize these institutes as higher education equivalent.

86 Toikoo, Keiko, *Travel Sketches of North Korea*, Jiusiki Eijia Publisher, Tokyo, 1982

87 Moo-Sook Min and Jae-Hee Ahn: 200.

88 Moo-Sook Min and Ja-Hee Ahn: 201.

except when they were mobilized to participate in voluntary labor.

There were segregation and hierarchy of roles between boys and girls. Girls took easy tasks, while boys took hard work or commanding jobs. Girls were always required to take orders from boys. The highest position was always to be filled with a boy, the second with a girl in co-ed schools.

After eleven years of compulsory education, about 16 percent of high school graduates advanced to universities and colleges, and a third of these became full-time students.[89] At least one vocational college was open in each city or county, comprising 600 colleges and accommodating about 180,000 students in 1987.[90] There were 46 teachers' colleges and the First and Second Pedagogical Universities, 77 factory colleges, 22 technological colleges and 16 agriculture and fishery colleges in 1982.[91]

The proportion of university and college students in the population was estimated at 1.46 percent in 1987.[92] Although there are entrance examinations for each college or university, the final decision for admission is to be made by local party committees which review teachers' reports in the elementary and secondary schools. In this admission procedure, the first requirement is the family background of the students, and the second is the loyalty and devotion of the students to the party. Academic achievements and potential come last.

North Korea reported that the proportion of women in universities and colleges was 35.2 percent in 1988. The proportion of women among university

---

89 See Insook Nam, *Nambukhan Yusung, Geuduleun Noogooinga?* 남북한 여성, 그들은 누구인가? (Seoul: Nanam, 1992); and Dongik Suh, *Bukeso Sanun Moseup*북에서 사는 모습 (Seoul: Bukhan Yungooso, 1987).

90 Yongrin Moon, "Gyoyook Chejewa Chedo," *Bukhangaeron*북한개론 (Seoul: Ulyoo-Sa, 1990): 393.

91 Bukhan Yungooso, *Bukhan Chongram*북한총람 (Seoul: Bukhan Yungooso, 1983):1284-1285.

92 Nicholas Eberstadt and Judith Banister: 76.

graduates, who enjoy a better reputation and brighter future in North Korea, was 28.8 percent, while the proportion of women among the college graduates was 40.2 percent.

Table 3.9) Proportion of Women among University and College Graduates

(in 1,000)

	Total	Men	Women	Proportion of Women
College Graduates	761	455	306	40.2 %
University Graduates	592	421	171	28.8 %
Total	1,353	876	477	35.2 %

Source : Eberstadt, N., and Banister, J., *The Population of North Korea*, 1992, p.76.

The distribution of female students by the field also re-affirmed sexual segregation: women were concentrated in humanities and literature, composing a third of all female students; the proportion of women in the Teachers' College that trained students for elementary school teaching was about 80 percent; the proportion of women in the Second Pedagogical Universities that offered a lower level of secondary school teaching jobs was 50 percent; the proportion of women in the First Pedagogical Universities for the upper level of secondary school teaching dropped to 30 percent.[93]

Discrimination against female students still prevailed in the universities and colleges. Female students were assumed to use honorary expressions to

---

93 Insook Nam:

male counterparts, while male students usually spoke using non-honorary expressions to women. Furthermore, female students were the ones who had to clean the class rooms.

> Women were pathetic in universities as well. In North Korea, there was no cleaner or sweeper in the universities and colleges. Cleaning should be done by students. Cleaning was done by female students. Moreover, there were many discharged-soldier students who were mostly conservative and conventional. These old ex-soldier students ordered young female students to do this and that, and used them just like their slaves. If any female student stood against them, they hold the hair of the female student and beat her.[94]

In the selection process for students who were going to study abroad, which is an extremely rare opportunity for North Koreans, women were also discriminated against. The criteria for student selection for the studies abroad were five: the family background, study performance, physical appearance, marital status and conjugal relationships. Men should be married and have excellent conjugal harmony, while women should be single. Married women could not hope for a study abroad. North Korea explained that investing in higher education for women was not worth it because women would spend most of their energy for the family after their marriage. That is to say that a woman should bare the burden of household chores alone, therefore they do not need to be provided with higher education.

---

94 Soon-Hee Im, *Bukhan Yusungui Sarm: Chisokgwa Byunhwa* 북한여성의 삶: 지속과 변화 (Seoul: Haenam, 2006): 35.

Masculine Men, Submissive Women

Traditional son preferences remained strong in North Korea. If her first child was a daughter, a woman usually felt guilty to her husband and in-laws. A woman refugee testified that her father refused to take a look at her when she was born, simply because she was a daughter.[95] Many first born or second born daughters tended to have names that had the word "Nam," meaning male or man. In Korea, both South and North, there was a saying that, if a daughter had a name with the word "Nam," she would bring luck of having brother – i.e., the next child of the family would be male.

The strong son preference resulted in an internalization of inferiority among girls. This sense of inferiority was also strengthened at school. Girls were taught to be feminine, moderate and submissive at school. These instructions continued to be imposed on women beyond the educational system. Women were instructed to accept inferior positions to men at work. Men were assumed to command, and women to be commanded. Menial tasks were to be done by women. Many foreigners often witnessed women doing all the manual work while men were sitting and playing cards.

At a Friday Labor, the hotel ordered its employees to remove all weeds at its play-ground. Unwittingly, I watched their weeding works. At first I thought the number of employees was unexpectedly large. However, soon I realized most of them were women. Where were the male employees? I found out most men were playing cards or taking nap under shade, or playing billiard at recreation room. I concluded that men were not doing the weeding work because they thought that kind of menial

---

95 Testimony of Young-Ran Hong, *Bukhan Yusungui Sarmgwa KKoom* 북한여성들의 삶과 꿈, ed. by Hangook Yusung Yungooso (Seoul: Sahoe-Moonhwa Yungooso, 2001): 98.

work belonged to women.[96]

The personality cult of the Great Mothers also inculcated women to be submissive to men. Kim Jong-Suk was depicted as the perfect woman with extraordinary talents and "virtuous" submissiveness to her husband. While men gladly accepted the Great Mothers as the model of ideal woman, most women were unable to follow suit of those perfect women. Men blamed women for their inability. The cult of the Great Mothers reinforced the traditional ideal of submissive wife and devoted mother.

> The Great Mother Kim Jong-Suk was in every sense a superwoman, multi-talented and perfect. We were educated like that. Kim Jong-Suk was capable of everything. She was an excellent sniper with gun, a best embroiderer with needle, a virtuous wife to husband, and a wise mother to her son. She had noble idea of self-sacrifice.... She was too great. Because of that education, I had determined to be just like her. Of course, I knew I could not be able to be perfect like her...[97]

> Men simply loved to illustrate the example of the Great Mothers. They often told women "Do just like the Mother of Chosun," "The Great Mother Kang Ban-Sok did such that...."[98]

Women were not allowed to smoke or drink. While a man's alcoholism was accepted as his habit, not necessarily a bad one, a woman's drinking was regarded as a sign of her promiscuity and indecency. Smoking was out of the

---

96 Tae-Young Lee, *Bukhan Yusung* 북한여성 (Seoul: Sil-Chun Moonhacksa, 1988): 249.

97 Moo-Sook Min and Ja-Hee Ahn: 211.

98 Moo-Sook Min and Ja-Hee Ahn: 213.

question. Alcoholic drinks and cigarettes were only for men.

In North Korea, the concept of masculinity incorporated physical strength, stubbornness, arrogance and domination. Gentleman-ship was, and is, rather foreign to North Korean men. One result of this machismo was the prevailing violence against women. Women who stood up against men were regarded to deserve blame or be beaten. Women should be polite to men, even to a stranger. One refugee witnessed that a woman was severely beaten by a stranger because she adamantly refused his absurd demand.[99]

Equal Work and Unequal Earning

While North Korea tried to pay "special attention" to the protection of women's labor, women became concentrated in agriculture, light industry, and "non-productive" labor such as health, education and caring jobs. As North Korea emphasized the importance of "productive labor," the authorities decided that wages for non-productive labor were lower than that of productive and heavy labor. Despite the principle of equal pay for equal work, women's earnings were lower than men's in general.

Considering the North Korean labor laws that prevented women from doing harmful work for the protection of motherhood and Kim Il Sung' emphasis on women's work, the two-digit proportions of women in mining and heavy industry appear rather extraordinary. However, North Korean laws have never prohibited women from doing hard work "voluntarily." On the contrary, the

---

99 Testimony by Jong-Hee Im. See, Gookto Tongilwon, *Gwisoonja Jeungunul tonghaebon Bukhancheje Byunhwa Siltae* 귀순자 증언을 통해 본 북한체제변화 실태: 190.

authorities have praised women who volunteered to do hazardous jobs as labor heroines.

Table 3.10) The Proportion of Women and the average Wages by Economic Sectors

(1985; wage unit DPRK won)

Industrial Sectors	Proportion of Women	Average Wages
Elementary Schools	80 %	70-100
High Schools	35 %	80-100
Technical Colleges	30 %	90-130
Universities	15 %	120-200
Light/Textile Industry, Office Workers	70 %	60-80
Health	70 %*	60-150
Heavy Industry	15 %	92-150
Mining	20 %	92-180

Sources: for the proportion of women in each sector (except health), Lee, Whan-Gu, *Bukui Silsanggwa Ho-sang* [북의 실상과 허상 (Seoul: Parkyoung-Sa, 1986): 267; for the average wages, Nae-Woe Tongshin, No. 448 (Nov. 8, 1985) and No.460 (Aug. 16, 1985); for the proportion of women in Health sector, from the testimony of a North Korean refugee (interview in 2003)

During the late 1950s,the "Stow Net Fishing Ship of Women [안강망여성호]" that was staffed by a women-only crew came into the spotlight in North Korea as the symbol of labor heroines. Stow net fishing was notoriously laborious and physically demanding. The ship had to anchor at one spot on the water for days and weeks. The Stow Net Fishing Ship of Women stayed out to sea for 300 days without docking. Because of the notorious working conditions on the ship, however, this practice was soon criticized and the female crew was discharged.[100]

In the Wiwon Coal Mine, Jagang Province, a squad of women rock-drillers was organized and sent to the end of mine shaft in the early 1960s. However, this squad also became famous, praised as labor heroines, then criticized and disbanded in 1965.[101] A woman crane driver in the Chollima Still Cooperative Plant was introduced in the Daily Labor as a dedicated labor heroine.[102]

As North Korea has relied upon ideological stimulation for labor incentives, these women labor heroines were invariably depicted as taking the jobs out of dedication to the nation. In many cases, however, women took laborious jobs out of economic concern. Although fishery was an extremely hard job for women even with the best technological support, many women volunteered for it: because the fishing company paid 20 kg worth of fish fortnightly. Women in heavy industry were also paid far better than women in light industry.

In the case of agriculture, farmers in general received their due by their average labor capacity [노력공수]. The average labor capacity refers to the standardized point of labor performance of a person per day. Adult women in general receive 0.8 points whereas men received 1 point. By this calculation of the average labor capacity, women earned less than men in collective farms as well.[103]

100 Whan-Gu Lee, *Bookui Silsanggwa Husang*북의 실상과 허상 (Seoul: Korean Publishing Corporation, 1985): 269.

101 Ae-Sil Kim, "Yusungui Kyungje Hwaldong," *Bukhan Yusungui Saenghwal Siltae* 북한여성의 생활실태 ed. by Bong-Sook Sohn (Seoul: Nanam, 1991): 209.

102 "Crane-gwa Hamkke 34 Nyun (34 Years with the Crane)", *Rodong Shinmoon* 로동신문 (October 29, 1987).

103 Miryang Youn, *Bukhanui Yusung Jongchaek* 북한의 여성정책 (Seoul: Hanul, 1991): 203.

Women were also discriminated against in promotions and job assignments. Even when women had scored higher than men at graduation, women were still assigned to lesser-paid and less-privileged jobs.

> Even among the graduates of the prestigious Kim Il Sung University, job assignments for men and women showed a stark difference. Women were hardly assigned to party positions. It was really frustrating to women. You know, in North Korea party positions were more powerful. Particularly the central party positions were the best of the best. Women never got there.... Women were very rare even in local party positions. Women could only be assigned to administrative job. But, you know, it was less prestigious than a party job. Graduating from Kim Il Sung University... and not being able to receive a party position. Many female graduates from Kim Il Sung University went into public media or a research institute... with no power...[104]

If a man after ten years of military service was assigned a job, he would certainly precede woman who kept the factories running for ten years. Even without military service, men in general were expected to be promoted earlier than women. Women have been inculcated to accept men's precedence as normal.

> It is a duty of women to bear and rear children, even though they are employed. While rearing the children, women cannot afford to work like men. Women have maternal leaves, too, you know. Therefore it is not so strange for women to be always under men.[105]

104 Moo-Sook Min and Jae-Hee Ahn, *Bukhanui Yusung Gyoyook-e gwanhan Yungoo*북한의 여성교육에 관한 연구, (Seoul: Yusung Gaebalwon, 2001): 219-220.

105 A testimony of a refugee. Re-quoted fromYoung-Ja Park: 295

Women's Sexuality

There have been two contradicting evaluations on sexual behavior of North Korean people. Some claimed that North Koreans had a rather liberal attitude towards sexuality and had no stigma for losing virginity before marriage. In fact this liberal view was accepted by many scholars and some North Korean refugees. However, many other refugees insisted that North Koreans were conservative on sexuality, and having pre-marital sex would cost dearly, particularly for women. These contradicting evaluations share some truth.

During the early stage of North Korean regime, the government exerted itself in destroying the old social order that confined women at home and that suppressed sexuality of people. As part of the effort to destroy old order, North Korea attempted to make marriage easily breakable, and the remarriage of widows and divorcees as a general norm. Communist leaders deserted their wives and remarried young socialites. During 1940s and 1950s, promiscuous behavior was common among communist leaders. That was regarded as part of the revolution.

The less-than-exemplary sexual lives of the leaders contributed to the liberalization of sexuality. However hard the leadership tried to keep the secret, rumors spread very fast among people: Kim Song-Ae became Kim Il Sung's mistress while Kim Jong-Suk was alive, causing implacable rancor in Kim Jong Il's emotion; Kim Jong Il took a famous but already married actress as a kept woman for himself and had his eldest son, Kim Jong-Nam; many cadres of the party also had young mistresses. Even worse, the refugees from North Korea heard of these so-called "pleasure groups" that consisted of pretty women aged from 18 to 25 and provided a range of services including sexual services, and singing and dancing performances.[106]

The old Korean saying that a hero never rejects a beauty or that a hero should afford a thousand women played another role in sexual behavior of men. Despite the effort by the leadership to crack down on corruption among party members, powerful men were assumed to have many women. Many young women became mistresses of party leaders, factory managers, or directors. Some women offered sex for promotion or a specific favor. The party occasionally carried out blitz operations for investigations on corruption and purged several party members on the grounds of corruption or immoral misdemeanor. However, it was not easy to incriminate anybody for personal affairs. When both parties consistently denied the accusation, the charges were dropped. If a married man had affairs with only one woman other than his wife, their relationship became the hardest to corroborate because the woman would believe his love and would never blame him. When a man had relationship with many women, he was easily caught and purged, because all the women might join in the accusation that he forced them to have sex.[107]

Furthermore, as economic development stagnated since the 1970s, North Korean people could not afford a life of leisure other than politically indoctrinating films and performances. Many youngsters, who tried to find something to throw off their oppressed instinct, resorted to sex, resulting in pregnancy out of marriage.

North Korean laws prohibit discrimination against children born out of

---

106 Kyungja Jung and Bronwen Dalton, "Rhetoric versus Reality for the Women of North Korea: Mothers of the Revolution," *Asian Survey 46* (2006, no. 5): 755.

107 Testimony from Mr. Kim who was a high ranking member of the National Security Department and fled to South Korea in 1989. Interview by Sejong Institute

marriage. Women have the right to choose whether or not to marry. In theory, therefore, an unmarried woman is free to give birth to and bring up children. In reality, however, the people strongly disapprove of children born out of marriage. It is almost unthinkable to North Koreans to have a child out of marriage.[108] When an unmarried woman was discovered to be pregnant, the family and the relatives, and often even the district authorities, coerced her to marry the father of the baby. If the man in question had been married, she was urged, in fact forced, to have an abortion.

North Korea had never outlawed abortion. However, the procedure required those who wanted an abortion to produce their ID and the reason of abortion. In the case of unmarried women, the authorities questioned the woman about who was the father and then purged or moved the father to a remote place. During the 1970s, there were many homicides of pregnant women: in fear of being purged, many men attempted to murder their pregnant lovers. In 1982, Kim Jong Il came to the rescue of those women and instructed the authorities to perform on-demand abortions without any question regardless of whether the woman was married or not. His instruction greatly reduced the number of murders related to pregnancy.[109] Many outsides viewed on-demand abortion without question as evidence of liberal view on women's sexuality.

This seemingly liberal view on sexuality, however, was not for women. A man's sexual activity out of marriage was to be regarded as a part of his masculinity: a man's sexual instinct was not supposed to be controlled. A woman's sexual relationship before marriage was to be deemed as promiscuous; women's

---

108   I have never encountered, or heard of, a North Korean who was born out of marriage.

109   Gookto Tongilwon, *Gwisoonja Jeungunul tonghaebon Bukhancheje Byunhwa Silta*: 95.

sexual desire was to be abstained.[110] When an affair between unmarried couple was revealed to the public, the woman would have to get married to the man; otherwise she would suffer from the stigma of "the past." The man would never suffer no matter what happens to the couple.[111]

Although the risk of being murdered was reduced, women's health risk was still very high: there was no anesthesia during abortion; personal hygiene conditions were miserable. North Korea never supplied women with contraceptive pills. For married women North Korea provided contraceptive roofs or rings that were to be inserted in the body by surgery for married women. For unmarried women, abortion was, and still is, the only method of birth control.

3.6 Under-Representation of Women in Politics

The Decline of the Women's Union

During the Korean War, the Women's Union successfully mobilized women into war efforts. In honor of the efforts of the Women's Union, the Chairwoman, Park Jong-Ae, was awarded the Stalinist Medal in 1951. The success of the Women's Union legitimized the expansion of its membership. The member-

---

110 Tongil Yungoowon (Korean Institute for National Unification), *Whitepaper on Human Rights in North Korea* (Seoul: Korean Institute for National Unification, 2003): 173.

111 Testimony by Jong-Hee Im. See, Gookto Tongilwon, *Gwisoonja Jeungunul tonghaebon Bukhancheje Byunhwa Siltae*: 190.

ship reached to 2.17 million in March 1958.[112]

At its third Congress, in 1965, the leadership of the Women's Union completely changed: Kim Ok-Soon, a partisan colleague of Kim Il Sung and the wife of another partisan general, became the Chairwoman; Kim Sung-Ae, Kim Il Sung's wife by second marriage, became the Vice Chairwoman; and other former partisan members as well as the wives of party leaders joined the union. The participation of these powerful women made the union even stronger, reaching to.2.5 million in 1962,[113] and 2.7 million in 1965.[114]

At the fourth Congress in 1971, the Women's Union made another leadership change: Kim Sung-Ae was elected to Chairwoman of the Union; and the secretariat was expanded to set up a Secretary General to assist the Chairwoman. The first Secretary General was then four-time parliamentarian of the Supreme People's Assembly, and other secretaries were the wives of the party leaders.

With influential leaders at the top, the Women's Union for several years enjoyed prestige and political influence. However, with the fall of Kim Sung-Ae, the Women's Union began to decline in its influence and membership.

Kim Sung-Ae was born in 1924 in Pyongnam Province. She met Kim Il Sung in 1946 while Kim Jong-Suk was still alive, and became his mistress. After Kim Jong-Suk died in 1947, she moved to live with Kim Il Sung. She gave birth to her first son in 1954. She was finally married to Kim Il Sung in 1963, almost a decade after the birth of her son. She gave birth to another son after marriage.

---

112 *Choson Chungang Yungam* (DPRK Central Yearbook) 1959: 157

113 *Choson Chungang Yungam* (DPRK Central Yearbook) 1963: 188.

114 *Choson Chungang Yungam* (DPRK Central Yearbook) 1966/67: 170.

She began her political activity as a chairwoman at a district women's union in 1954. After her marriage, she soon climbed up to become the Vice Chairwoman of the DWU in 1965. Armed with a few years of experience in running a national organization, she was elected to Chairwoman of the Central Committee of the DFU in 1971.

As the Chairwoman of the Women's Union with 2.7 million members and a powerful secretariat, and also as the wife of Kim Il Sung, Kim Sung-Ae for a few years exercised political influence and rivaled the influence of Kim Jong Il. She accompanied Kim Il Sung in official events and received foreign visitors as the First Lady. As the Chairwoman of the DWU, she also delivered many addresses and reports to the Union and other women.

The *Choson Chungang Yungam* 1971 (DPRK Central Yearbook of 1971) printed the full text a report delivered by Kim Sung-Ae with her name apparent.[115] The report was presented to the 25th anniversary of the Women's Union in 1970. It was the only document in the *Choson Chungang Yungam* that was printed under a person's name other than Kim Il sung and Kim Jong Il.

In the1972 and 1973 *Choson Chungang Yungam* also printed the name of Kim Sung-Ae along with Kim Il Sung in the section of chronicling Kim Il Sung's activities. She was referred to as "Comrade Kim Sung-Ae, the wife of Kim Il Sung." Since North Korean publications usually avoid recognizing personal names, except Kim Il Sung and Kim Jong Il, the recognition of her name in the Central Yearbook suggests her huge political influence.

However, her glory lasted only briefly. Since the 1974 *Choson Chungang Yungam* onwards, her name disappeared forever. With the rise of her step son,

---

115 *Choson Chungang Yungam* (DPRK Central Yearbook) 1971: 465–474.

Kim Jong Il, she gradually retreated into a nominal role. Even when the Women's Union held its Congress, she could not deliver an address as the Chairwoman. The General Secretary of the Union assumed the role of the reporter and moderator. Furthermore, the Women's Union itself faced a grave set back. With the fall of its Chairwoman, the Women's Union also had to be reduced in its influence and membership.

At its 5th Conference in June 1983, the Women's Union changed its regulations, and limited its membership. Until then all adult women could join the Women's Union regardless of their membership in other organizations. But after 1983, women with membership in other organizations were not allowed to join the Women's Union. This effectively brought the decline of the Women's Union. In North Korea, every person should join at least one organization by work and by age. Children from elementary school to high school are to join the Chosun Scouts; youngsters from ages eighteen to thirty join the Kim Il Sung Socialist Youngster's League; the factory workers join the Chosun Trade Union; the farmers join the Chosun Farm Workers' Union and so on. Women without any affiliation are only those housewives without employment. In North Korea, at least nominally, housewives without employment were rare until the economic debacle of the 1990s. After limiting its membership to those without affiliation, membership was reported to be 200,000 in 1987.[116] In a word, the erstwhile powerful Women's Union became a "powerless organization of elderly women aged between 50 and 55,"[117] and the "organization of housewives who have no

---

116 Wan-Joo Bang, *Choson Gaegwan* 조선개관 (Pyongyang: Foreign Languages Publishing House, 1987): 74.

117 Testimony of Mr.Lee who was born in 1974 in Kiljoo, North Hamkyung Province. Interview by Sejong Institute (November 7, 2002).

jobs and who are not related to the military members."[118]

The Women's Union also changed its executive organization. The secretariat came to deal with purely managerial work, the powerful secretaries changed into vice presidents without real power, and the Secretary General became the real driving force for the Women's Union. The Chairwoman, Kim Sung-Ae, became a titular figure until she was finally replaced by Chun Yun-Ok in 1998.

After Kim Jong Il became the heir-apparent, the major task of the Women's Union became the education of women to be loyal to the future leader under the slogan of accomplishing the *Three Revolutionary Tasks*. In rhetoric, the *Three Revolutionary Tasks* means that people should keep on revolutionizing their thoughts, technique and culture even after the socialist revolution was completed. In reality, the *Three Revolutionary Tasks* demanded people to be thoroughly armed with the *Juche* Thoughts and the personality cult of the Kim family. Inculcating the people with the *Juche* Thoughts and idolization of the Kim family were the fundamental purposes of the *Three Revolutionary Tasks*.

For women, the *Three Revolutionary Tasks* meant the personality cult for the Great Mothers, the mothers of Kim Il Sung and Kim Jong Il. Following the model of the Great Mothers was the essence of becoming a revolutionary woman. As soon as the book titled *Kang Ban-Sok Nyusarul Ddara Baewooja* (강반석 녀사를 따라배우자: Let's Follow the Model of Lady Kang Ban-Sok)[119] was published in 1967, the Women's Union launched intensive education campaigns for its members.

The Report of the Central Committee of the Women's Union to the 30th

---

118 Testimony of Ms. Lee who was born in 1971 in Wonsan, North Kangwon Province. Interview by Sejong Institute (February 26, 2003).

119 *Kang Ban-Sok Nyusarul Ddara Baewooja* 강반석 녀사를 따라배우자 (Tokyo: Chosun Chungnyun, 1967).

Anniversary Conference of the DWU in 1976 reveals the meaning of revolutionizing the thought: women were demanded to read one hundred times a hagi-
ography of Kang Ban-Sok, Kim Il Sung's mother.

Table 3.11) Three Revolutionary Tasks of the DWU (30ᵗʰ Anniversary Report)

Revolution	Contents of the Tasks
Thought	Working-Classization and Revolutionization of the Whole People 1) Carrying out the Political Education Campaigns i) to strengthen the study of *Juche* Thought ii) to study *Let's Follow the Model of Lady Kang Bansuck* one hundred times iii) to love labor and to have a collectivist mind 2) Strengthening the DWU Organization
Technique	To Fight against the Limitation of Nature and to Guarantee Independent and Creative Lives for Workers Ensuring that all Women Participate in the Technical Innovation Struggle i) to make innovations in light industry and the service sector ii) for female technicians, to produce innovative suggestions that will reduce the gap between heavy and light labor iii) for female workers in collective farms, to learn how to operate farming machines
Culture	To Educate Future Generations to be *Juche* Communists and to Make all people Intelligent Educating Mothers to be Fit for Bearing and Teaching Children to be *Juche* Communists

Source: Lee Tae-Young, *Bukhan Yusong* [북한여성], Shilcheon Moonhack, Seoul, 1988, pp.177-178.

Women in the Supreme People's Assembly

Since its inception, North Korea has taken measures to mobilize women into society. One of the efforts was to have more female representatives at all levels of peoples' committees and assemblies. As a result, the proportion of women in the Supreme People's Assembly (SPA) remained in two digit numbers, except once. Also two women were elected as Vice Chairpersons of the SPA. However, the SPA is more symbolic than real in political representation.

Although the SPA was, according to the Constitution, the supreme sovereign organ of the DPRK, its function was only to approve the decisions of the Party, and its meetings last less than a month during its four year period of terms. The SPA opened its session once every year, only for two days on average. The SPA was not, in reality, genuinely representing the will of the people because voters were cast for or against a single candidate nominated by the United National Front. Since the WPK was in full control of the United National Front, the representatives to the SPA were chosen by the WPK.

Many women who were elected as Representative to the SPA were labor heroines. Until 1990, there were 47 women Representatives who were elected more than three times, among whom 25 were labor heroines.[120] While becoming the party cadre required familial connection in addition to personal capability, becoming a Representative was dependent on personal devotion and achievements.

---

120 Miryang Youn, *Bukhanui Yusung Chongchaek*북한의 여성정책: 174-180.

Table 3.12) Women in the Supreme People's Assembly

	Year	Total Number of		Number of Women		Proportion of Women	
		Reps [1]	St-Reps [2]	Reps	St-Reps	Reps	St-Reps
1	1948	572	34	69	1	12 %	3 %
2	1957	215	12	27	2	13 %	6 %
3	1962	383	27	35	3	9 %	11 %
4	1967	457	18	73	1	16 %	6 %
5	1972	451	19	113	2	21 %	11 %
6	1977	579	19	120	2	21 %	11 %
7	1982	615	19	121	2	20 %	11 %
8	1986	655	15	138	3	21 %	20 %
9	1990	687	15	138	2	20 %	12 %

1) Reps refers to Representatives
2) St-Reps refers to Members of Standing Committee or Standing Assembly
Sources: SPA, "The Election Result and the Composition of Representatives," Reports to the first session of each term.

To supplement the nominal role of the SPA, there was the Standing Committee or the Standing Assembly which exercised the SPA's authority when the SPA was out of session. The number of members in the Standing Committee or Assembly varied term by term. Until 1989 there were only 7 women who were selected to the Standing Committee, including Park Jong-Ae and Kim Sung-Ae.

The other five women were: Kim Deuk-Ran who was born to a destitute tenant farming family during the Japanese colonial period, began to study after the Independence, worked at a farm and became a labor heroine, and became Vice Chairperson of the SPA; Kim Ok-Soon who was a guerrilla warrior with Kim Il Sung during the colonial period and the wife of guerilla general Choi

Gwang, and became the President of the Women's Union at its 3rd conference; Huh Jong-Sook who was one of the most intelligent female communists at the time. Huh was born in Seoul, graduated Ewha Women's University, studied in the United States and China, and was fluent in five languages. Her intelligence and expertise in languages made her one of the most well-known women in Korea; Nam Soon-Hee who was a scholar and Dean of Pyongyang Teachers' University; and Yuh Yun-Gu who was the daughter of a famous leftist-nationalist, Yuh Woon-Hyung, and studied at Moscow under the auspices of Kim Il Sung.

Among these seven women, Kim Sung-Ae and Yuh Yun-Gu could be regarded as selected by personal connection, although Yuh played an important role in inter-Korean politics because of her father's fame. Other five women had their own distinguished achievements. In general, Representatives of the SPA are selected by their achievements and devotion to the nation and the WPK.

Women in the Worker's Party of Korea

As in any communist country the WPK is most important power organ of the DPRK. The proportion of women in the WPK's membership has not been fully reported, but it is estimated at 30 to 40 percent.

When the WPK was inaugurated, the Congress and the Central Committee played key roles in decision-making. However, the party organization and its internal power structure experienced several shifts: at its 3rd Congress in 1956, the Political Committee of the Central Committee became the key organ; when the Secretariat was established in October 1966, the Secretariat that was under direct control of Kim Il Sung almost monopolized power; at the 6th Congress in 1980, the WPK changed the Political Committee into the Politburo, and established a Standing Committee within the Politburo. The Standing Committee of the Politburo that was composed of only three men became the core of all power. After the deaths of Kim Il Sung and Oh Jin-Woo, two members of the Standing Committee, only one man, Kim Jong Il, represents the Committee.

The Party Congress, the supreme organ of the Party according to the Party Covenant, was supposed to be held once a year until 1980. In reality, the Congresses had been held irregularly, only to finalize the power struggles within the party. At its 6th Congress in 1980, the WPK changed its Covenant to provide that the Congress would be held once in every five years. However, the Party Congress has not been held for 26 years since its 6th Congress.

The Central Committee that was to exercise the authority of the Congress between the Congresses was supposed to be the second highest organ of the party. The Central Committee consisted of regular members and candidate members, of which the numbers varied term by term. The proportion of women in the Central Committee has been 2.3 percent and 6.5 percent. The female members in the Central Committee include most of those women in the Cabinet and the SPA. However, unlike the Standing Committee of the SPA or the Cabinet where most female members had distinguished achievement, the members in the Central Committee of the party includes many women who had only extraordinary familial connection to Kim Il Sung and Kim Jong Il All the members of the Kim family and the wives of the highest party leaders were included.

The Politburo, the core of the communist power, also consisted of regular members and candidate members. The total number varies, but it was never more than 20. Only one woman, Park Jong-Ae, was elected as a regular member of the Politburo, at the 3rd and the 4th Congress; and three other women served as candidate members during the 6th Congress.

After the Secretariat was established only one woman, Huh Jong-Sook once served as a Secretary. Since her death in 1991, there has been no report of new woman Secretary of the Party. Despite the pledge of sexual equality, wherever real power came from, the proportion of women dropped in the end.

Table 3.13) Women in the Central Committee of the WPK

Congress	Regular Members			Candidate Members		
	Total	Women	Proportion (%)	Total	Women	Proportion (%)
1st (1946)	43	2	4.6 (%)	–		
2nd (1948)	67	2	3.0 (%)	–		
3rd (1956)	71	2	2.8 (%)	–		
4th (1961)	85	2	2.3 (%)	50	3	6.0 (%)
5th (1970)	107	7	6.5 (%)	55	6	10.9 (%)
6th (1980)	169	6	3.6 (%)	103	8	7.7 (%)
6th (1990)	180	6	3.3 (%)	148	8	5.4 (%)

Sources: Gukto Tongilwon (NUB), *Choson Rodongdang Daehoe* [조선로동당대회자료집], Vols.1-4: Also see Miryang Youn, *Bukhanui Yusong Chungchaek*, 1991, p. 183.

Women in the Cabinet

During its existence, North Korea changed its political system several times. For a while, it had a system in which the cabinet exercised the authority of policy making and implementation together. Then it divided policy-making from implementation, and made the cabinet a purely policy implementing entity. Recently, by the constitutional amendment of 1998, the cabinet regained the policy making authority.

North Korea had always kept a large number of ministry-level organizations: since 1945, it had 300 ministry-equivalent positions among which only 6 were women. Compared with the proportion of women in the SPA, the proportion of women in the cabinet is disproportionately low. However, these six women cabinet members were all qualified by their performance and excellence.

The most prominent woman member was Kim Bok-Sin, a Deputy Premier. She first obtained a good reputation as a manager of a military uniform and textile supply factory during the war, and was accepted to the Central University for Party Cadres. She was reported to be an excellent technocrat in industrial management and administration. She successively filled various posts in the cabinet such as Minister of Textile Industry (1967-1972), Chairperson of Trade Committee (1982-1986), Chairperson of External Economic Relations Committee (1986-1990) and Minister of Light Industry (1990-1998). She served as Deputy Premier for 21 years, from 1977 to 1998. However, partly because of her age, she disappeared after 1998.

It is worthwhile to note that the posts that the position that these women held in the cabinet were not typically women's job: trade, finance, culture and propaganda, justice, and agriculture. Yoon Ki-Jong served as the Finance Minister for 21 years, from 1977 to 1998. She was reportedly a genius in finance. Huh Jong-Sook, the only woman party Secretary, was also appointed as the Minister of Justice in 1957. Park Jong-Ae became Minister of Agriculture in 1957, and Park Young-Sin became the Minister of Culture in 1962. Another female Minister of Finance, Im Kyung-Sook, lasted only for two years, from 1998 to 2000.

3.7 Coping Strategy of Women

Complaisance with Reservation

As the high proportion of women in employment indicates, most women complied with the call of the working-classization. There were several explanations for this complaisance. First of all, the history of Korea restricted the people from questioning. People in North Korea had experienced a long history of Confucian order and decades of cruel colonial rule. Complaisance to social order had long been considered as a matter of life or death. Secondly, women had been discriminated against for so long that they came to accept inequality as natural. And third, the North Korean system forced women to be employed.

The people were assigned jobs as soon as they graduated high school. The freedom of the people to choose whether or not to work or where to work was not granted. The people had the right and duty of labor, but not the right of choice under the Socialist Constitution and the *Socialist Labor Law*. The job assignment was mandatory. Only married women and the retired could be excused of employment. However, most married women had to be employed because of the ration system. The amount of food rationed to the unemployed was small enough to force many people to be employed.

Not only food, but also other necessities were linked with employment. People were demanded to produce, as well as money, "goods ticket [구매권]" or "supply card [공급카드]" for the purchase of industrial goods. Money alone did not enable people to buy goods. However, these tickers and cards were distributed through the work places. In order to buy a decent dress without much trouble, therefore, a woman had to have a job.

Most women in North Korea also preferred employment to "voluntary labor. Unemployed housewives and dependants, most of who had retired, were either demanded to participate in voluntary labor without pay or in house industry work-teams.

Voluntary Labor in fact refers to a kind of forced labor, which enjoined all the unemployed to engage in manual labor without pay, and even without provision of food or the necessary equipment for work. In North Korea, every person, including the highest cadres of the WPK and Cabinet members, is required to engage in manual labor, at least once a week, six to eight hours a day, in order to revolutionize and working-classize themselves. Most party cadres and government officials join the labor on Friday, naming it as Friday Labor [금요노동].

Voluntary labor for the unemployed is more systematic and forcible. Housewives were urged by the Women's Union to work in road and drainage repair, rice planting or harvesting, and often in a large-scale construction work. At least 730 housewives in Hyesan City joined voluntarily in a large scale housing construction project.[121] As many as 3,000 housewives joined in mining works in Gum-Duk Mine, Ham-Nam Province, as part of voluntary labor.[122] Many housewives also worked voluntarily for the extension project of Kim-Chaek Steel and Iron Plant in 1988.[123] This voluntary labor is in reality compulsory: those unemployed who are not able to participate in voluntary labor have to produce proper documents for the exemption, or be punished as anti-revolutionary.

---

121 *Chosun Nyusung*, February 1980: 34–35.

122 *Chosun Nyusung*, May 1988:

123 *Chosun Nyusung*, March 1988: 26–28.

However hard and taking long hours, the voluntary labor was not reward-ed either by money or by the entitlement for pension. Usually the "voluntary labor" implied long and manually demanding works, the voluntary labor was excluded from the entitlement for social security such as pension and insurance. People's abhorrence of the voluntary labor was rather sensible.

Home Industry Work-Team

Despite the mandatory job assignment, the ration system, and the volun-tary labor, many women chose not to be employed. In rural areas where the food rationing was not applied,[124] 70 to 80 percent of married women remained at home.[125] The proportion of unemployment among married women became even higher with the decline of the economy during the 1980s.[126]

Since the launch of its Second Seven Year Plan (1978-84), the North Ko-rean economic growth rate dropped to 2 percent per year. Economic decline caused many big companies to stop running, creating a situation that where employees were only nominally employed and left idle. With the increase of de facto unemployment, many married women were allowed to stay at home and be housewives.

124 In North Korea, the collective farms had the right to keep a portion of their product to themselves after harvest. The families that belonged to collective farms were allocated grains and produces in bulk twice a year. People working in industries were rationed once or twice a month, in principle. After the decline of the economy, the rationing becomes irregular.

125 Testimony of Hyung-Soon Kang, Gookto Tongilwon, *Bukhan Juminsaenghwal Siltae Chosa* 북한 주민생활 실태조사 (Seoul: Gookto Tongilwon, 1989): 16.

126 Testimony of Hyung-Soon Kang, Gookto Tongilwon, *Bukhan Juminsaenghwal Siltae Chosa* 북한 주민생활 실태조사 (Seoul: Gookto Tongilwon, 1989): 44.

North Korea tried to utilize the labor capacity of housewives by providing part-time works. As the authorities regarded housework and child-care as natural women's work, making all housewives into employed workers did not seem practical. In many cases even the local industries were not able to coerce housewives to take jobs as workers. Therefore North Korea created a new sort of part-time job for housewives: the home industry work-team.

Since the government disproportionately emphasized heavy industry, North Korean people had always been in severe need of consumer goods. Although the advocates for focusing on consumer goods production were purged during the 1960s, the chronic shortage of the consumer goods attracted the government attention after the 1970s. The idea of the home industry work-team emerged from this condition. While utilizing the unemployed housewives, North Korea attempted to increase the production of consumer goods without deducting the resources from heavy industry.

The home industry work-team [가내작업반] refers to a small group that produces consumer goods with flexible work hours and no fixed work place. Sometimes those work-teams work at the homes of the members, sometimes at a small parcel of land or at an office annexed to a collective farm or a factory. Women who are good at knitting can organize a knitting work-team, while staying at home. Those work-teams are supposed to recycle the waste from the respective factories or farms. In reality, most of the materials necessary for production are improvised by the members. Some women recycle their old sweaters; and others bring materials from the black market. After production, each team is required to submit 80 percent of its products to the respective authority. The remaining 20 percent of products is to be divided among the members. This type of work-team has been in existence since the 1950s, but becomes legally recognized by *the Socialist Labor Law*.

The *Socialist Labor Law* of 1978 stipulated that "all local government bodies and the relevant state organs, enterprises and social cooperative organizations should ... organize home industry work-teams and home cooperatives so that women who do not go to work may join them if they wish" (Article 31). These "women who do not go to work" are unemployed, and excluded from pension or other benefits as workers.

Kim Jong Il, already in full control over the country during the 1980s, further institutionalized the home industry. He instructed the party to mobilize housewives into the production of consumer goods on August 26, 1983. The government responded by accelerating its effort to mobilize women in the home industry work-teams.

During the National Consumer Goods Exhibition, Kim Jong Il instructed the participants to improve the recycling of wastes and increase the production of consumer goods on August 3, 1984. Since then, consumer goods have been referred to as "8.3 People's Consumer Goods" or simply "8.3 goods." The home industry work-teams also came to be called as the "8.3 work-teams;" and the payment by the work-teams to the authority as "8.3 fund."

In principle, the work-teams were supposed to produce consumer goods out of the factory or farm waste and submit the products to the authority. In reality, however, people had to provide the resources by themselves, and avoided submitting products to the authority. Because of the severe shortage of consumer goods, people realized that selling all the products on the black market was more profitable than submitting a large portion of them to the authority. The state-set prices were so often less than a tenth of the market prices. Therefore the people in the work-teams began to pay the authority in cash, the amount of money equitable to 80 percent of their products by the state-set prices. Therefore people called the payment as "8.3 funds," instead of 8.3 products. If a woman wanted to stay at home without working at all, she could be excused by paying the "8.3 fund."

Many women preferred participation in the work-team to official employment. Participating, at least nominally, in the work-team provided women a better chance of earning money and having free time. Some affluent women came to stay at home altogether by paying the "8.3 fund" and pretending as a member of a work-team. While the work-team was intended to mobilize women in social production, women responded in the end by their own way, regardless of the government intention. As the North Korean economy declined even further, the "8.3 fund" was widely used as the excuse for the people who wanted to be officially "unemployed" and be engaged in trades. The home industry work-team, in the end, became the seed of the trades that during the "Arduous March" enabled women to support their family.

Chapter IV

The Arduous March
and
the Hour of Women

4.1 Kim Jong-Il Regime

The New Leadership

The collapse of the eastern European communist regimes and the Soviet Union during the late 1980s and early 1990s compounded the problems of the already declining North Korean economy. Even though North Korea claimed to be self-reliant economically, it had benefited from "friendly trade" and cooperation among the communist regimes. The cut off, or severe reduction, of these benefits led North Korea to a crisis of survival.

In order to overcome the economic crisis, North Korea at first tried to open its economy to the outside. It designated the Rajin-Sunbong region a special economic zone, and tried to induce foreign investment. It soon became clear that the Rajin-Sunbong project was a failure because of the lack of infrastructure such as transportation, water, electricity and communication facilities, and because of the ambivalent attitude of the government towards the opening.

In 1993 North Korea admitted the failure of its seven-year economic plan for 1987 to 1993, and set a three-year buffer period to rearrange the goals for the next economic plan. During the buffer period, North Korea endeavored to increase the production of light industries and agriculture in order to mitigate the severe shortage of consumer goods and food.

While its economy was slipping into crisis, Kim Jong-Il tried to strengthen his power base as heir apparent. His efforts to assure "coronation" were first directed to gain control of the military power. Unlike his father, Kim Jong-Il had not had any real experience in military affairs so that he and his father were naturally concerned about the response from the military leaders. The father and son contemplated that it was urgent to secure a military position for the son while Kim Il-Sung was still healthy and strong. Kim Jong-Il was elected at the 19th Central Committee of the WPK on December 24, 1991 as the Supreme Commander of the People's Army. Based on the party support, he was also approved to be the Chairman of the National Defense Commission (NDC) at the SPA in 1993. After his inauguration as the Supreme Commander of the People's Army, he promoted more than 1,000 officers to the rank of general, ensuring their loyalty for him.

During the late 1980s and the early 1990s, the US government noticed that North Korea was developing nuclear weaponry. By 1994, the Clinton administration of the US was even contemplating a pre-emptive strike. However, South Korea opposed any action that might trigger another Korean War. After years of negotiations, North Korea agreed to hold a summit meeting with the South on July 25, 1994 as a part of a deal. However, the summit was never realized because the Great Leader died on July 8, 1994, just two weeks before the scheduled meeting.

Despite the economic debacle and the death of the head of the state, North Korean leadership determined to "properly mourn" the late leader prior to crisis management. The government declared three years of "national mourning," without official succession of the headship of the state. The references of "Supreme Leader" and "Great Leader" [수령; 위대한 지도자] were, and are, reserved for Kim Il-Sung alone. Kim Jong-Il continued to be referred to as the "Dear Leader [친애하는 지도자]." Without head of the state, the government was run by the legacies of Kim Il-Sung. Every policy or government decision was attributed to the precepts of Kim Il-Sung.

Many outsiders suspected this abnormal political situation as a sign of acute power struggle within the party. Others tried to explain that Kim Jong-Il decided to wait for a better environment for inauguration as ruler. North Korean officials who met foreigners claimed that "most pious leader" Kim Jong-Il was mourning for his late father, as any good and pious son of Korea should do, for three years. During the *Chosun* dynasty, the son should wear hoarse cloth made of hemp, live in a hut in front of the grave, and mourn every day and night for three years after the parent died. Whatever was the case, many North Korea watchers called this anomalous situation as the "Legacy Politics by Kim Il-Sung [유훈통치]."

During the mourning period, North Korea was also devastated by natural disaster for two consecutive years. In a sense, the "natural disasters," the flood of 1994 and 1995, were not born of nature. North Korean authorities had encouraged people to cultivate whatever land possible to produce more grain. The result was deforestation and loss of soil. The flood was long expected by many.

The Arduous March began. Arduous March is a euphemism for suffering and starvation of the people. The Arduous March originally referred to the suffering and retreat for one hundred days (to be exact, 110 days) of Kim Il-Sung and his partisan colleagues during the period of December 1938 to March 1939. During the period, Kim Il Sung and his partisan unit suffered from the biting cold of the Manchurian winter, starvation, and the persistent and ruthless pursuit of the Japanese forces. Many members of his group died during the period.

Kim Il Sung admitted that the period was the hardest time for all his struggles. He often recalled the experience with bitterness. He said people who had experienced starvation knew how valuable rice and the peasants were. He declared that people without the experience of starvation would never know the meaning of revolution.[1]

Derived from the Long March (1934) of Chinese communists under the leadership of Mao, North Korean authorities described the hardship of Kim Il Sung's unit as the "March" towards ultimate triumph of socialism. Although it was named "March," since it ended in a glorious return to Korea after Liberation, it was arduous and tormenting. To North Koreans, therefore, the "Arduous March" meant the suffering during the revolution and the glory of the success.

When North Korea suffered from famine, the authorities referred to the suffering as another "Arduous March." That label implied that North Korea would conquer the famine and construct a glorious future in the end. The "Arduous March" became the party slogan in 1996 to overcome the economic debacle. As Andrew Natsios discovered, the North Korea media was quoting again and again the passages from the memoir of Kim Il Sung about starvation and revolution.[2]

However, food shortage led many people to starvation in reality. During the 1990s, 0.6 million to 1 million North Korean people, roughly 3 to 5 percent of the population, died of starvation.[3] North Korea became the only significantly industrialized country to experience a peacetime famine.[4] The government, for the first time since its inception, appealed to the international organizations for food aid in 1995.

---

1 Kim Il Sung, *Segiwa Dobulo* 세기와 더불어 (Kim Il Sung Memoir: With the Century), Vol. 7 (Pyongyang: Choson Rodongdang Chulpansa, 1996): 154.

2 Andrew S. Natsios, *The Great North Korean Famine* (Washington DC: USIP Press, 2001): 83.

3 Stephan Haggard and Marcus Noland, *Famine in North Korea: Markets, Aid, and Reform* (New York: Columbia University Press, 2007): 1.

4 Andrew Natsios: 7.

During the national crisis, Kim Jong-Il relied on the "military-first-politics." The military-first-politics means, according to a North Korean definition, a "politics designed to place importance on the military and to strengthen the military."[5] Although this phrase appeared for the first time on May 26, 1998 in *Rodong Shinmun*, many North Korean watchers pointed out that Kim's activities had been disproportionately concentrated on military affairs since his father's death. By focusing on and mobilizing the military, Kim managed to rebuild social order and keep the North Korean regime intact.

Kim Jong-Il was unanimously approved by both the Central Committee and the Central Military Committee of the WPK as the Secretary General of the WPK on October 8, 1997. This was another anomaly. By the Party Covenant, the Secretary General should be elected by the Party Congress. However, the Congress has not been held since the 6th Congress in 1980. Instead of holding the Congress, the WPK took the formality of "unanimous approval" from the Central Committee and the Central Military Committee. Kim Jong-Il now secured his official position in the party and the military.

It seemed high time to elect a new head of the state and to normalize the nation. Instead, North Korea adopted a new "Kim Il-Sung Constitution" named after the deceased leader in 1998. The new Constitution abolished the office of the President of the DPRK and designated the Chairman of the Standing Committee of the SPA to perform some of the administrative and ceremonial functions formerly reserved for the head of the state. The Chairman of the Standing Committee of the SPA was to represent the state, receive foreign envoys, negotiate treaties, and to appoint and recall envoys. In the new Constitution the highest

5 Sang-Jin Ko, "The Fundamental Characteristics of Great Leader Kim Jong-Il's Military-First-Politics," *Chulhak Yungoo* 철학연구 (Pyongyang: Gwahak Baekgwasajon Chulpansa, 1999, no.1): 17.

office in the republic was the Chairman of the National Defense Commission (NDC), which position had been held by Kim Jong-Il. In a word, this new Constitution created two heads of the state: one ceremonial and diplomatic; and the other the real power. The Constitution declares Kim Il-Sung as the "eternal President of the Republic, implying that there will be no office of the President of the DPRK afterwards.

> The DPRK and the entire Korean people shall uphold Great Leader Comrade Kim Il-Sung as the eternal President of the Republic, defend and carry forward his ideas and exploits, and complete the *Juche* Revolution under the leadership of the Workers' Party of Korea. The DPRK Socialist Constitution is the Kim Il-Sung Constitution; it legally embodies Comrades Kim Il-Sung's *Juche* ideology and achievements.[6]

In 1998, the government regained, at least partly, its control over the people and issued new ID cards for citizens. Although North Korea recorded eight consecutive years of negative economic growth rate, from 1990 to 1998, the economy showed signs of recuperation in 1999. North Korea also opened one of its most famous attraction areas, the Mountain Keumgang, to South Korean tourism in 1998, as a way of earning foreign currency.

In June 2000, Kim Jong-Il made a grand appearance to the world by holding a historic summit meeting in Pyongyang with the President of South Korea, Kim Dae-Jung. The next year, Kim Jong-Il announced the end of the "Arduous March" and promised to build a "Strong and Prosperous Nation [강성대국]." North Korean media repeatedly emphasized "a new thinking" and pragmatic

---

6 Kim Il-Sung Constitution, Preamble.

approaches to the economy for the Strong and Prosperous Nation.

In July 2002, North Korea enacted a package of macroeconomic policy changes. The July 2002 reform package included consumer prices increases, wage hikes, currency devaluation, ration system devolution, and the introduction of the concept of "revenue" in the management of factories. However, the inauguration of the Bush administration in 2001 in the US began to cloud the prospects. The Bush administration adopted a tougher policy towards North Korea, and named North Korea as one of the "Axis of Evil" in the State of the Union address on January 29, 2002. In October 2002, the US Assistant Secretary of State James Kelly paid a visit to Pyongyang, and accused North Korea of breaching the Agreed Framework by secretly enriching uranium. The result was the second nuclear crisis on the peninsula that was escalated into the nuclear test of North Korea in October 2006. Although North Korea boasted of itself as a nuclear power, international isolation and the confrontation with the United States were leading North Korea to a rather gloomy future. All the while the North Korean people were suffering from chronic food shortages.

New Legal System

North Korea had introduced constitutional amendments at an average interval of approximately 20 years. It had its Constitution enactment in 1948, and amended in 1972 and 1992. The 1992 Socialist Constitution was said to have been amended for a new era so that the revolutionary achievements and experiences of the past twenty years could be legally established and the great project of *Juche*-oriented revolution could be successfully completed. The 1992 Constitution inserted a new Chapter 4 (National Defense) that created the National Defense Commission (NDC) as a new state organ.

After Kim Jong-Il was officially inaugurated as the Secretary General of the party, North Korea amended its Constitution again in 1998, only six years after the previous amendment. The 1998 Constitution was named the *"Kim Il-Sung Constitution."* The Constitution added a long Preamble that declared Kim Il-Sung's immortality, claiming that Kim Il-Sung would live and work with the people eternally. *"The Great Leader Comrade Kim Il-Sung Lives Forever with Us"* became the most often heard slogan of North Korea. According to Chapter Six, Section Two of the *Kim Il-Sung Constitution*, the NDC was the highest military supervisory organ with state sovereign power and an organ for overall management of national defense, securing the real power for the Chairman of the NDC. While the Constitution designated the SPA Presidium as the highest sovereign organ at the next section, Section Three, the real power house was obvious, the NDC. However, the new Constitution made little change in the citizens' rights.

The citizens' rights were almost the same as under the 1972 and 1992 Constitutions, except for a new addition of the freedom of residence and travel in Article 75. However, as all the refugees testified, the freedom to choose where to live and travel was only on paper. People had to produce proper documents to travel in the country. Traveling abroad was not an option for ordinary North Koreans, except when they left illegally at the risk of their lives. The Constitution also repeated the guarantee of sexual equality and the promise of special protection for mothers. Since the rights of people were severely violated by the famine, all these guarantees in paper became fictional.

After Kim Jong-Il was selected as the Secretary General of the WPK in

1997, North Korean government decided to retake the control over the people. The first measure to control the people was the enactment of *the Law on Citizen Registration* on November 26, 1997.[7] While the citizen registration had been established by the Cabinet Resolution during the 1950s, it was now to be regulated by the law with 19 paragraphs. This law was to restrict the mobility of the people and re-establish administrative authorities.

There were three kinds of ID cards: Birth Certificate, Citizen Card and Pyongyang Citizen Card. Citizens aged seventeen and above were to be issued the Citizen Card, and those living in Pyongyang the Pyongyang Citizen Card. This different ID card reveals the regional disparity in North Korea. As many refugees said, residents in Pyongyang were the privileged. For ordinary people, visiting Pyongyang was an extravagance that required specific travel permit.

---

7 **Para.3)** Citizen Registration is carried out by the People's Security organs of the district of the citizen's residence. Citizen Registration of the citizens residing in foreign nations is carried out by the DPRK Consulate to the nation.

Para.4) Citizens shall register their residence to the local People's Security Authorities by submitting the application for residence registration. Citizens shall report their name, sex, date of birth, place of birth, the address of residence in the application for residence registration.

Para.7) The Birth Certificate, the Citizen Card and the Pyongyang Citizen Card are the warrants confirming the DPRK citizenship of the holder.
Those who register birth are issued the Birth Certificate, those who are age seventeen and above the Citizen Card, and those who are age seventeen and above and reside in Pyongyang the Pyongyang Citizen Card.

Para.9) Parents shall register the birth of their children within 15 days of the birth by submitting the application for birth registration. The application for birth registration includes name, sex, date of birth, place of birth, and the address of residence.

Para.10) Citizen shall submit the application for Citizen Card and Pyongyang Citizen Card within 15 days after their 17th birth day to the People's Security organs of the district of their residence. The applications for Citizen Card and Pyongyang Citizen Card include name, sex, date of birth, place of birth, and the address of residence.

Para.14) Those who move their residence to other district shall register the removal by submitting the application for removal registration. The Application for removal registration includes name, sex, date of birth, place of birth, the address of residence, and the address of the new residence.

Para.15) Citizens who registered their removal shall register their new residence within 15 days of the removal registration.

North Korea had not established a single code of family law until 1990. Familial relations were covered by many different laws, including the *Sex Equality Law* of 1946. The *Socialist Family Law* of 1990[8] was the first coherent code of familial relations, albeit very simple and short, consisting of six chapters and 54 paragraphs in total.

The *Socialist Family Law* re-confirms the abolition of the traditional family register by omitting provisions for family register. Many paragraphs are mere repetition of previous laws. Marriage is declared to be the foundation of a family (Paragraph 2), and the family the basic unit of the society (Para.3). However, the law newly provides with the right of inheritance (Para.5 and Chapter 5), recognizing private ownership of some property or goods. People have the right to free marriage, and polygamy is prohibited (Para.8). The marriage age is seventeen for women and eighteen for men, but "the state shall encourage youths to marry after devoting themselves long enough to their nation and people, and to society and the collective" (Para.9), still echoing late marriage policy. Marriage is concluded by marriage registration, and conjugal relation without marriage registration is prohibited (Para.9). State intervention in a very intimate personal affair like cohabitation of an unmarried couple is guaranteed by the law. Even without this paragraph, cohabitation of an unmarried couple has been effectively prevented by the short supply of houses and the well-organized civil surveillance system anyway.

Divorce is to be decided only by the court (Para.20). In case of divorce, children under the age of three shall be brought up by mothers, unless unavoidable circumstances require otherwise (Para.22). The relationship between

8 See Appendix 3.

step-parent and step-children is assumed to be equivalent to a blood relationship, and the parental relationship between the natural parent and the children is to be terminated once the step-parental relationship is established (Para. 29). Consequently, many divorcees may lose their parental rights when their ex-spouses who reside with their children remarry.

Despite North Korea's claim that it accomplished socialist revolution, many paragraphs reverberate of the Korean custom of extended family, imposing the duty to support the members of the family on the family itself. Education of the children is an important duty of parents, and the parents must bring up their children as revolutionary and new communist humans (Para.27). Offspring must support their parents when the parents cannot work (Para.28). If the parents are all dead, grandparents have the duty to support the grandchildren (Para.35). In return, grandchildren must support their grandparents when they cannot work, or they have no other relatives to support them (Para.38). Siblings also have the duty to support their disabled or sick sisters and brothers (Para.36). Relatives, sisters or brothers, or other members of the family must support inactive members of the family, e.g., minors, the elderly, or the disabled (Para.37). Those who do not support members of the family may face punishment by the court (Para.54). The Socialist Family Law is, in essence, an amalgam of old Korean custom and socialist institution, not a progressive step beyond the *Sex Equality Law*.

In 2002, North Korea adopted a new Inheritance Law, expanding Chapter 5 of the *Socialist Family Law*. The *Inheritance Law* declared that "To protect personal property of individuals is the consistent policy of the DPRK. The State protects inheritance rights of people to personal property" (Para.2). The precedence to inheritance was the spouse, children, adopted children, step-children, unborn child, the parents, adopted parents, and step-parents (Para.17). There is no discrimination against women in inheritance right. Since most properties including land, house and vehicles belonged to the state and the collectives, the range of inheritable properties was limited to movable consumer goods. However, many people succeed in obtaining the usage right of the properties of the deceased, making such property rights practically inheritable.

North Korea first adopted the *Civil Code* in September 1990 and amended it in 1993 and 1999. Unlike the civil codes in capitalist countries, North Korean *Civil Code* deals mainly with property and economic relationship. Therefore the North Korean Civil Code is not a general statute for private relations, but a combination of property law, commercial law and economic law. Familial matters are dealt with by the *Socialist Family Law* and the *Inheritance Law*.

North Korean *Civil Code* is based on the principle of collectivism. Although the state and local government, cooperative enterprises, collective farms and other public entities as well as individuals have legal capacity, the Code gives the state and the society priority. Individual interests come last (Article 9).

The basic principles of the *Civil Code* are the reinforcement of the socialist planned economy, the socialist ownership of the productive goods, especially protection for the socialist ownership system, democratic centralism, collectivism and socialist law-abidingness.[9] As the Civil Code is basically an economic law, women's issues are not included.

There were a flood of enactment during the 1990s and 2000s. It was an effort the regain control over the people while the economic decline. A US lawyer, Marion Spina, further argued that the enactments were reflecting the intention

---

9 Sang-Yong Kim, "Basic Principles and Main Contents of Civil Codes of Korea, China and North Korea," *Buphak Yungoo*법학연구 Vol. 13, No. 2(Seoul: Law Study Institute, Yonsei University, June 2003): 37.

of the North Korean government to establish the rule of law in North Korea and catch up with the international legal standard.[10] However, the *Socialist Family Law* was a retreat from the *Sex Equality Law*, lagging behind many of the international legal practices. Certainly, formulating many laws is no guarantee of equality or progress. Revolutionary sentiments of the 1940s in legislation were forgotten in North Korea.

4.2 The Great Famine and Its Social Impacts

The Great Famine

North Korea has relied heavily on chemical fertilizers and the extensive use of electrically driven irrigation in agriculture, both of which were dependent on imported oil, because of the inauspicious natural conditions such as short growing seasons and limited arable lands surrounded by endless steep mountains. After the collapse of the Soviet Bloc, North Korea could not maintain its agricultural production as it had before. The shortage of oil and electricity also led industries to stop operating: two thirds of factories reportedly stopped operating. People stayed at home regardless of whether they were employed or not, because there was no reason to go to the idle factories. Both agriculture and the industry were almost stopped producing. With the steep decline of agricultural and industrial production, the Public Distribution System (PDS) became in-

---

10 Marion P. Spina, "Brushes with the Law: North Korean and the Rule of Law," KEI, *On Korea: Academic Paper Series*, Vol. 1 (Washington DC: KEI, 2008): 75–97.

creasingly paralyzed.

North Korea had established the PDS by the Cabinet Resolutions No.96 and No.102 of 1957. The PDS supplied all the people except those who belonged to collective farms with rations of grains, meat and cooking oil. The ration by the PDS does not mean the in-kind supply of grains or goods. The state procured grains and other necessities from the collective farms and industries, and then distributed them to the people at very low, in fact nominal, prices. The PDS in this sense was the state subsidies for basic necessities.[11] Therefore, it was possible, and later became common practices, to buy food outside of the PDS. Since the collective farms were allotted grains per year after the harvest, some members of the farms actually sold grains in black market at high prices even before the famine.

The PDS was based on twelve hierarchical classes,[12] with the Kim family at the top and prisoners at the bottom. Prisoners were assigned, in normal times, 200 grams of grains daily, which was substantially less than needed.[13] However, the exact composition of the twelve classes has not been officially reported. It has been estimated based on the reports of the North Korean refugees. Therefore the estimate of the grouping and the allocations were varied by researchers. In general, miners, defense workers, heavy-industrial workers, and fishermen received the highest amount, 900 grams a day. The next groups were high-ranking government officials and military personnel, receiving 800 to 850 grams. Office

---

11 Therefore, it was possible, and later became common practices, to buy food outside of the PDS.

12 In a strictly theoretical term, the word "class" is inappropriate, since North Korea claimed to abolish the private property and class. However, many North Korea watchers regard the hierarchical structure as the class system.

13 Andrew Natsios: 93. However, with exacerbation of the famine, the allotment of rations to prisoners was reported to stop altogether.

workers and light industry workers received 600 grams. The aged and the children received less than 400 grams.[14] However, actual rations were far less than numeric allocations.

Most refugees from North Korea reported that until the 1970s they had not experienced starvation, although the rations were hardly abundant. However, the authorities began to deduct four-days-amount of rations each month since 1973 under the name of "reserved rice for war." Further, the authorities announced the deduction of three-days-amount of rations as the "patriotic rice saving" in 1987 when the Soviet Union reduced its assistance to North Korea. This further deduction forced people to live without a full week of rations for each month.

In many countries, 300 to 400 grams of grains a day per capita would be enough for the people to survive. People can supplement their nutrition with meats, dairies, eggs, vegetables and fruits. However, in North Korea, the main diet was the grains. The shortage of the sources of fat and protein made the North Korean people very vulnerable to the deduction of grains.

The deduction did not stop there. In 1991, the government initiated a *"Let's eat two meals a day"* campaign. Many refugees reported that for at least some segments of the population, the PDS began to fail to supply food on regular basis since 1991.[15] North Korean official acknowledgement of food emergency began in the summer of 1995. North Korea attributed this food emergency to natural disaster, the two consecutive years of flood in 1995 and 1996. However, an extremely high incidence of "stunting," the unusually low height-for-

---

14 Andrew Natsios estimated the allocation amount from 900 to 200 grams. Marcus Noland estimates 800 to 100 grams. The two researches had different groupings and allocation estimates. Andrew Natsios: 93; Stephan Haggard and Marcus Noland (2007): 54

15 Stephan Haggard and Marcus Noland, *Hunger and Human Rights: The Politics of Famine in North Korea* (Washington DC: US Committee for Human Rights in North Korea, 2005): 14.

age condition, among children of North Korea suggested that food crisis had begun well before 1995. The reported prevalence of child stunting was greatly higher in North Korea than in Laos, Cambodia or in Bangladesh, where national income per capita and the literacy rate of the people were estimated lower than North Korea.

Table 4.1) Indicators of Malnutrition in Children Under 5 Years

Country	Year	Nutritional Measure (Percentage)		
		Severe Underweight	Moderate/Severe Wasting	Moderate/Severe Stunting
Cambodia	1990-95	7	8	38
Laos	1990-95	12	11	47
Vietnam	1990-95	11	12	47
Bangladesh	1990-95	21	18	55
India	1990-95	21	18	52
Nepal	1990-95	16	11	48
Pakistan	1990-95	13	9	50
Sri Lanka	1990-95	7	16	24
North Korea	1998	32[1]	19	57

Source : World Food Program, 1999; UNICEF. Re-quoted from Nicholas Everstadt, *The North Korean Economy: Between Crisis and Catastrophe* (New Jersey: Treansaction Publishers, 2007): 135.
Note [1]: Under 7 Years of Age

The PDS became more erratic with time. In 1993, the authorities stopped supplying foods to many remote areas. For several years from 1994, as refugees testified again and again, many people began to die of hunger. In Moosan coal mine area, around 140 people died of starvation among 200 geological investi-gation squad members and their families.[16] According to a survey of North Ko-rean refugees carried out by a South Korean NGO, almost a third of the family members of the surveyed died during the period from August 1995 to October 1998.[17] Among 10,127 family members of the 1,855 surveyed refugees, 2,991 people died during four years. Although the refugees were likely to come from the worst-off members of North Korea, the death rate was astonishingly high.

However, the death toll was not evenly distributed to all classes and re-gions. The people from the mistrusted classes and from the Northeast region[18] starved first. Haggard and Noland argued that the real cause of massive death tolls of particular groups of people was the state failure. In the socialist system, the state directly determines the entitlement of people for food, job and other social security. Those who died of starvation were not entitled for food by the state decision. The entitlement failure was thus the state failure to distribute food equitably.[19] Similarly, Andrew Natsios named the state decision to cut-off food subsidies to the Northeast region in 1994 and 1995 as "triage."[20]

Regardless of whether the government triaged some people or not, those who were cut off food subsidies had to rely on themselves for survival. The most common one-time coping methods at the early period of the famine were

16 Good Friends, *Bukhansramduli Malhanun Bukhan Iyagi* 북한사람들이 말하는 북한이야기 (Seoul: Jungto-Pub-lisher, 2000): 20.

17 Good Friends, *Bukhan Sikryangnangwa Bukhan Ingwon* 북한 식량난과 북한인권 (Seoul: Jongto Chulpansa, 2004): 32.

18 Northeast region is located far away from Pyongyang, and has very little arable land. Northeast region has been relied on transported grains from Southwest region. If food is not consciously allocated and trans-ported to the region, people in the Northeast region are to face severe shortage of food.

19 Stephan Haggard and Marcus Noland (2007): 22.

20 Andrew Natsios: 91.

either selling family effects or getting money from better-off relatives, or both. Starving people sold clothing, furniture, ceramics and even the house itself. Some people who had managed to keep the family heirlooms and antiques despite the long communist rule began to sell them as well.[21] Those who had wealthy relatives within and outside of North Korea visited or wrote for help. Among them those who had relatives abroad, including in South Korea, were the luckiest because they could obtain foods and US dollars. However, family effects or the support from relatives soon dried out.

After the cash, either from selling their belongings or from relatives, dried out, many people began to consume wild foods that were not normally part of the diet. These foods are collected from country side. Peasants had long been passed the knowledge of wild foods that were edible when desperate. Wild greens and plants' root were thoroughly consumed. Many people mixed staple grains with inedible material such as rice straw or the powered bark of tree to extend their quantity of the meal. A survey targeted young North Korean wanders showed that 75 percent of the respondents had consumed wild foods.[22]

Consumption of wild foods caused severe indigestion, constipation or diarrhea, or food poisoning. Some could survive these dire conditions. Many people, however, died from these diets. Even with the possibility of food poisoning and death, starving people continued to wander the field to find any wild greens and roots.

The collapse of the PDS and the starvation of the people shook the society. Facing the choice of life or death, people began to ignore most laws and orders.

---

21 North Korean antiques began appearing in South Korea in 1996. Andrew Natsios: 85.

22 Good Neighbors (2004): 37. The surveyed were 482 young refugees from North Korean to China. They were all teenagers.

Since the factories or offices were unable to provide food or money, people absented themselves from their jobs and wandered the field for food. As people moved around, the thick nets of social organizations lost their control over the membership. Law and order were widely ignored.

Crumbling "Organization Life" [조직생활]

While people were going out to collect wild foods or sell their belongings for food, the strictly controlling "organization life" crumbled. North Korea has maintained an extremely exhaustive social organization system. Every person has to join at least one social organization from the age of seven onwards. When a child enrolls in second grade in elementary school, usually at the age of seven, he or she has to join the Juvenile Corps [소년단]. Although every child joins the Juvenile Corps, the timing of joining is different among the children, to a great degree depending on the family background. Privileged children join the Corps on February 16, the birthday of Kim Jong-Il, with a grand ceremony. The next selected children join the Corps on April 15, the birthday of Kim Il-Sung, also with a big ceremony.

The joining ceremonies are part of the many national events celebrating the birthdays of the father and son. The ceremonies are held in front of a huge crowd of visitors consisting of party cadre members, leading figures in the local or central government, military commanders, war veterans and revolutionary heroes. After the children bow to express loyalty for the party and the Kims, the visitors tie a red scarf to the neck of each child one by one. The red scarf is the symbol of the Juvenile Corps. Children wear the red scarf almost everyday and on every official occasion. This ceremony itself infuses the children with pride and sense of loyalty. Remaining children join the Corps on June 6, the anniversary of the Juvenile Corps with a simple ceremony of bowing. The difference in the timing and the scale of the ceremony of joining the Corps causes stratification and jealousy among the children.

The Juvenile Corps operates like an autonomous students' association and carries out its own tasks like raising rabbits, collecting scrap metal or iron and assisting farming. The members of the Juvenile Corps are required to practice marching in file on Saturday and attend daily evaluation meetings. The activities and performance of each child are thoroughly evaluated by the teachers and the party instructors. The record of the activity evaluation remains for life and affects the future of the child.

When the children reach at the age of 14 and enter middle-high school, they join the Kim Il-Sung Union of Socialist Youths (Youth Union). The procedure of joining the Youth Union is similar to that of the Juvenile Corps, but more complicated and difficult. If a youth is admitted to the Youth Union, he or she removes the red scarf of the Juvenile Corps and is issued with the Youth Union membership card. Members of the Youth Union are instructed to regard the membership card as their socio-political life which is more important than their physical life. Therefore members tend to wrap the card with water-proof plastic and keep it in a wallet. Damaging or losing the membership card is a grave matter, invoking a severe criticism from the leaders, and sometimes causing future disadvantage.

Except the age of the members, the Youth Union is similar to the Juvenile Corps, in that it operates as an autonomous students' association of the school and carries out its own tasks like organizing ideological study meeting. The activities and performance of the students are also reviewed and recorded by the teachers and the party instructors. The evaluation record plays an important role in the decision of where to send the student after high school graduation.

Those who are age eighteen and above can apply to join the WPK. While joining the Juvenile Corps and Youth Union is compulsory, joining the party is voluntary and highly selective. The applicant to the party submits an application form and two recommendation letters of the members of the WPK. Then the local party committee decides whether or not the applicant is admitted. If an applicant is admitted, he or she serves as a candidate member for a year. After a year, his or her performance is reviewed by the committee. If the result of the review is satisfactory, he or she obtains full membership to the party. The party member then leaves the Youth Union, and serves the party organization.

Those who are not party members remain in the Youth Union until the age thirty. When a non-party member reaches to the age of thirty, he or she moves to an organization related to his or her occupation. Farmers join the Farming Workers Union of Korea (Farmers Union), workers and office workers the Workers Union of Korea and unemployed housewives the Women's Union. Those who do not belong to any of these organizations, like retired and elderly people, are to join the People's Squad [인민반]. In principle, those People's Squads compose all the residents in the area. However, since others attend the organizational activities in the Unions, only retired, elderly and seriously ill people actually attend the People's Squad meetings.

All these organizations require their members to attend lectures, study meetings and daily evaluation meetings. Lectures and study meetings are to educate the speeches of Kim Il-Sung and Kim Jong-Il and instruct the party policy to their members. If one misses any of these meetings without prior permission, he or she could be accused of slackened discipline and laxity of morality. This accusation could cause other criminal charges. Therefore, the "organization life [조직생활]," as North Koreans call the organizational activities, is the core tool of control and surveillance for the people.

During and after the famine, however, it became impossible for many people to continue the mandatory organization life. People began to skip the meetings and lectures. Instead, people roamed around the country to obtain whatever foodstuffs possible. Because it was a matter of life and death, the mighty organizations could not prevent the people from skipping the meetings. The organization life became nominal. With the crumbling organization life, social order also decayed.

Decaying Social Order

Not only did people skip the organizational activities, they also absented themselves from work without leave. When only 30 percent of the factories and industries were actually operating, the employees anyway had nothing to do and nothing to obtain in the factory. Some came in the morning and soon left their work place. Some simply did not show up at all. Some stayed out of work for months, some few days a month.

Food shortage increased the mobility of the people. Many people traveled, irrespective of whether they procured proper document for travel or not, to the rural areas to obtain foods. Also several hundred thousand people crossed the national border to China. During the famine period and immediately after, hunger and the search for food were the major factor to push people to China.[23] However, people continued to go to China even after the famine became less severe, in search for better life, or in avoidance of suppression or persecution from the North Korean regime.[24]

Some people succeeded in obtaining food from their relatives by travel. Others had to rely on begging or foraging. Among the refugees who left North Korea before 1993, only 6.9 percent reported they went begging. However, among the refugees who left North Korea after 1994, 21.5 percent said they went begging.[25] Also many people sold their family belongings in exchange of foods.

Increased mobility of people also gave rise to a prevalence of corruption and bribery. In order to travel, North Korean people needed to carry written permissions. Facing the rapidly increasing demand of travel permits, many bureaucrats and party members received money in return for the permits. Sometimes they received the reward in kind, like tobacco, sugar, or other consumer items. Those who could not afford the bribe had to risk arrest and imprisonment. If a person was picked up by the police or security personnel while traveling without a permit, he or she could be beaten, arrested or have all luggages confiscated. In many cases, people avoided arrest by handing out goods or money as bribes. Even when the travelers had proper paper, many realized soon that paying bribes was easy and less costly. Bureaucrats, the police, party members, security guards, and other authorities demanded and accepted bribery. For them, bribery

23 Good Friends (1999): 14.

24 Yoonok Chang: 14-33.

25 Hyun-Sun Park, *Hyundai Bukhansahoewa Gajok*현대북한사회와 가족 (Seoul: Hanul Publishing House, 2003): 148.

was their way of survival. Bribery became the general norm of social life. According to a survey targeted 521 North Korean refugees in China, 51.2 percent of them experienced arrests by the authorities, among which 29.6 percent were released by bribery.[26]

(Woman from Kyungsung, North Hamkyung Province, age 53) All the security guards and patrolmen confiscated my goods whenever they saw me selling them. I cried and begged them, who were aged like my son, to return at least half of the goods. But they did not care, and forced me out. One day, I noticed that they overlooked other young women's selling. Later I realized that those women had connection with the security guys. Those women paid bribe like tobacco and liquor in advance.[27]

The social welfare system including education and health-care also crumbled. Although North Korea nominally maintained the eleven year free compulsory education system, nurseries and schools demanded the parents to pay for the children. Doctors and nurses also illegally traded medicines that were provided for public health system.

(Man age 52, former nursing home manager) In the past, North Korea had maintained free education and free health-care system. However, even in the past, pupils had provided voluntary labor without pay. Elementary school pupils had had to work for ten to fifteen days in the farms or other places. Also school had burdened the parents with many items for education, like notebooks, papers, paints and even cement. After the economic crisis, the burden became bigger. It was not free

26 Good Friends, *Bukhansahoe, Mooussi Byunhago Itnunga?* 북한사회, 무엇이 변하고 있는가 (Seoul: Jungto Chulpansa, 2001): 222-223.

27 Good Friends, *Onului Bukhan, Bukhansui Naeil*오늘의 북한, 북한의 내일 (Seoul: Jungto-Publisher, 2006): 44.

education. Parents had to go to markets to provide their children with notebooks, pencil and so on. Market prices were outrageously high... For health care, the state had levied one percent of wage for social welfare, and provided free treatment. Now, they said there was no medicine at clinics or hospitals. Now we could be treated only with our money.[28]

Nursery and school management also became insolvent. Since state provisions for these institutions were stopped, nurseries and schools were unable to provide heating, sanitation, or lunch. Donations or provisions by the parents were in short supply. Moreover, many teachers in famine stricken area were absent either because they were ill, or because they were traveling for food. Parents who could not afford these school demands made their children to drop out. Some schools were almost closed.

(Woman, age 39, former worker at textile factory) There was nothing provided by the state to nurseries. Towels, tooth paste, soap and papers were all brought from home. Food and food coupons also were brought from home.[29]

(Woman, former Head of a People's Squad, age 36) Because teachers also were not paid for months, they suffered from famine. Many teachers handed in their resignation in order for trades. Although North Korea educated people that trades was bad capitalist seed, the state had to tolerate trades activities after the crisis. However, teachers were supposed to teach students the right things, the state strictly forbade

28 Hyun-Sun Park, *Hyundai Bukhanui Gajoke Gwanhan Yungoo: Gajok Jeasaengsangwa Gajokgoojorul Chungsimuro* 현대북한의 가족에 관한 연구: 가족 재생산과 가족구조를 중심으로 (Seoul: Ph. D. Thesis, Ehwa Woman's University, 1999): 173-174.

29 Hyun-Sun Park (1999): 176.

teachers from trades. Therefore teachers were more desperate.[30]

According to a survey of 1,072 North Korean refugees in China, 75.5 percent of them answered that many students skipped school because of hunger, and 38.8 percent answered that one or more children were engaged in trades, instead of going to school, for the survival of the family.[31]

Crimes and prowlers increased. Stealing, robbery, pick-pocketing and gang crimes threatened people. In particular, the increase of child prowlers caught the eyes of the outside world. They were called "Flower Swallows [꽃제비; kkot-chebie]." Many youngsters, at the age of about early teens, just roamed around the country, rummaging through garbage sites for left-over foods, or stealing food at the market. Sometimes they became gang robbers.

The origin of the name "Flower Swallows" is not clear. Korean Chinese people explain that swallows came from "snatch away" [잽이: chebie] that has the same pronunciation with swallow in Korean, and that flowers came from the Chinese word "bagger" [화자: hua-zi] that literally reads flower child. Therefore, Flower Swallow means snatching, pick-pocketing, or stealing bagger. Others reckon that, in Korean slang, "swallow" meant a gigolo or a man living with money exploited from women. The word "flower" was added to emphasize the young age of the prowlers. According to a novel published in North Korea in 2001, the word Flower Swallow came from Russian words "КОЧЕВНИК" or "КОЧЕВОЙ" that sound like "kkot-Chebie."[32] The word КОЧЕВНИК means no-

---

30 Hyun-Sun Park (1999): 175.

31 Good Friends (2001): 23.

32 Ki-Jong Chung, *Yulbyung Gwangjang* 열병광장 (Pyongyang: Monye Chulpansa, 2001): 95.

mad, and КОЧЕВОЙ nomadic. This novel explains that the word "Flower Swallows" has been in use since the Soviet occupation of North Korea immediately after the surrender of Japan when many Koreans suffered from utter poverty because of colonial exploitation.

Whatever is the origin, this romantic name is contradictory to the reality of the children. Many foreigners filmed the pathetic situations of the Flower Swallows in the markets or railroad stations. They did not have families or homes. They slept together in and outside of train stations, market places and huts. They wore stinking tatters. They ate anything they could touch, including waste foods. They often stole or rob. Many refugees testified that they experienced being robbed by the Flower Swallows.[33]

Often the authorities cracked down these Flower Swallows and sent them to the 9.27 Camp that was reported to be established to accommodate young roaming orphans and prowlers by the instruction of Kim Jong-Il on September 27, 1997.[34] However, because this camp did not provide enough food for the youngsters, most of them escaped and returned to the life of Flower Swallow.[35]

Hamhung City, which was located in the middle of North Hamkyung Province and was worst inflicted by famine, had one of the largest and busiest railway stations in North Korea. Around the Hamhung Station were a large number of Flower Swallows.

Hamhung City was the world of Flower Swallows. Disabled one, or disfigured one... There were sometimes three or four year old Flower Swallows as well. I saw

---

33 Good Friends (2001): 225.

34 "Hyesan 927," Good Friends (2000): 162–183.

35 Good Friends (1999): 52.

a five year old sister holding hand of her three year old brother and looking down all the way to find any fallen foodstuffs. That scene was really heart-breaking.[36]

Family Breakdown

As the increase of the Flower Swallows clearly shows, famine and the collapse of the PDS resulted in the breakdown of the families. Many children stayed out of the home because their parents were either missing or dead, or deserted them. According to a survey, while 6.9 percent of refugees who left North Korea before 1993 experienced either death or disappearance of one or more of their family members, 20 percent of refugees who left North Korea after 1994 experienced that kind of loss of family members.[37]

A survey of 1,027 North Korean refugees in China reported that 29.5 percent of the refugees had at least one dead and 86 percent at least one missing among their family members during the period from August 1995 to September 1998.[38] The primary reason of the missing was to search for food. One refugee reported that by the end of the 1990s 30 to 40 percent of married couples had to separate in order to survive. Other refugee testified that an apartment complex in Hoeryung City became almost an empty ruin in 1998 because most of the residents left their home to search for food.[39]

---

36 Hyun-Sun Park (1999): 246.

37 Hyun-Sun Park (1999): 174.

38 Good Friends (2001): 22.

39 Soon-Hee Im, *Bukhan Yusongui Sarm: Jisokgwa Byunhwa* 북한여성의 삶: 지속과 변화 (Seoul: Hae-Nam, 2006): 80-81.

The first pattern of family breakdown came from the death of a member. The old or the weakest member died first. When between 0.6 million and one million people died because of famine, many families shared the common experience of loss.

> (Woman from Bukchung, South Hamkyung Province, age 41) My husband and mother-in-law, father-in-law and my youngest daughter died after suffering from starvation for three years. My eldest son was serving in the army. Among six family members, only my elder daughter and I survived.[40]

> (Woman from Leewon, South Hamkyung Province, age 28) In North Korea, I was married with a daughter of age four. I and my husband were employed, but were not paid for years. My family was starved. We had to eat grass roots or the bark of trees.... My husband had long been suffering from gastroenteric disorder. Those coarse foods were too difficult for him to digest. He became seriously ill, but we could not obtain any medicine. He died without ever being treated.[41]

The second pattern of family breakdown was family separation or missing person's case. This pattern usually came from the efforts to obtain foods. Sometimes families actively chose to separate the family as a survival strategy. One or two family members went and stayed with better-off relatives, and others scattered around the country on their own. Also, many people left for relatives in rural areas or in China. In most cases they returned home after a long, risky travel. However, some just stayed where they could survive, either by begging, working, or stealing. Even those people returned home had to travel again be-

40 Good Friends (1999): 93.

41 Good Friends (1999): 98.

cause foods lasted for only a short while. Some roamed around wherever they could beg for food and survive, like Flower Swallows.

(Woman from Hamhung, North Hamkyung Province, in her mid-50s) During the famine, my husband and second son died. The remaining four family members decided to sell the house and split the money. My two children and a brother-in-law went to live with my sister-in-law. I came to China to depend on my brother.[42]

(Woman, age 39) Fortunately, my family survived together. However, many families were breaking. The wife went to her natal parents, the husband to his, and the children deserted at railway station.[43]

(Man from Chungjin, North Hamkyung Province, age 35) I lived with my wife, two daughters and one son. One day my wife left home in search for food. She never returned. I don't know whether she is dead or alive somewhere else, or whether she deliberately deserted us or not.[44]

According to the aforementioned survey, 32.3 percent of missing cases were reported to be caused by the member's travel to obtain foods, 32.1 percent by the member's travel to China, 27.4 percent by the member's becoming the prowler or Flower Swallow. In some cases, family members accidentally separated in China or border cities.

The third pattern of family breakdown was divorce or separation of married couples. During the famine many couple filed for divorce. In some cases,

---

42 Hyun–Sun Park (1999): 245.

43 Hyun–Sun Park (1999): 246.

44 Good Friends (1999): 100.

one spouse committed adultery while the other party was traveling to obtain foods. In other cases the wives filed for divorce on the ground of the husband's economic incompetence. When divorce cases increased, the North Korean authorities decided to impose heavy fine for divorce, making divorce more costly. However, the heavy fine did not deter divorces. Many couple decided to separate without legal procedure.

> (Man from Jaeryung, North Hwanghae Province, former member of the WPK) Divorce is in fact impossible. The state would not allow divorce. It is very costly too. If a couple hated to live together, they would simply separate. Legal divorce will be only one or two in 10,000 cases...[45]

After the separation, many women crossed the border to China and married to other men without registration. A survey that was carried out in the three Prefectures in north-eastern China, three quarter of refugees in these areas was women.[46] The high proportion of female refugees resulted from the fact that women could be married, or trafficked, to Chinese men and thus obtain shelters in China. Among the female refugees, a large numbers of women married in China, either by force or fraud, or by their own choice, after leaving their husbands in North Korea.

The fourth pattern of family breakdown was the desertion of the children. Marriage breaks often resulted in the desertion of children by both parents, producing a large number of Flower Swallows. In many cases, the desertion was out of desperate effort to survive.

---

45 Interview by the Sejong Institute (December 12, 2002).

46 Good Friends (1999): 23.

(Woman from Kiljoo County, age 27) My husband was killed by his best friend because of money. I had to find ways to survive, so I headed for China with my infant bay. The baby began to cry, because she was hungry. However, since I was starved as well, my breast was all dried up. I could not feed her. She cried loudly. I had to cross the border river. It was impossible to cross the river with a crying baby. So I left her in front of a house, wishing the family of the house would take her. I succeeded in crossing the river, and married to a Chinese man.[47]

(Man from Chongjin City, age 35) I had wife and a daughter of age three. My wife left me a short note to say goodbye, and disappeared. My daughter cried everyday looking for her mother and foods. I could not feed her. One day, I took her to a busy railway station. I handed a note to my daughter. In that note, I wrote: "She is an orphan. Anybody who takes care of her will be blessed." Then I came to China.[48]

The last, and the worst, pattern of family breakdown was the whole family suicide. Some couples chose to kill their children first, and kill themselves afterwards. In 1997, a doctor's family of six members in Hamhung City committed suicide, in order to avoid making the children Flower Swallows.[49]

---

47 Among those who answered the survey, 6,841 were male, 21,100 were female. Good Friends (1999): 103–104.

48 Good Friends (1999): 102.

49 Soon-Hee Im (2006): 84.

4.3 The Plight of Women

Increased Burden of Labor

From the beginning, North Korean leadership has demanded women to shoulder both the burden of household chores as traditional housewives and the burden of employment as socialist workers. As mentioned earlier, Kim Il-Sung made it very clear that household works belonged to women. While the proportion of women in the labor force increased, women's burden as home-makers remained the same. The double burden of women was not light even during the best periods. With the economic crisis, moreover, women had to shoulder new burdens of coping with extreme conditions.

First, the shortage of electricity and energy created new burdens of labor, like carrying water and coal to houses. Women living in high-storied apartment houses had to walk up and down the stairs to carry barrels of water from the ground, because there was no running water or elevator. Women living in detached houses also had to go to the communal wells, draw water and then bring the water to home. Some husbands helped their wives in carrying water, but most did not. Carrying water was part of home-making, and thus women's job.

(Woman from Jagang Province) My apartment house was large and clean. It was nice. However, like many others, we did not have running water. The apartment building supplied running water for one or two hours a day. But because of the weak pressure of water, only houses on ground- or second- floor could receive the water. We lived on the 6th floor. I had to walk up and down, from ground level to the 6th floor, with heavy barrels of water. After the birth of my first child, I needed a huge amount of water everyday. I had to carry water twenty times a day. You could hear the sound of water pump from the ground. That was the signal of running water. Then I had to rush down to take water. Water supplying hour was so short that soon it ended. If you do not hurry up, you cannot get water. Often I had to carry my baby on my back while I went down to take water.[50]

Also women had to make briquette out of coal-powder. Ordinary people relied on home-made briquettes for heating and cooking. There had been briquette factories, but these almost stopped running after the economic crisis because of the shortage of the electricity and inadequate transportation. However, making briquettes was easier than collecting firewood and twigs. In rural areas people had to find firewood and twigs for heating and cooking. Many husbands took the responsibility of making briquettes and collecting firewood. However, cleaning the mess during and after the process of making briquettes was the responsibility of wives.

In North Korea, every family had to make briquettes for heating and cooking at home. Every family had a machine for briquettes. In autumn, there was always huge commotion to make briquettes. Everybody looked dark-black, their noses and faces were black. And the houses and the roads were all black with the dust of coal-powder. There were briquette factories, of course. However, the factories could not supply enough briquettes because there was no train to transport large amount of coal to the factories....[51]

Second, many social institutions for children, the sick and the elderly

---

50 Hankuk Yusong Yunguso: 187–188.

51 Hankuk Yusong Yunguso: 165.

became nominal only, leaving their erstwhile clients under the care of women within the family. Women as mothers and daughters-in-laws had to spend hours to look after children and the elderly. If a member of the family fell ill, women had to wander around for hours to find herbs for cure, because medicines were hardly available for ordinary people.

Third and most importantly, with the collapse of the PDS, women had to rely on their own wit to find foodstuffs. Feeding the family was the responsibility of the wives, irrespective of whether the husbands earned means to obtain foodstuffs or not. Many women went out to collect edible wild greens, plant roots and barks of trees. Sometimes people died because they took poisonous greens by mistake. Collecting edible greens and cooking them required enormous amounts of physical effort, carefulness and creativity.

Women also cultivated plants wherever they had access to. Planting vegetables in kitchen gardens was routine daily work. Even in apartment buildings in urban areas, women grew small animals like chicken or rabbits, or vegetable on their balconies. In rural areas, women went far away to cultivate more greens.

When people all over the country tried to till lands everywhere, deforestation and soil erosion became the cause of chronic natural disaster. The government attempted to forbid the tilling of steep hills and mountains, but to no avail. Finally the government demanded people to plant trees simultaneously with cultivating vegetables and pay money for land use. The burden of planting trees and paying the fees were burdensome for ordinary people. Therefore people developed new evasive tactics like disguising the size of the land they were cultivating and paying bribes.

People made private patch field in steep hills where the gradient reached up to from 30 to 60 degrees. Since these hills had never been cultivated before, people had to remove trees, rocks and wild bushes. Often they had to remove a huge base rock as well. They had to do all these jobs only with small weeding hoes and pickaxes… There was no irrigation system, of course. People had to go to nearest river or reservoir for water. With chronic malnutrition, cultivating wild land was an extremely exhausting work nearly costing life.[52]

This exhausting work was mostly done by women. These menial jobs were supposed to be done by women. Many foreigners reported the anomaly of North Korea: one may easily watch that while women worked in the fields, men tended to play cards in the shade.[53]

Many women became the breadwinners of their families. Although the state and the industries stopped paying wages and salaries, men were assumed to go to work. It was women who went out to sell things and earn money to support the family. Between 70 and 80 percent of dealers in markets were women.

(Man from Kaesung, born in 1971) In North Korea, I was (illegally) trading tobaccos. I mean, I smuggled tobacco from China. Then I passed them to women. I would not do that kind of (menial) thing like selling tobaccos at market. That was women's job. Most of trades at markets were dealt with by women.[54]

(Woman from Wonsan) Most of dealers at markets were women. It was women's job. We called the women "locusts." Whenever one shouted loud "Security Guards

---

52 Good Friends (2004): 63.

53 Whenever I traveled rural area in North Korea, I witnessed the same.

54 Interview by Sejong Institute (November 12, 2002).

are coming," then those women just ran all over, like locusts.[55]

Selling things at markets was a rather enviable occupation. Many women could not afford the luxury of sitting-to-sell. Those who could not obtain a vending booth or space at a market place, either because they could not pay fees or because their goods did not suit the market, had to visit from house to house or travel to remote places to sell their goods. These peddlers had to walk for a long time, because of the inadequate transportation. Ironically, the inadequate transportation was the source of the trading profits. All these conditions compounded women's already heavy burden of labor.

Deteriorating Health

All the hard work that women performed required sufficient provision of nutrition. However, in reality, women were less nourished than men. In addition to the general shortage of foods, there were other factors exacerbating malnutrition of women. First, the authority distributed food, if any, mainly to employed men. According to a report by a United States intelligence organization, North Korea rationed 150 grams of grain a day only to men who were involved in heavy labor in the north-eastern and north-western areas in 1997. Women in those areas were not rationed at all.[56] Second, women tended to refrain themselves from eating in order to feed their families first. Women were inculcated

---

55 Interview by Sejong Institute (February 26, 2003).

56 Soon-Hee Im (2006): 83

with the patriarchal code of behavior that demanded women to be devoted to their husbands and sons first.

The official newspaper of the WPK, *Daily Rodong*, ran a report in commemoration of the International Women's Day (March 8), in which the hardship of women during the Arduous March was unusually vividly depicted. The Daily Rodoong also praised the devotion of women who "gave way even a bowl of porridge to their husbands and children." The sacrificial devotion of women for their family led women to more hazardous health conditions.

> The impact of the unexpected shortage of foods, electricity and fuel came to women first... Our women gave way even a bowl of porridge to their husbands and children. They made lunch boxes, out of wild vegetables, for their husbands and children and nothing for them. Without revealing the fact that their lunch boxes were empty, they brought their empty lunch boxes to work, and continued to run the machines.[57]

> (Woman, former teacher, age 47) We most valued a bowl of rice. Because of the shortage of rice, most people had to eat corn. If a family managed to obtain some rice, rice was assumed to be for the head of the family (husband) and corn for other family members. When one took their young children to the distribution centers, children said "father's food is coming" if rice came. If corn came, children said "mommy's food is coming." Everybody took that for granted. Some families made it a rule that the husbands' bowl should be spooned out first. Even though the husband and wife were both employed, the husband always had the priority. If the wife stayed at home, she would have a bowl of porridge out of the scorched corn from the bottom of the pot.[58]

---

57 *Rodong Shinmoon* (March 8, 2000).

58 Hyun-Sun Park (2003): 340.

As a result, the degree of malnutrition of mothers and children was alarmingly severe. According to the survey by the DPRK Central Bureau of Statistics under the auspices of the United Nations Children's Fund (UNICEF) and World Food Program (WFP), a third of mothers measured were suffering from malnutrition, with Mid-Upper Arm Circumference (MUAC) of less than 22.5 cm. A MUAC of less than 22.5 are at high risk of having a low birth-weight baby. There is also a correlation between MUAC and Body Mass Index (BMI). A BMI of less than 18.5 is considered to be incompatible with leading a healthy life. A MUAC of 22.5 approximates a BMI of 18.5.[59] Malnutrition of mothers also worsened malnutrition of babies because 70 percent of mothers gave babies only breast-milk.[60]

Inadequate maternity care also worsened women's health. Since contraceptive pills were non-existent, most women relied on uterine loops that were provided by local clinics free of charge. As was mentioned earlier, uterine loops were made of metallic material, and often caused side-effects like back pain and sterilization. Moreover, while uterine loops were supposed to be replaced in every three or four years, most women were ignorant of the fact and kept one for more than a decade.[61]

Despite their problems, uterine loops were better than abortions for the health of women. Since uterine loops were provided only for married women who already had borne a child, unmarried women had no access to contraception. As pre-marital sexual relationship was regarded as a laxity of socialist

---

59 UNICEF, *Nutrition Assessment 2002, DPR Korea*: 25.

60 UNICEF, *Nutrition Assessment 2002, DPR Korea*: 3.

61 Interview with Choi Bong-Rye, who fled from North Korea in 1987 with her family of eleven members, and Im Jong-Hee.

morality, many unmarried women resorted to abortion in case of pregnancy. Because of the lack of medicines and energy, in most cases surgeries were done without proper sanitation and anesthesia. Abortion was not even considered to require any anesthesia.[62] Poor sanitation and lack of medicine caused excruciating pain and long lasting side effects for women who had abortion.

While the government had enforced birth control to reduce births during the 1970s, it encouraged women to have more children when the economic crisis caused sharp decline in birth rates during the late 1990s. The government held the Second Mothers' Conference [제2차 전국 어머니대회] in 1998, praising multiple births and motherhood. Also there were reports that Kim Jong-Il instructed the government to encourage women to have many babies. After the instruction, hospitals and clinics began to reject the request for abortion. Therefore, those women who were determined not to have more babies had to secretly call doctors, pay bribes, and endure makeshift surgeries at home. In one case, a woman's fetus was aborted with a heated iron skewer. She suffered from the aftermath, and became sterilized.[63]

Women's health was also threatened by the lack of proper sanitary napkins. Disposable sanitary napkins were almost unheard of. Most women could not afford clean cotton gauze either. They had to rely on threadbare clothes, mostly of synthetic fiber. This poor condition of women was spotted in 1997 when North Korea secretly dispatched a married couple to South Korea for espionage. Although well educated and privileged in North Korea, the spy couple could not obtain sanitary napkins. They instead bought diapers for baby after a

---

62 Interview with Choi Bong-Rye, who fled from North Korea in 1987 with her family of eleven members, and Im Jong-Hee.

63 Soon-Hee Im (2006): 94.

little confusion. After their arrest, the husband confided that they had no idea of disposable sanitary napkins. Because of unhygienic conditions, gynecological disorders were spreading.[64]

> In North Korea, if anybody can have cotton cloth as sanitary napkin, she is very lucky. Sanitary napkins made of soft gauze were sold during the mid 1980s, for two or three years only. A small number of mothers who were learned visited drug stores or hospitals, and obtained cotton cloth, and cut it into small sizes. Others use harsh papers or threadbare cloths.[65]

In addition to the lack of medicines and the collapse of medical infrastructure, women's health further deteriorated because of insensitivity of women to their body. Women were ignorant of gynecological symptoms and unaware of the importance of early diagnosis of cancers. Symptoms like coughing, anemia, dizziness, vomiting and diarrhea were all regarded as natural with their coarse diet. They were concerned about the health of their husbands and children, but hardly of themselves. To a great extent, this insensitivity of women to their health was the result of psychologically embedded social order of male-dominance and subordination of women.

Trafficking of Women

The North Korean government reported to the United Nations Commis-

---

64 Soon-Hee Im (2006): 95.

65 Hankuk Yusong Yunguso: 164.

sion on Human Rights that it thoroughly destroyed the trafficking of women and that there was no case of trafficking for the last five decades in 2001. However, surveys on North Korean refugees in China consistently revealed that the trafficking of women became prevalent since the economic crisis began.

In China, particularly in rural areas, traditional preference for sons has led to an acute shortage of marriage-age Chinese women. The shortage of marriageable women resulted in the thriving of the trafficking of women. Marriage brokers and pimps provided those Chinese men who could not find Chinese women with North Korean women with relatively cheap prices. In a word, there was a huge demand for Korean women in rural areas for brokers or human traffickers. For desperate North Korean women who needed shelter and food, this demand meant easy access to China. As a result, the proportion of women among North Korean refugees living in the three northeastern Provinces in China reached up to 90.9 percent,[66] and the proportion in the Yenbien Korean Autonomous Prefecture was 62.2 percent,[67] making up to 75.5 percent of refugees in these areas in 1999.[68]

In some cases, the parents sold their daughters in desperation. In other cases, young women chose to be sold to China in order to send money for their families. In extreme cases, women were kidnapped from their home by gang groups. However, in most cases, women fell victims to human trafficking either by force or deception. As soon as women crossed the border to China in search for foods, they were trapped by marriage brokers and pimps. Although they

---

66 Good Friends (1999): 198.

67 Good Friends (1999): 172.

68 Good Friends (1999): 14.

were sold as "wives," in most cases these North Korean brides were treated like slaves. They were abused physically and sexually by the Chinese families. Moreover, they were still in danger of repatriation if they were detected by the Chinese authorities.

(Woman from Hoeryung, North Hamkyung Province, age 24) One day my mother told me: "We are going to starve to death however hard we work. We have no other option. You should go to China and send us money." My mother took me to a broker and sold me at the price of 10,000 Won. I do not bear grudge against her. How desperate she was. I understand her.[69]

(Woman from Chungjin, age 26) One day my mother told me: "Women should get married anyway. I heard that there were many women who married to Chinese men. You should go to China, find a husband, and live well." We did not have any other way to survive.... Soon I visited a woman who was engaged in trade (human trafficking), and asked her to take me.[70]

(Women from Chungjin, age 24) I came to China to earn money with two other girls. We are working as barmaids. Soon we realized that we three were sold to the bar keeper at 2,000 Won.

(Woman from Ryongyun, Hwanghae Province, age 34) I came to China to find my cousin. As soon as I crossed the border, I was kidnapped by a gang, and taken into a car. I do not know where I was traveling by the car.... In the end I was sent to a house. There was an old man of his sixties in a room. The family was relatively wealthy, but the father had a stroke, and became half-paralyzed. So the family

69 Good Friends (1999): 61.

70 Good Friends (1999): 64.

bought me at 2,000 Won to take care of him.

(Woman from Sunggan, Jagang Province, age 28) I crossed the border with a strange middle age woman. When we tried to find the road, we were abducted by men. I was sent to some city, and then sold to a man at the age of 39. He was alcoholic and compulsive gambler. He was impotent. He was also beating me. I might be soon dead because of his violence. The parents of the man bought me hoping their son would be changed after having me. It did not work. If I would be caught by the authorities, the family should pay a huge sum of fine. So the family let me go.

Many human traffickers were watching the border river and kidnapped women. Others lured women into secured houses pretending they were providing with safe haven, and then sold them. A survey estimated the price of North Korean brides between 500 and more than 4,000 Yuan (Chinese currency). The mean price of women was roughly 1,900 Yuan (approximately 244 US Dollars), but half were sold for less than 1,700 Yuan (218 US Dollars). Prices varied depending on the age and the beauty of the women and the fact whether the women had dependants with them or not. Young, pretty and single women were sold at high prices.[71]

The North Korean government has claimed that it abolished prostitution. However, food crisis also led some women to prostitution. Throughout the human history, women resorted to prostitution when they were desperate during and after wars or severe economic crisis. Many North Korean women were also forced to sell their bodies for their survival. Many women loitered around the busy railway stations and solicited men with sex for money. Women traveling

---

71　Yoonok Chang: 23.

for trades often provided sex for the police in order to avoid arrests. The authorities had attempted to exterminate prostitution, and punished those who were involved in prostitution with pubic execution until 1998. However, prostitution persisted, and the authorities loosened the punishment to imprisonment for between three and six months.[72] Many people say sarcastically that sexual morality and state-set price are gone long-long time ago.[73]

4.4 The Hour of the Women

Development of Coping Strategies

As one-time coping methods of the people dried up, people had to invent longer-term coping strategies. One was moving out to other regions or to other nations. Urban people were first hit by the famine, they moved to rural areas and around farms.

Rural areas had some advantage over urban areas in several reasons. Since collective farms allotted grains to farmers first before selling the grains to the state, farmers managed to keep their grains. In addition, families had access to fields to cultivate. Every family tilled whatever land they could use outside of the collective farms, like small kitchen garden or paddy fields a little away from houses. When one travels in North Korea during spring or summer, he or

---

72 Soon-Hee Im (2006): 106-107.

73 Testimony of Mrs. Kim from Kyungsung (August 21, 2003); Mrs. Kim from Jasung (October 8, 2003) and others. Interview by Sejong Institute.

she will see small fields cultivated with vegetables and beans everywhere, even on rooftops and on very steep hillsides. Farmers pilfered fertilizers distributed to collective farms for their own fields, making the productivity of the private fields far higher than that of the collective farms. The vegetables and grains yielded in these private fields went to markets. Therefore, the people in rural areas were relatively better-off than urban lower class workers.

Many people chose to leave the country. Several hundred thousand North Korean people crossed the border to China, alarming the world that a possible massive refugee crisis was developing. The river that bordered China and North Korea is not deep, and freezes during winter, making China the easiest nation to enter. Some went to Russia, and others went on further to Mongolia, Thailand, Myanmar, and Laos.

According to the Ministry of Unification of South Korea, around 300,000 North Koreans were illegally residing in China in 2004. Other estimates by the Good Friends, a South Korean non-Governmental organization, put the figure between 140,000 and 200,000 in 1999.[74] The condition of North Korean refugees was horrible by any standard: they were subject to the mercy of Chinese-Koreans; if they were lucky, they could work like slaves for food and miserable shelter; if they were unlucky, they were arrested and repatriated to North Korea where they could face the charge of national treason; women were trafficked to brothels or to forced marriages. Although the number of North Koreans illegally residing in China began to decline since 2000, the plight of these refugees became more precarious overtime. Chinese surveillance of the border region has intensified since 2002 following a number of incidents in which

74 Good Friends, *Doomangangul Gunuon Saramdul*두만강을 건너온 사람들 (Seoul: Jungto Chulpansa, 1999):13-14.

North Koreans entered and occupied foreign embassies and consulates in search for shelter and asylum.[75]

The legal restriction to the moving residence did not discourage people to move, either within North Korea or to a third country. The Citizens Registration System began to be nominal until 1998 when North Korea introduced and enforced a new Citizen's Registration system.[76]

The most conspicuous coping strategy was "trades" or "sales" [장사: *changsa*] as North Koreans call it. In the beginning, people began to expand their onetime-selling into constant economic action. In North Korea, people simply say "trades" for a variety of mercantile activities. Some sold home-grown vegetables at markets. Some traveled to a remote village to sell consumer goods. Some pilfered items from their factories and sold them to neighbors. A woman refugee testified that she had pilfered lye from a factory, and sold it to neighbors. Later, she traded grains by misappropriating from collective farms and then selling to people.[77] All these activities were referred to trades.

The barrage of trades brought about the flourishing of markets. Farmers markets have existed since the inception of North Korea in the form of traditional village markets. During the 1940s they were called as the people's market. They became three- or five-day interval village markets during the 1950s. In

75 Yoonok Chang with Stephen Haggard and Marcus Noland, "North Korean Refugees in China: Evidence from a Survey," *The North Korean Refugee Crisis: Human Rights and International Response*, ed by Stephen Haggard and Marcus Noland (Washington DC: US Committee for Human Rights in North Korea, 2006):14.

76 After the mass starvation situation began to subside in 1998, North Korea introduced a new Citizen's Registration system as an effort to regain its control over the people. Andrei Lankov, *North of the DMZ: Essays on Daily Life in North Korea* (Jefferson and London: McFarland & Company, 2007): 179

77 Hankuk Yusong Yunguso, *Bukhan Yusongdului Sarmgwa Kkoom*북한여성들의 삶과 꿈 (Seoul: Sahoe-Munhwa Yunguso, 2001): 39–56.

1958, the North Korean government approved the existence of the markets, and changed them into ten-day interval farmers markets. However, the government regarded the market as unofficial and undesirable, and attempted to restrict the activities. Nevertheless, with the chronic shortage of consumer goods, farmers markets gradually increased in numbers and sizes. During the 1980s when Kim Jong-Il and the government launched the 8.3 consumer goods production campaign, farmers markets flourished to deal with these consumer goods. They came to deal with not only agricultural products, but also all sorts of industrial products. The state had approved a limited number of farmers markets for the trade of agricultural products. However, people kept opening markets regardless of the state approval.

With the collapse of the PDS, people's dependency on these markets intensified. By 1993, the markets were open daily, forcing the government to give quasi-official sanction to the markets and began to tax traders at rates ranging from 30 won per month to 2 or 15 won per day, depending on the size of the space that the individual occupied.[78] In the late 1990s, there were 300 to 400 markets countrywide, one or two in every county and three to five in every city. Most markets open everyday, making them permanent market places. People who grew vegetables came to markets to sell. People who wanted to trade their belongings for food also came to markets. People could find almost anything in the markets, including grains, bicycles, cars and other smuggled goods, most of which were banned items. Grains like rice and corn were banned, but were nevertheless sold at markets. There is a saying that "You can buy all but the horn of a cat at the market" [고양이 뿔 외에는 다 있다], because cats do not have horns.

---

78 Andrew Natsios: 99.

Markets became the centers of economic activities for most North Korean people.

Often the state attempted to restrict markets. Unofficial markets were regularly cracked down. Approved farmers markets were also sometimes raided for the banned items. Nevertheless, people continued to return to markets. There were at least one big and many small markets in every big city. The Jangsoo Market in Pyungsung, South Pyongan Province and the Sunam Market at Chungjin were two of the markets well known even to South Koreans. The Bosung Market in Kaesung and the Sungchon Market in Hamhung were also prosperous.[79]

The government was forced to tolerate a variety of behaviors that it had not tolerated before. The government introduced a "New Economic Management System" on July 1, 2002, which came to be called 2002 economic reform. This reform contains many measures that involved a break with the past. It decentralized the decision making and allowed wider range of autonomy for the economic activities of industries. The new system also introduced the concept of revenue for the industries. Until 2002 all the companies were instructed to produce designated goods to the certain quantity, and received materials and wages according to the assignment. Now the companies could receive their share according to their revenue, or profit. The government also increased the state-set prices into real market-price levels and introduced the independent profit system for the industries.

Although North Korean authority avoided referring to the package as reform measures, many North Korea watchers outside were debating over the pos-

---

79 Good Friends (2006): 56–63.

sibility of economic reform and opening of North Korea. Many were skeptical, because the reform measure needed the expansion of supply first, which North Korea was unable to make. Some were hopeful, because any sign that the North Korean regime recognized the necessity of reform would be welcome.

In line with the economic reform, the government allowed markets to sell industrial products as well as agricultural products, and changed the name from "farmers market" to "market," deleting the restrictive adjective in March 2003. Precisely what kind of products were allowed to be traded in the market was not clear. However, a researcher concluded that those products that had been legally obtained, but banned at the farmers markets were allowed to be sold. Industrial products by enterprises or imported goods were granted at markets. Other goods obtained by illicit means continued to be banned.

However, in reality, most goods were on sale at markets without questioning the legality of the source. As a result, goods or foods obtained by misappropriation or pilfering were easily found at markets. Prices began to be decided by market. Many North Korean watchers agreed that this situation was at least partial marketization.

Table 4.2) Items on sale in Farmers Markets

	Sources of the Products	Legality of the Source	At Farmers Markets	At Markets
Individual Products	Kitchen Garden Products	Legal	Granted	Granted
	Home-grown Small Animal or Home-made Foods	Legal	Granted	Granted
	Collateral Products from Collective Farms	Legal	Granted	Granted
	Home-made Industrial Products	Legal	Banned	Granted
	Unauthorized Patch Field Products	Illegal	Banned	Banned
	Unauthorized Large Cattle	Illegal	Banned	Banned
Official Products	Official Sectors (Collective Farms & Enterprises)	Legal	Banned	Granted
	Misappropriation from Official Sectors	Illegal	Banned	Banned
Imported Products	Imported by Official Sectors	Legal	Banned	Granted
	Smuggled	Illegal	Banned	Banned
International Aids	Misappropriation by Individuals or Enterprises	Illegal	Banned	Banned

Source: Yang, Moon-Soo, "The Formation and Development of Markets in North Korea: With Focus on the Product Goods Market," *Comparative Economics Study*, Vol.12 No.2, Seoul, 2005, p.10, Table 2. Fifth Column was added by the writer.

In North Korea, individuals do not have the ownership of real estate like houses and land. Individuals only have the right to use the property. In reality, however, people buy and sell their houses. During the famine some people bought several houses. Real estate transactions came to markets as well.

(A Flower Swallow) A blind couple had lived in our neighborhood. The husband died of hunger. The wife and daughter sold their house only for 20 kg of corn-flour.

There were many families like this. Families first sold their clothes and furniture, and then other belongings, and finally sold their house. In contrast, some people bought several houses.[80]

(Woman age 39) After marriage, first I lived with the in-laws for a while. But I did not get along with the in-laws. So my husband and I set out a new home. We bought an apartment by bribe. Houses were in principle to be allocated, not bought. However, allocation took so long. Most people just sold and bought in secret.[81]

With this partial marketization of economy, many people began to run their own businesses. Some people opened small restaurants or beauty parlors at home, without registration or signboard. Some people ran illicit distilleries and made liquors. Some people ran home industry with several sewing or knitting machines. People who managed to run these home industries soon amassed a fortune and became new "capitalists." Trades [장사] seem to be paving the way for marketization of North Korea.

"North Korean Market Forces Have Female Faces"

The collapse of the PDS and the flourishing markets forced many women to become the breadwinner of the family. Men were still employed or enrolled in industries and factories in nominal terms. However, since most factories stopped operating and paying wages or salaries, men were in reality unem-

---

80 Good Friends (2000): 146.

81 Hankuk Yusong Yunguso: 85.

ployed. With unemployed and unwilling husbands, it was up to women to keep the families alive. Men were so concerned about their face and "dignity" that they could not do the menial jobs like foraging roots or vending small things in markets.

It was women who had to go out and find food however they could. If a woman was competent, her family had a chance to survive the famine. More and more men became dependent on women. A man's survival depended on the existence and competence of his wife. A male refugee explained the death of his brother-in-law as the result of his sister's death years earlier. "Without wife, how could a man survive at that time?"[82] Andrei Lankov also introduced a woman refugee's remark on "man's role" in North Korean families.

> "Well, in 1997-98 men became useless. They went to their work places, but there was nothing to be done there, so they came home. Meanwhile, their wives traveled to distant places to trade and kept the families going."[83]

The situation is reminiscent of the post-war memoir of Countess Fritz-Krockow. In her memoir, the Countess of Prussia derided men for their inability to support their families after the World War II.

> These Prussians, these German men! So marvelously competent – you could conquer half the globe with them. Pride of office... mission... duty... honor... victory! And then in defeat they were suddenly no good for anything, not even stealing

---

82 Testimony of Mr. Kim who was a member of the WPK and Director of a Research Institute on Chemicals in North Korea. Interview by Sejong Institute (March 21, 2003).

83 Andrei Lankov: 323.

spinach, and it was up to us women to make sure the children got fed. [84]

Women engaged in a variety of activities: running illicit restaurants at home; vending vegetables or Korean fast food to markets; smuggling grain and consumer goods from China; peddling consumer goods; and participating in informal, or private, production activities like a new form of home industry work team and private farming. All these activities in non-state (illicit) economy were described variously as "sideline activities," "micro-enterprises," or "off-farm activities."

Women were over-represented among these market traders and small-time entrepreneurs. Andrei Lankov, a North Korean watcher, commented this development as a creeping, but irreversible revolution towards capitalism.[85] He also noticed that the marketization of North Korea was driven by women.

But the new North Korean capitalism of dirty market places, charcoal trucks and badly dressed vendors with huge sacks of merchandise on their backs demonstrates one surprising feature: it has a distinctly female face. Women are over-represented among the leaders of the growing post-Stalinist economy – at least on the lower level, among the market traders and small-time entrepreneurs.

This partially reflects a growth pattern of North Korean neo-capitalism. Unlike the restoration of capitalism in the former Soviet Union or China, the "post-socialist capitalism" of North Korea is not an affair planned and encouraged by people from the top tiers of the late communist hierarchy. Rather, it is capitalism from below, which grows in spite of government's attempts to reverse the process and turn the

84 Christian von Krockow, *Hour of the Women* (London: Faber and Faber, 1993): 98.

85 Andrei Lankov: 315–319.

clock back.[86]

Women engaged in all kinds of activities including running small businesses at home, producing and selling small items at home and even smuggling.
North Korean people called all these activities as simply trades. However, the
trades composed of basically three activities: services, trade and production.
Services included running small canteens, beauty parlors and inns and providing
repairing, cleaning, and other domestic convenience services. Trades included
retailing, vending at markets, peddling around the country, call-sales and smuggling. Production included domestic-manufacturing and private farming. Some
women remained in small scale vending or peddling. Some managed to run a
large business. Most women were involved more than one of these trades.

> (Woman, age 30) I did everything: I brewed liquor and sold it; I bought products
> smuggled from China and forwarded them to others; I dealt with US dollar trans-
> actions; I sold sea-cucumbers and so on. I think I have been involved in all the
> things that we call trades. When Chinese merchants came with industrial products,
> I bought goods from them, and then forwarded them to others. The items were dai-
> ly necessities like foods, clothing, cosmetics, lighters and electric bulbs.[87]

Through these trades, i.e., providing services, trading and producing whatever goods they could, women managed to keep their families alive. The survival of most families depended on women. Women were to a great extent the
savior of the family.

---

86 Andrei Lankov: 323.

87 Hyun-Sun Park (2003): 210.

New Entrepreneurs of Service Industry

Service industry has been in existence in North Korea since its inception. However, all the facilities and people engaged in service belonged to official sector. When North Korea presented its population by occupation, it categorized its people as state workers, coop workers, officials, and farmers. Officials referred to employees in the non-productive sector, where service industry belonged. Restaurants, public bath-houses, inns and cleaners were operated under the control of Convenience Service Management Office [편의봉사사업소/편의봉사관리소]. According to North Korean definition, "domestic convenience service" [가내편의봉사] composed of: processing service that includes domestic food-processing and domestic production of small items from wastes; repairing service that repairs daily necessities, clothing and shoes; and sanitary service like cleaning, washing and beauty-treatment.[88]

The employees in convenience service sector were paid their wages just like other workers irrespective of their quality of service. Despite the low quality, service sector has been always in short supply and high demand. Because of the high demand, women in service sector managed to obtain extra-benefits from customers, making their job profitable. Employees at restaurants could take small food-stuffs or good left-over for themselves. Employees at beauty-parlors often stole chemicals for hair-permanent and provided service in private. They were rewarded with other goods or money. North Koreans refer these jobs as "jobs-with-eggs" [먹을 알이 있는 일].[89]

---

88 *Choson Tae Baekgwa Sajon* 1조선대백과사전1 (Pyongyang: Baekgwa Sajon Chulpansa, 1995): 62.

89 Miss Kim from Hoeryung, North Hamkyung Province. Interview by Sejong Institute (June 27, 2003

During the late 1980s when the economic decline and the shortage of consumer goods became apparent, many women began to run their private service businesses. Instead of reporting for duty, service sector employees used their skills for private profit.

The first were private restaurants, food stalls and inns opened near the markets. Since home-processed food was allowed at markets, food-stalls were the first to appear at the markets. Women who could afford a large stall in or near the markets also sold instant Korean foods like noodles, rice cake and dumplings. Others simply prepared simple food at home, and sold them at the markets.

(Woman from Hoeryung, North Hamheung Province, age 27) My mother sold bread at the market. She made 50 to 100 breads a day. My mother always hoped to sell them all, but I wished the opposite. If she could not sell them all, I could eat one. Since we could not afford a stall at the market, we sold them on the ground.[90]

Women who had houses large enough to put in some tables began to run (illicit) restaurants. These restaurants sold rice, noodles, meat stew, and sometimes home brewed liquors without sign boards. Home brewing is of course illegal, and punishable with long imprisonment. However, home brewed liquors were one of the most profitable items for the restaurants.[91] Private restaurants were concentrated particularly near college town. Since college students were not fed enough at dormitories, they came to the private restaurants and ate bean

---

90 Miss Kim from Hoeryung, North Hamkyung Province. Interview by Sejong Institute (June 27, 2003)

91 Interviews with many Refugees by Sejong Institute: including Ms Lee (Feb.26, 2003); Ms Lee (Apr. 4, 2003); Ms Kim (Aug. 21, 2003); Ms. Kim (Oct. 8, 2003); Ms Bae (Apr. 7, 2004) and others.

curds and rice.[92] For those who ran these restaurants, bribery to the authorities was a must. Those who had more than one room at the house often used their house as inn for mainly Chinese merchants.

> (Woman from Moosan, age 73) Chinese merchants stayed in the private houses about 10 to 15 days until they fully received the money for their goods. They stayed at my house, too. When they came with huge bunch of goods, and gave us rice in return for their lodging, nothing could be better than that. Just a bag of rice... That was more than enough.[93]

Women with deft hands opened beauty-parlors. Providing services of hair cut and perm did not require many equipment or capital. There were two or three official beauty parlors in every district in North Korea. However, these official parlors were in bad shape because of the shortage of electricity and beauty materials, particularly chemicals for hair permanent. In general, North Korean women tended to have their hair perm in every six months. The shortage of shampoo also made women prefer short and permed hair to long and straight hair. Illicit beauty parlors were armed with smuggled chemicals for hair perm, and attracted women. These beauty parlors provided with eye-brow tattooing as well. After 2001, eye-brow tattoo became popular among women, and many women refugee had eye-brow tattoos.[94]

> (Woman from Hamkyung Province, age 61) In North Korea hair permanent was

---

92 Good Friends (2006): 49.

93 Hankuk Yusong Yunguso: 314.

94 Ms. Lee from North Hamkyung Province. Interview by Sejong Institute (April 4, 2003).

enormously popular. Perhaps that was because there was no accessory for hair-do. They could afford only hair permanent and hair cut. There was always a long queue before the parlor. Women who wanted hair-permanent often gave me additional presents. Therefore my family was relatively well-off.[95]

Some women worked as domestic maids for wealthy Chinese families living in North Korea. These activities were referred to private labor [개인로동],which the government long attempted to abolish, and which is still illegal. Therefore these women had to pretend to visit close friends when they went to work. During the farming season, private farmers also employed women for the season.

> (Woman from Hamkyung Province, age 61) In farming season, farmers needed to thin out the rows of cabbage. Then they called women to thin them out with payment. Those women took the (rooted) cabbage to home. Some women ate the cabbage, some sold at the markets.[96]

In 1989, the North Korean government pronounced the Regulation on the Production and Distribution of the 8.3 People's Consumer Goods [8.3 인민소비품 생산과 처리에 관한 규정] and the Regulation on the Management of the Home Work-Team and Sideline-Team, and the Domestic Convenience Service Businesses [가내작업반, 부업반 관리운영 및 가내편의봉사사업에 관한 규정]. By these two regulations, North Korea attempted to control private labor and private service industry. Although the contents of the two regulations are not available to

---

95 Hankuk Yusong Yunguso: 155.

96 Hankuk Yusong Yunguso: 163.

outside world, a 1997 regulation suggests the terms of the domestic convenience service business.

The 1997 Regulation on the Domestic Convenience Service Businesses in the Free Economic and Trade Zone [자유경제무역지대 가내편의봉사사업 규정] aimed at establishing order in domestic convenience service and ensuring the benefits of the people (Para.1). Although the jurisdiction of this regulation was limited in the special economic zone, the Rajin-Sunbong area, it could be applied to other areas, albeit in a stricter manner. The regulation requires people those who want to run the business to report to the authority and to be permitted for the business. It also provides the authority with the power to control the price and other activities as well as to levy the state payments. Despite the government efforts to control and restrict service businesses, women were still running businesses, paving a new way for capitalism.

Women Merchants

Among what North Koreans call trades, trades proper or mercantile activities have the most various patterns: vending, consigned sales, peddling, callsales and smuggling. Vending at markets was the most common among women. Women comprised 70 percent of vendors in these markets.[97] Those women who managed to obtain designated booths at the markets, with appropriate payments to the authority, came to the markets on average 7 or 8 o'clock in the morning. Others had to come as early as 3 or 4 o'clock in the morning to take their places

---

97 Soon-Hee Im, *Sikryangnangwa Bukhanyusongui Yukhal mit UisikByunhwa*식량난과 북한여성의 역할 및 의식변화 (Seoul: Korean Institute on National Unification, 2004): 82.

for the day.[98]

    Those who had designated booths often engaged in consigned sales. Those who could not afford booth or those who did not have courage to sit and sell at the markets forwarded their products to these booths, with less profit. Having a booth, therefore, meant easy gain as well. Vendors who sold industrial products that had been banned at the markets until 2002 were often called "locust vendors"[메뚜기 장사], because they had to rush to hide with their bundle like locusts whenever the authorities were coming.

    (Woman from Gaechun, South Pyongan Province, age 40) When I sat at my booth, people from rural area came to me with eggs that they got from the chickens raised at home. Then I sold the eggs by the piece. If others brought red pepper powder to me in bags, I sold the power by small quantities. So I could earn money just sitting there.[99]

    (Woman from Wonsan, age 33) I sold clothing at markets. Because clothing is industrial products, it was banned at markets. But clothing was the most demanded products. Since it was banned at market, we had to sit on the ground displaying pieces of clothing. That is locust vending. Whenever somebody shouted "Security guys are coming," we had to jump up and run away, like locusts. After the security guys disappeared, we returned to sell the things again. I did the same.[100]

    Peddling also required physical strength and wits. Peddling was profitable because of the poor transportation system of North Korea and travel restrictions.

---

98 Testimony of Ms. Lee. Interview by Sejong Institute (August 14, 2003).

99 Testimony of Ms. Joo. Interview by Sejong Institute (November 5, 2003).

100 Testimony of Ms. Lee. Interview by Sejong Institute (February 26, 2003).

There were huge price differences market by market, region by region. Any consumer goods were profitable because of the price differences. A bundle from a backpack would make three times or more in profit. North Koreans call peddling "racing" and the peddlers "race-runners" [달리기 선수].[101] There were several well known "race-runners" between cities: the Saebyul-Chungjin race runners were those who traveled back and forth between Saebyul County and Chungjin City. They bought rice, corns and beans at Saebyul then sold them at Chungjin. When they returned to Saebyul, they carried chemical seasoning stuffs, clothing and other industrial products with them.[102] Peddlers sometimes sold the products at the markets themselves, but mostly forwarded them to local vendors. Often peddlers engaged in call-sales on demand as well.

(Woman from North Hamkyung Province, age 25) I borrowed money from my mom, and began my trade business. I had an acquaintance at a chemical factory, who stole lye from the factory. He sold the lye at a low price, 15 Won per unit. Then I went to remote villages to sell the lye at the price of three or four times higher than my payment. It was hugely profitable. I earned 1,000 Won.[103]

(Woman from Hamheung, age 53) After my husband died...I quitted my job and returned to the knitting part of the 8.3 work-team. The knitting at the 8.3 work-tam earned me 200 Won a month, among which I could keep 70 Won to myself. It was higher than normal wage. Later, I began trade, leaving my name registered in the 8.3 work-team. I went to the border area like Namyang, Onsung and Hoeryung and bought consumer goods smuggled from China. And then I went to Hamhung and

101 Testimony of Ms. Bae. Interview by Sejong Institute (April 7. 2004).

102 Good Friends (2006): 90–91.

103 Hankuk Yusong Yunguso: 49.

sold them at double or triple price.... By the trade, I became very wealthy.[104]

Travel restrictions by the government also made peddling profitable. In North Korea traveling around the country requires official documents. Travel without official documents is a crime punishable with imprisonment. Those who were capable of obtaining documents, or those brave enough to take risks, were engaged in peddling. Until the 1980s, obtaining travel permit was extremely difficult. However, since the famine obtaining, or buying, the documents became easier than before. North Korean refugees in general testified they "bought" the documents legally. Bribery became so common that most people confuse the corrupted practice with legal procurement.

(Woman from Danchon, age 36) Traveling requires documents. In the past obtaining the documents was very difficult. But recently it became easier to buy. One may pay money (bribe) to security guys or the railway station personnel. If one uses car for trade, one should pay the driver. In the end, buying documents in advance and paying money to the people cost almost the same. Therefore, in these days people prefer buying documents to paying bribe.[105]

Smuggling in grain and industrial products was the second most common strategy, despite its danger. In smuggling, however, men outnumbered women, because it required physical strength as well as connections. Smuggling in goods from China did not require cutting-edge technology or heavy armor as depicted in western movies. The North Korean version of smuggling in general

104 Hankuk Yusong Yunguso: 136.

105 Testimony of Mrs. Bae. Interview by Sejong Institute (April 7, 2004).

is very primitive. It was done mostly by carrying a large backpack and at the largest scale by using a truck or two, so physical strength and bribery was more important than technology. When smuggled goods were sold in the markets, it was women who did the selling, becoming the "locust vendors."

Some people engaged in smuggling out natural resources and antiques to China. Since North Korea's economic decline, many antiques including some national treasures have been smuggled to China. Small antiques are easy to carry and sell at high prices. Many women from Kaesung, the capital of the ancient Koryo kingdom, were either directly involved in or heard of the antique smuggling. The North Korean government has tried to stop the smuggling but with little effect. Underground resources were also sold to China. However, smuggling these items is so risky that the number is relatively small – but relatively high compared with ordinary people of other countries.

(Women from Sunbong, North Hamkyung Province, age 37) I sold antiques to China. When others heard that I was dealing with antiques, those who had some old items rushed to see me. I bought them conditionally. If I could sell them I would pay more. Otherwise, they had to return my money. I sold hanging scrolls, celadon porcelains, vanity boxes carved with mother of pearl, ink-stones, and even a Japanese ceramic.[106]

Women Producers

With the flourishing of the markets individual productive activities also

---

106 Testimony of Mrs.Lee. Interview by Sejong Institute (April 4, 2003).

increased rapidly. Most rural families cultivated vegetables in their kitchen garden or in a small patch field around their houses. This agricultural production was acquiesced by the state. Facing famine women tried to expand their small land: they cultivated steep hills and barren wasteland far away from their home. A woman in Saebyul County was reported to cultivate land of 0.5 acre that was located at 16 km away, and two rivers across, from her residence.[107] They also raised small animals like chicken, rabbits, and goats. Since big cattle like cow was under strict control of the state, people could grow only small livestock.

> (Woman, age 47) We filled the shortage with sideline activity. Since we lived in a detached house, we had a small garden. We raised chickens, dogs and rabbits. That activity could be done while I was still employed. In fact, the money from the sideline activity was much larger than my salary. Dogs and rabbits were not necessarily fed very much. They could be fed with dried grass or left-over. The price of a rabbit was as much as my salary for a month.[108]

In addition to agricultural production, a variety of productive activities developed among women. Many women made small consumer goods like socks and gloves at home. The 8.3 home industry work-teams became the pretext for these individual productive activities. Instead of delivering goods to the authorities, people paid money, the "8.3 fund," in order to remain unemployed. The amount of the 8.3 fund varied region by region. The products made by the 8.3 work-team were in principle to be sold collectively at the 8.3 Direct Shops [8.3 직매점]. However, most women chose to sell their products by themselves. A

---

107 Good Friends (2006): 70.

108 Hyun-Sun Park (2003): 212.

woman bought an automatic knitting machine and managed to sell her product per piece at a price higher than average monthly wage of workers.

(Woman from Samchun, South Hwanghae Province, age 46) I learned knitting at home. I learned it very hard. And then I bought an automatic knitting machine. With the machine, I produced a large quantity of knitted clothing. I designed the clothing very prettily. In North Korea, clothes are in general not so pretty. Fashionable clothes could be sold at a very high price. I received 100 Won per piece, while average wage was just 60 to 80 Won a month.[109]

Some bought smuggled shabby second-hand cloths in bulk, and repaired them into new products. Second-hand bulk cloths were sold, illegally, at the international ports like Haejoo, Chungjin and Nampo. People bought a sack of cloths at 5,000 to10,000 Won. After reparation, women sold them by pieces at far higher prices. However, it was impossible to check the bulk-sack before purchase, overall revenue from the reparation was reported to be about 30 to 60 percent of original payment.[110] Some women took usable wastes from the factory, and made shoes at home.

(Woman age 27) I was employed to a shoes factory. I took some waste materials (rubbers) from the factory, and made shoes every night at home with my threadbare clothes. After I needled old clothes into shoe shape, I put the rubber and then steamed it. Then the rubber became solid, and the shoes completed. The shoes were sold at 10 Won. It was equal to one kilo gram of grains.[111]

---

109 Testimony of Mrs.Kim. Interview by Sejong Institute (December 19, 2003).

110 Good Friends (2006): 48.

111 Testimony of Ms Kim. Interview by Sejong Institute (June 27, 2003).

Some manufactured bean-curds or liquor in a specialized way, and sold them to other trades people. While normal food-vendors at markets made one frame of bean-curds a day, these (illegal) specialists made five to six frames a day. They sold the curds to private restaurants, inns and sometimes to factories.[112] In fact, women made everything with almost useless wastes. Their creative adaptation to the famine sustained the family and the society.

4.5 Changing Society and Women

Cowering Husbands, Assertive Wives

During the Arduous March, North Korean economy was in fact reshaped into a quasi-market economy. The marketization process was led by women. While the economic role of wives vastly increased, the attitudes of the husbands rarely changed. The idle husbands demanded their working wives to cook and clean for them. Women began to question the authority, and ridicule the incompetence, of their husbands.

Many disparaging terms have emerged for incapable husbands. Women name the unwilling husbands "ten thousand dollar door lock [만원짜리 열쇠]," "hanging-painting [걸그림]," "woof-woof [멍멍이: the sound of dog barking]," and "daytime light bulbs [낮전등]" and so on. "Ten thousand dollar door lock" means that men are good only for keeping the house from minor burglary.

---

112 Good Friends (2006): 49.

"Hanging-painting" means that men are as good as a decorative painting. "Woof-woof" means almost the same as the "ten thousand door lock," but more despising because it refers to dogs. "Daytime light-bulbs" means men are useless or unnecessary like light bulbs in sunny daytime. Because of the shortage of electricity, North Korean people can hardly imagine lighted bulbs at daytime. These names are far from "master," which North Korean women were educated to call their husbands.

(Woman age 36) Even when I finished my work very late, I had to cook the meal afterwards. Sometimes my husband came to me while I was working and asked. "Is the meal ready?" "No" "Why not? Hurry up. I am hungry." Then I rushed to cook the rice. He was just like a *Nolboo* (a Korean folk-tale character who is malignant and takes pleasure from the misery of others). In North Korea, husbands are "daytime light-bulb" [낮전등]. Do you need a light-bulb at bright day-time? They are useless. Sometimes we call husbands "hanging-painting"[걸그림] that was hung at wall for decoration. Some call them as "woof-woof " [멍멍이] that guards the house.[113]

(Woman from Hamheung) We call husbands as "woof-woofs." Men are weak in their will to survive. They are like dogs that guard the house. If a wife became sick and tired of supporting her stupid "woof-woof," she left him bringing with her children. The woman and children can survive. The "woof-woof" soon dies. There are lots of these "woof-woofs."[114]

(Woman age 42) In North Korea, everything is done by women. We call men as "woof-woof" or "ten thousand dollar door lock"[만원짜리 열쇠]. They are good

---

113 Testimony of Ms. Lee from Chungjin. Interview by Sejong Institute (August 14. 2003).

114 Hyun–Sun Park (2003): 245.

only at guarding the house. Men can not earn money. They are incapable of supporting the family. Women walk so hard and far away that their feet were bleeding in order to find things to support the family. But men stay idle at home. So many young girls are avoiding marriage.[115]

(Woman age 40) In the apartment complex where I lived, most women were engaged in trades. They sold a pair or two shoes at the markets and bought one or two kilo grams of grain. The wives were working to death. The wives braved out the piercing coldness and the scorching heat. But the husbands never gave a hand to their wives. The wives had to take water from well, cook the rice, wash the laundry and clean the house. Everything was to be done by myself. Furthermore, since he was the head of the family, I scooped out his bowl first with best grain. While we ate corn, he ate rice.[116]

(Man age 56) In theory, the WPK is supporting the lives of the whole people. But in fact everything is done by wives. Wives support the family. Men are dependent on wives these days. My sister died years before the Arduous March. Who would support my brother-in-law then? He died of hunger.[117]

With the faltering authority of the husbands, many women began to choose to simply run away from abusive husbands, which was extremely rare until the 1980s. Many women refugees testified that they left their husbands because of abuse. It is a striking difference from the defectors during the 1970s and early 1980s, when most women chose to stay with their abusing husbands. In official terms, the divorce rate has remained less than 0.2 in every 1,000

---

115 Testimony of Ms. Kim from Jasung. Interview by Sejong Institute (October 8, 2003).

116 Testimony of Ms. Joo from Gaechun. Interview by Sejong Institute (November 5, 2003).

117 Testimony of Mr. Kim from Hoeryung. Interview by Sejong Institute (March 21, 2003).

marriages. However, refugees invariably testify that divorce by desertion and separation are rapidly increasing. Since 2002, two thirds of refugees arriving in Seoul from North Korea have been women, among whom half are not married. Regardless of the fact whether they were married or not, however, most women came alone, or with children only. Women with husbands are rather minority. Those who married but came alone tend to claim that they had divorced. It was discovered soon, through further questions, that they had been separated or simply run away, without legal procedures of divorce.

There came a sign of change in the attitude of young women. While marriage had been regarded as a mandate for a longtime, young women began to regard marriage as only one of their options. Nearly half of unmarried women refugees reported that they chose not to get married because they had to support husbands as well as themselves.

> (Woman age 31) I did not get married. I choose not to. In North Korea women have to support the whole family after marriage. Wives went to trades. Everyday, wives carry huge bags on their back and walk all over the country, shouting "but this, but that..." Or they sell bread at the markets. Oh, no. I don't want to do that. I can't. That's why I choose not to marry.[118]

A women's choice of husband is also changing. Until the 1980s men with KWP membership were the best grooms; in the 2000s, men capable of trade are the most popular choice. Since most party members are more severely monitored by the authorities, they are in most cases unable to engage in trade, and therefore poorer. Party membership, which for a long time was the symbol of

---

118 Testimony of Ms. Kim from Onsung. Interview by Sejong Institute (March 7, 2003).

power and privilege, became an unattractive qualification.

(A former member of the WPK) In the past women regarded the members of the WPK as manly and masculine and adored them. Now women begin to think that earning more money is better than being a member of the WPK. It is one of the evidences that the WPK is losing confidence and trust from the people.[119]

Another new trend also appeared. Some wealthy women with the experience of marriage are reportedly getting married to younger and never-married men, which is still very unusual even in South Korea. Wealthy old men marrying young girls have been found throughout history, but the opposite has been almost non-existent in Korea.

(Woman age 42) Young girls are avoiding marriage. Only old women are galore. When young men are discharged from the army, they often find nobody to support them. Their families were dispersed or dead because of the famine. Young girls are drawing back from them. So many young and never married men choose married women with children as their wives. If a woman has enough means to live with, she can marry a young man regardless of whether she was married, or she has children. Young men live with women elder than them by 5 to 6 years. They choose to live as dependants to their wives.[120]

---

119 Testimony of Mr.Choi from Euijoo. Interview by Sejong Institute (December 5, 2002).

120 Testimony of Ms. Kim from Jasung. Interview by Sejong Institute (October 8, 2003).

Growing Capitalist Minds

While they fought against the famine, women developed a sense of market economy and the capitalist mode of live. North Korean people had been inculcated with the dogma that capitalism was evil and that those who traded products for private profits were poisonous villains. Although many people were at first forced to engage in trades for survival, they came to change their perception on market economy. Many refugees report that most people these days consider those people who were engaged in trades as clever.

(Woman age 36) I think it is already market economy. A real market economy. Now if we hear that a person died of starvation, we think the dead one was lazy and stupid. If anybody is clever and industrious, even any neighbor would ask him to run a business together. "Although you don't have money, you are diligent and industrious. I will provide money for the business. You can use your body for transportation and other physical labor. After we sell the goods, we can share the profits" like that.[121]

(Woman age 25) If you give money, you can get in the (prohibited) Rajin-Sunbong area. Nothing is impossible with money…. North Korea is in a transition stage from socialism to capitalism. Trades are the basic of market economy. Clever people are very quick to detect what will be most profitable. And then they change what they sell. I sold lye, rice and oil consecutively, among which I earned most with oil.[122]

(Woman age 39) Although North Korea is still socialist in its appearance, it develops sort of capitalist minds to a great extent. North Korea has long attempted

---

121 Testimony of Ms. Lee from Chungjin. Interview by Sejong Institute (August 14, 2003).

122 Hankuk Yusong Yunguso: 51

to mould socialist personality among its people, but to little avail.... Now many
people live in capitalist mode of life. Those who depend on the PDS seem to me
almost non-existent. Everybody lives on trades.[123]

According to the 1998 interview by the Good Friends, 57 percent of North
Korean refugees in China resorted on foraging and consumption of inferior
foods like grass roots and tree barks, and 46 percent engaged in barter or trades.
The proportion changed greatly in 2004. According to the survey by the Good
Friends in 2004, 92.5 percent of the refugees answered that they were engaged
in trades. Half of the refugees answered that almost 90 percent of North Korean
households were engaged in trades.[124]

Markets are basically categorized into four: producer goods market, consumer goods market, capital and financial market and labor market. In socialist
countries, these markets do not exist by nature. In socialist economy, all the productive factors are allocated by the state according to the central plan. Products
are also distributed by the plan. The emergence of the four markets, therefore,
means the development of marketization and a transition towards capitalist
economy.

Yang Moon-Soo argues that these four markets are all emerging in North
Korea.[125] The markets become typical consumer goods markets. Producer goods
markets are emerging. The "Socialist Exchange Market" was open by the direction of Kim Jong-Il, which deals with raw materials and parts for the companies.

---

123 Hankuk Yusong Yunguso: 94–95.

124 Re-quoted from Marcus Noland and Stephan Haggard (2007): 175.

125 See Moon-Soo Yang, "The Formation and Development of Markets in North Korea: Focusing on the
Products Market," *Pigyo Kyungje Yungu* 12, no. 2 비교경제연구 (Seoul: Korean Association of Comparative
Economic Studies, 2005): 1–53.

In the past companies had to rely on the allocation by the economic plan for the raw materials and necessary parts. Companies are now allowed to exchange materials and products with other companies in the Socialist Exchange Market. Outside of the Socialist Exchange Market as well, companies are allowed to procure materials from markets. Also, there is a primitive pattern of financial markets developing. With many people engaged in trades, the demand for financial supply increased. There appear "money owners"[돈주] who provide money for the traders and take interests. Some money owners are reported to lend money to companies and even to state enterprises. The most important development is the emergence of labor market. Many North Korean people provide their labor for daily wage outside of the official employment. Some worked as domestic maids, some as private drivers, and some as private-employees.[126] This "private labor" remains in illicit activities. However, as the markets have developed against the government's effort to control them, labor market has potential to grow further. The development of markets may lead to promote capitalist minds among North Korean people.

Unchanging Politics

The society underwent a substantial change during the Arduous March. However, the politics remained unchanged. Because of Kim Il Sung's death and the three-year mourning period, the general election for the 10th Supreme People's Assembly was held in 1998, three years later than due year. The gen-

---

126 Good Friends (2006): 186.

eral election for 11th SPA was held in 2003, after five years as regulated in the Constitution. In the 10th and 11th SPA, the proportion of women representatives remained exactly the same as the 9th SPA, recording 20.1 percent. The total number of the representatives was the same, 687, and the number of women representatives was also the same, 138, as the 9th SPA in 1990. It seems that the North Korean authorities were paying no attention to political representation of women since the 1970s. The proportion of women remained constant. The consistency of the number of women representatives may reflect the indifference about the political representation of women in the nominee selection procedure. It may result from the simple selection criterion "the same as the last election."

The number of women among the standing committee and the deputy chairpersons was also the same. In fact the proportion of women in the standing committee was declined slightly, only because the total number of the standing committee was increased by 2, from 15 to 17. The number of women in the standing committee remained two. It was the same in 1990.

In addition to the standing committee, there was a college of chairpersons, consisting of a chairperson and two deputy chairpersons. The college was to chair the Plenum of the SPA. One woman has remained as deputy chairperson since 1990. Won-Gu Yuh, the sister of the late Yun-Gu Yuh and the daughter of Woon-Hyung Yuh, replaced her sister as vice chairperson after her sister had died. One woman remained in service in the Standing Committee since 1990. Mi-Young Ryoo, the wife of a famous Teakwondo association leader who had defected South Korea during the 1970, had inherited her husband's political seat in the Standing Committee. Yuh and Ryoo both advanced into the leadership position by the family background.

Another seat for woman in the Standing Committee was reserved for the chairperson of the Women's Union. Since Kim Song-Ae was replaced by Yun-Ok Chon in 1998, Yun-Ok Chon became a member of the Standing Committee in 1998. However, Chon was also replaced by Soon-Hee Park in 2000 as the Chairwoman of the DWU, her seat in the Standing Committee was also taken by Park. Until the general election for the 12th SPA was held, which is due in November 2008, Ryoo and Park would take seats in the Standing Committee.

Since there has been no Party Congress since 1980, the changes in the Central Committee of the WPK were not revealed exactly. However, through the North Korean media, some changes could be detected. Most changes came from the death of the party cadre members. Many first generation of the revolution are dying of old age. A small number of new names came to be mentioned as the member of the Central Committee. However, no new female politician has emerged in the Standing Committee. In the Cabinet as well, no female minister has been reported after the departure of Yung-Sook Rim.

There is, however, an unnoticed change in progress. The Women's Union is reviving. While women were busy in trades, they were not affiliated with any social group but the DWU. The membership in the DWU is reported to have increased to 1.2 million by the end of 2002.[127] Facing an increase of women unemployed and uncontrolled, North Korean authorities issued a new guideline that urged the DWU to reinforce its activities in 1998.

The DWU, once denigrated as an "old and weak grandmother's organization,"[128] is returning to the core of social organizations. Kim Sung-Ae resigned

---

127 Testimony of a former advisor to the Headquarters for Special Guard. Interview by Sejong Institute (May 27, 2003). There were numerous testimonies about the increase of the DWU members during the late 1990s and 2000s.

128 Testimonies from the Interviews by Sejong Institute: Mr. Kim from Pyongyang (May 27, 2003); Mr. Lee from Kiljoo (November 7, 2002); and Ms. Lee from Wonsan (Feb. 26, 2003).

from the presidency of the DWU in 1998 after the three year mourning period for her deceased husband passed. Since then the presidency became rather managerial, and Park Soon-Hee has been incumbent since 2000.

Women's activities in the economy have not brought forth the expanded influence of women in politics until now. However, with women's roles and activities in surge, women may gain more power in politics in the future. After the matter of survival of the family is resolved, women may turn to their attention to their representation in the politics, too.

Chapter V

Conclusion

Chapter V. Conclusion

The Revolution

The period from Liberation to the end of Korean War was the era of revolution for women in North Korea. They were referred to "women" as a group by the communists. They were identified as a category with distinct interests. The communists announced that women were equal with men. The communists attributed the exploitation of women to the feudal custom and capitalist division of labor. The communists also demanded women to work outside of the home and wage a war for anti-feudal, anti-capitalist revolution. The prerequisite of the emancipation of women, it was repeated, was the participation of women into the labor.

A flood of laws promised equality. The *Law on Agrarian Reform* of 1946 provided women with land in their own rights, not in tandem with their fathers, husbands or sons. Poor peasant women became land owners for the first time in their lives. At least in theory, peasant women could be independent economically from their husbands. The *Sex Equality Law* of 1946 proclaimed equal rights of women with men. Women were guaranteed equal rights in every sphere of the state, political, economic and cultural life. The *Labor Law for Workers and Office Employees* of 1946 stipulated the principle of equality at work and the principle of equal pay for equal work regardless of the sex. Women were expected to be the workers like men, with equal rights. The *Constitution* of 1948 also confirmed the guarantee for equality between the sexes: All people have equal rights in every sphere of life such as political, economic, social, and cultural. Specifically, women were again declared to have equal rights with men in every sphere of life.

In addition to the laws, almost all the reform measures also paid attention to women. The women's organization was the first to inaugurate as a social organization in North Korea. The government also tried to provide social conditions for working mothers including the nurseries and kindergartens. Although the number of kindergartens and nurseries was miniscule, the concept of the state responsibility to provide child-care facilities for working women was novel in Korea.

In comparison, conditions for women in South Korea remained similar to the colonial period. Despite the constitutional promise of equality, women had been denied equal rights in the family such as parental rights in the case of divorce and legal capacity in employment contracts by the *Civil Code* until 1977. The *Labor Standard Law* left the work conditions to be decided by the work contract between the companies and the employees. By the work contract, many women were discriminated against in payments, promotion and dismissal. The South Korean government limited land reform to "farming" land, and carried out confiscation and allocation of land with compensation. Therefore, most poor peasants, not only women but also men, were unable to obtain land. Economic independence of women was hardly considered in the economic development strategy.

Although North Korean legislation did not guarantee equality in reality, all these laws were the announcement of the government's and the communists' intention to build a socialist society. During the early period of the regime, Kim Il Sung and the communists made all-out efforts to promulgate laws that would stimulate and sustain the social revolution in North Korea. Even with some faults, the *Sex Equality Law* and the *Labor Law* were decades ahead of the South Korean counterparts.

In response to the call for emancipation, North Korean women rapidly entered the society and the labor force. More than a fifth of adult women joined the Women's Union by the end of 1947. The Women's Union sent some hundred thousands of women to political rallies and to vote in elections. Mass gatherings of women, which were unthinkable under the Confucian tradition, became familiar. The successful organization and expansion of the Women's Union could be attributed to the experience of nationalist movement that had legitimized women's organizations and to the social fervor for the construction of a new sovereign and independent state. Women became an indispensable part of the nation-building. Women participated in politics as well. Since its first ever election in North Korea in 1946, women has recorded double-digit numbers of proportion in representatives to the people's committees and assemblies of all levels. Women representatives in political arenas also became not-unusual figures.

During the revolutionary era, women became a major force in the society. They eagerly responded to the call for revolution, participated in social campaigns and rallies, entered the politics, went to the polls, and joined the Women's Union. They were the actors of the revolution.

However, the revolution ended with the Korean War. During the War, every effort was forwarded to the war effort. Construction of new nation nurseries and kindergartens had to be halted. All the new laws, decrees and orders were for supporting the war and the soldiers. The pursuit of constructing a new nation was also suspended. The Korean War, nevertheless, contributed to the North Korean revolution by destroying the old social order, displacing a huge number of people, and by removing possible opposition forces. In that sense the war was a continuous part of the revolution.

The Retreat

After the war, North Korea announced the resumption of its socialist revolution. However, the socialist transformation of the economy was accompanied with the dictatorial changes in the politics. As Kim Il Sung established his dictatorship, the society should learn and exercise the feudalist practices of loyalty to the ruler.

North Korea proceeded with nationalization of industries and agriculture. In 1958, North Korea completed collectivization of agriculture and of most industries. Only a small number of private sectors survived. The minuscule number of private sectors soon disappeared, and North Korea claimed the complete of socialist revolution.

During this economic transformation process, the proportion of women in the labor force rapidly grew. The number of female workers reached up to 500,000 in 1960, which was almost tripled from 170,000 in 1956.[1] The proportion of women in the industry increased to from 33.3 percent in 1961 to 48 percent in 1976.[2] Half, sometimes more than half, of the workforce has been women since the 1970s. Statistically, therefore, women became the working class.

This *"working-classization"* of women became possible by coercive

---

[1] *Choson Chungang Yungam* (DPRK Central Yearbook) 1961: 116.

[2] *Rodong Shinmoon*로동신문 (July 30, 1976).

measures such as mandatory job assignment and the Public Distribution System (PDS) that provided people with ration of food and necessities. All the people ought to either be assigned job by the authorities or enroll with a higher education institute as soon as they graduated from high school. The employment or enrollment was the prerequisite for the entitlement of the PDS. Therefore, people without employment or enrollment were denied ration. To a great degree women were forced to be working-classized.

However, women were concentrated in the light industries, personal services, health care, and elementary education. The labor force was segregated by sex. Most of women's jobs rewarded less than men's. The division of labor by the gender, as in capitalist society, resulted in unequal earnings between men and women. The principle of equal pay for equal work might not be breached, but was evaded. The female working-class was not fully freed from exploitation even in this self-claimed socialist system.

While the North Korean economy was transforming into the socialist system, Kim Il Sung came to exercise an absolute power over the people. Beginning in the mid 1960s, the mention of activities of specific person other than Kim Il Sung and his family almost stopped appearing in official publications in North Korea. In the early 1970s, Kim Il Sung's son, Kim Jong Il, was designated as heir apparent to the power. With the effort to legitimize the power succession from father to son, the personality cult for the Kim Il Sung family began. Learning about the Kim family was a part of the "*revolutionization*" of the people.

How to depict the "greatness and achievements" of the Kim family had nothing to do with facts. It depended on the desired value system of the North Korean leadership, especially Kim Il Sung. The hagiographies of the Kim family reflect virtues that Kim Il Sung valued very high: loyalty to the leader and to the state; sacrifice and devotion for the nation; filial piety to the ancestors; and "femininity" for women.

In alleged memoirs and biographies, Kim Il-Sung and Kim Jong-Il always presented themselves as filial sons. When he returned to Korea after the Liberation, Kim Il-Sung publicly visited his hometown, and made an emotional scene of tearful reunion with his grandmother, demonstrating his filial piety.[3] After the death of his father, Kim Jong-Il allegedly refused to be inaugurated as the Party Secretary for three years in order to keep the traditional three-year-lasting mourning and self-restraint period. Their demonstration of filial piety, in turn, was implicitly demanding loyalty from the people.

His ideal woman was embodied in the description of his mother and his wife, the Great Mothers. The Great Mothers were depicted as loyal and submissive to their husbands, devoted to the nation, enduring all the hardships with sacrifices, and wise in bringing up their children. His mother, Kang Ban-Sok, never complained to the in-laws, and took the blame when the siblings of her husband made mistakes. His wife and the mother of Kim Jong Il, Kim Jong-Suk was also extremely respectful to her husband. At any time and in any place, she respected her husband as the Commander-in-Chief and the Great Leader of the nation, and always answered "yes, Sir."

The task of "*revolutionization*" urged women to learn about and emulate the Great Mothers, which ended in inculcating women to be submissive to men. Men were regarded as the head, the main breadwinner, and the protector of the family. Women were considered to be secondary supporters for the family and subjugated to men. All the household chores and caring of children were to be

---

3 Charles K. Armstrong "Familism, Socialism and Political Religion in North Korea," *Totalitarian Movements and Political Religions* 6, no.3 (London: Routledge, December 2005): 389.

done by women regardless of whether they were employed or not. Although women constituted half of the labor force, women were instructed to accept inferior positions to men at work. Men were assumed to command, and women to be commanded. Menial tasks were to be done by women.

The *"revolutionization"* of women, in the end, reinstated the traditional virtues of noble women in the *Chosun* Dynasty. At the same time, North Korean Revolution that had started with a fanfare in 1945 ended in the retreat into a dynasty.

To Markets

Although the social norm on women returned to old fashioned oppression, women continued to work inside and outside of the home. Women participated in the labor force, as either employees or "volunteers," while shouldering the sole responsibility of household work and child care. In order to obtain entitlement for the Public Distribution System (PDS), many women chose to be employed.

However, with chronic shortage of consumer goods during the 1980s and 1990s, many women turned to the home industry work-teams that produced consumer goods with flexible work hours and no fixed work place. Engaging in the home industry work-team was regarded as unemployed, and denied entitlement for the PDS. Despite the disadvantage of losing the entitlement, many women found that engaging in the home industry work-team was more profitable than employment. They produced consumer goods and sold them to markets. Although the home industry work-team was supposed to submit in kind 80 percent of its products to the authorities, many members of the work-team chose to submit cash instead. The cash paid instead of the products became to be referred to the "8.3 fund."

Consumer goods were sold in farmers market. Farmers markets have existed since the inception of North Korea in the form of traditional village markets. During the 1940s they were called people's markets. They became three- or five-day interval village markets during the 1950s. In 1958, the North Korean government approved the existence of the markets, and changed them into ten-day interval farmers markets. However, the government regarded the market as unofficial and undesirable, and attempted to restrict the activities. Nevertheless, with the chronic shortage of consumer goods, farmers markets gradually increased in numbers and sizes. During the 1980s when Kim Jong-Il and the government launched the 8.3 consumer goods production campaign, farmers markets flourished to deal with these consumer goods. They came to deal with not only agricultural products, but also all sorts of industrial products. The state had approved a limited number of farmers markets for the trade of agricultural products. However, people kept opening markets regardless of the state approval.

By engaging in the home industry work-team, women began to contact markets. While most men were supposed to be employed, the "dependant" wives went to markets to sell and buy goods. In a sense, the home industry work team unwittingly provided women with opportunities to experience the market economy. Women became the major actors in markets in North Korea.

North Korea was suffering from the slow down of its economic growth from the 1970s. Its economy deteriorated and its GDP was reduced by half in the 1990s. Two thirds of the industries were reported to stop operating. The PDS became erratic, forcing the people to further rely on markets. When North Korea experienced a famine that killed 0.6 million to 1 million people, roughly 3 to 5 percent of the population in the mid-1990s, the PDS collapsed, resulting in the flourishing of markets. While the North Korean government beautified the economic debacle as the "Arduous March," some North Korean watchers analyzed the expansion of markets as the marketization process.

During the Arduous March, many women became the breadwinners of their families. Although the state and the industries stopped paying wages and salaries, men were assumed to go to work. It was women who went out to markets to keep the family alive. Between 70 and 80 percent of dealers in markets were women. Women were over-represented among these market traders and small-time entrepreneurs. The marketization of North Korea was driven by women.

Women engaged in all kinds of activities including running small businesses at home, producing and selling small items at home and even smuggling. North Korean people called all these activities as simply "trades" [장사]. However, the trades composed of basically three activities: services, trade and production. Services included running small canteens, beauty parlors and inns and providing repairing, cleaning, and other domestic convenience services. Trades included retailing, vending at markets, peddling around the country, call-sales and smuggling. Production included domestic-manufacturing and private farming. Some women remained in small scale vending or peddling. Some managed to run a large business. Most women were involved in more than one of these trades.

Many people survived the famine by relying on markets. In spite of predictions by many North Korean watchers that it would soon collapse, the North

Korean regime also muddled through the economic debacle. To a great extent, one of the important resources that enabled North Korea to muddle through was the marketization of the society, which was driven by women. In this light, women were the main force that sustained the North Korean regime during the Arduous March.

Towards Genuine Liberation

While women were actively incorporated in the markets, men were rather reluctant to adapt to the changing environment. While they became dependent on their wives for their survival, men did not share the burden of housework. A nominally employed husband usually idled his day at home and demanded his wife to prepare supper when she returned home from long and laborious trade business. If a tired wife answered back impolitely, her husband often gave her lesson with domestic violence.

The economic dependence and domestic violence of men gradually caused women to change. Many young women become reluctant to get married because they do not want to have a dependent husband. Many married women develop many degrading names to express their anger towards incapable husband. Instead of the head of the family, many women call their husbands as "woof-woof" or "day-time light bulb," implying the uselessness of their husbands. In a word, women began to refuse to be subjective wives.

North Korea proclaimed that it succeeded in socialist revolution in 1972. There would be no oppression in socialist society because private property, the cause of exploitation, was abolished. North Korea also claimed that women were emancipated by the guidance and instructions of Kim Il Sung. According to North Korea, the liberation of women was given by the leadership.

Liberation by the leadership might be effective in changing laws and decrees, and providing social facilities. However, liberation by the leadership was destined to be driven by the leadership. In North Korea, the leader, Kim Il Sung, cherished male-dominating traditional concepts. While the government declared that women were fully emancipated, women were instructed to be submissive to their husbands. It was in reality subjugation, not liberation of women. Liberation would be gained by women themselves and on their own terms.

Since the beginning of the North Korean regime, many women have struggled to obtain equality and liberation. They responded to the leadership and the environment. As they had eagerly responded to the call of revolution during the revolutionary period, they actively engaged in the marketization of North Korea during the Arduous March. When a new environment required, they would change their coping strategies.

However, not all responses of women were consciously chosen for their liberation. Before the Arduous March, women in most cases had complied with the leadership and acquiesced in the oppressive social norms. Although women had been the actors in the North Korean revolution, their actions had been often instinctive and responsive. They had never voiced or demanded the change of the gender relations in the society. In a sense, women had been as much indifferent to changing the gender relations as men.

During and after the Arduous March, however, many women began to question the existing gender relations. Although they did not explicitly demand the change in gender relations, they began to move towards change. Their expressions and behaviors to men gradually contradicted existing gender relations.

It may be only the beginning of the long process of transforming gender relations. Transforming gender relations encompasses changes in all aspect of life, not only in the political, economic and social structure but also in the perceptions of the people. Changing perceptions of the people has been a very slow and challenging process.

Nonetheless, many signs of change in the expression and behaviors of North Korean women are the first step for transformation of gender relations. Furthermore, it is women who started to move towards change, not the leadership. In this light, women in North Korea are opening a window for genuine liberation for themselves, albeit a small and obscure window.

Appendices

Appendix 1

List of Interviews Carried out
by the Sejong Institute

Appendix 2

List of Books Based on
Testimonies of the Refugees

Appendix 3

Major Laws related to
the Status of Women

Appendix 4

A Note on the Rape
in the North Korean Penal Code

Appendix 1

List of Interviews Carried out by the Sejong Institute

	Name[1]	Sex	Date of Interview	Occupation	School	Area[2]	Birth Year
1	YC Choi	M	11.12. 02	Trade	College	Kaesung	1971
2	SC Lee	M	11. 7. 02	Farmer	High S[3]	Hambook Kiljoo	1971
3	CG Lee	M	11. 21. 02	Train Driver	High S	Pyungnam Sungchon	1965
4	DH Choi	M	12. 5. 02	Marine Product Center Manager	High S	Pyungbook Euijoo	1960
5	DG Kim	M	12.12. 02	Second Lieutenant	High S	Hwangnam Jaeryung	1958
6	YG Soon	M	12. 18. 02	Instruct at a Revolution Site	High S	Pyongynag	1957
7	SK Lee	M	12. 27. 02	Foreign Trade	College	Yanggang Kapsan	1956
8	YJ Kim	F	1. 23. 03	Narration Teacher	High S	Pyungbook Pakchon	1969
9	CR Joo	M	2. 14. 03	Rolling Mill Technician	College	Hambook Hoeryung	1951
10	KH Choi	F	2. 21. 03	Trade	College	Hambook Hoeryung	1967
11	OS Lee	F	2. 26. 03	Trade	High S	Kangwon Wonsan	1967
12	MS Kim	F	3. 7. 03	R-Station Chief Announcer	College	Hambook Onsong	1969
13	DS Kim	M	3. 21. 03	Director of Chemical Ins.	College	Hambook Hoeryung	1947
14	SH Kim	M	3. 26. 03	Foreign Trade (Czech)	College	Jagang Kanggye	1950
15	MS Lee	F	4. 4. 03	Rolling Mill Technician	College	Hambook Sunbong	1963
16	YN Lee	M	4. 18. 03	Student	College	Hambook Moosan	1979
17	BW Kim	M	4. 24. 03	Central Gov't Worker	College	Pyongyang	1959
18	GI Chung	M	5. 16 03	Trumpeter	High S	Hwangnam Haejoo	1977
19	YC Kim	M	5. 27. 03	HQ of Special Guard	College	Pyongyang	1966

	Name[1]	Sex	Date of Interview	Occupation	School	Area[2]	Birth Year
20	SI Kim	M	5. 20. 03	Sales Manager	College	Hambook Hoeryung	1965
21	KM Chang	F	6. 3. 03	Army Sergeant	High S	Hambook Chongjin	1972
22	SH Kim	M	6. 13. 03	Bureau Chief (Gov't)	College	Hambook Chongjin	1945
23	HK Kim	M	6. 20. 03	Laborer	Technical College	–	1961
24	SY Kim	F	6. 27. 03	Laborer (Shoes)	High S	Hambook Hoeryung	1973
25	CS Park	M	7. 4. 03	Resources Management	High S	Hambook Hoeryung	1951
26	IK Hwang	M	7. 8. 03	Resources Instructor	High S	Hambook Saebyul	1963
27	SH Kim	F	8. 21. 03	Artistic Propaganda	High S	Yanggang Kapsan	1973
28	KN Hwang	F	7. 18. 03	Nursery Governess	High S	Hambook Chongjin	1941
29	GI Chae	M	7. 25. 03.	Oriental M. Doctor	College	Pyungnam Moonduk	1967
30	C. Kim	M	8. 8. 03	Mine Laborer	High S	Nampo	1974
31	ES Lee	F	8. 14. 03	Rail Station Announcer	College	Hambook Chongjin	1964
32	CW Kim	M	8. 28. 03	Pianist	College	Pyongynag	1971
33	JJ Kim	F	9. 3. 03	– (Dependant)	High S	Hambook Kyungsung	1970
34	YJ Kim	M	9. 10 03	Volleyball Player	High S	Pyongyang	1979
35	JK Kim	M	9. 17. 03	Railway Worker	High S	Pyongyang	1956
36	SY Suh	M	10. 15.03	Laborer	High S	Kangwon Wonsan	1963
37	SH Choi	M	9. 26. 03	Foreign Trade	High S	Pyongyang	1964
38	CM Shin	M	10. 1. 03	Mine Laborer	High S	Hambook Chongjin	1952
39	SE Kim	F	10. 8. 03	Farmer	High S	Jagang Jasung	1958
40	HC Choi	M	10. 15. 03	Army Personnel	College	Pyongyang	1962
41	SO Joo	F	11. 5. 03	– (Dependant)	College Drop out	Pyungnam Gaechon	1960

	Name[1]	Sex	Date of Interview	Occupation	School	Area[2]	Birth Year
42	TY Han	M	11. 12. 03	Mechanic	High S	Hamnam Danchon	1961
43	MA Yang	F	11. 19. 03	Inspector at Brick Factory	Technical College	Pyungbook Pihyun	1964
44	H. Han	M	11. 26. 03	Laborer	High S.	Hambook Chongjin	1969
45	CS Kim	M	12. 5. 03	Provincial Gov't Worker	High S	Hwangnam Haejoo	1957
46	GC KIm	F	12. 19. 03	– (Dependant)	College	Hwangnam Samchon	1956
47	SH Kim	F	1. 8. 04	Laborer	High S	Hambook Myungchon	1961
48	HY Kim	F	1. 16. 04	Instructor to Nampo Port	College	Hambook Kiljoo	1962
49	YO Park	F	1. 31. 04	Foreign Trade	Technical College	Hambook Moosan	1978
50	GC Huh	M	2. 18. 04	Laborer	High S	Hambook Chongjin	1972
51	HC Lee	M	2. 27.04	Gymnastic	High S	Hambook Chongjin	1974
52	MH Kim	F	3. 31. 04	Instructor at Glass Factory	College	Hambook Chongjin	1942
53	SH Bae	F	4. 7. 04	Trade	College	Pyungnam Hoechang	1965

Note 1: Used Surname and Initial only for the protection of the identity of the interviewees (Initials may also be a pseudonym sometimes).

Note 2: The place where the interviewee last resided within North Korea.

Note 3: High S means High- Middle School [고등중학교]. In North Korea most adults are graduated from High-Middle school because of the 11 year-lasting compulsory education system.

The names of ten other interviewees are excluded upon their request of anonymity.

Appendix 2

List of Books Based on Testimonies of the Refugees

1. Chosun Ilbo-sa, Bukhan, *Geu Choongkyukui Silsang* 북한 그 충격의 실상 (Seoul: Chosun Ilbo-Sa, A separate-volume Supplement for *Wolgan Chosun*, Jasnuary 1991).

2. Dongik Suh, *Bukeso Sanun Moseup* 북에서 사는 모습 (Seoul: Bukhan Yungooso, 1987).

3. Geukdong Moonje Yungooso (Institute of Far Eastern Studies), *Bundan Ban-Segi Nambukhanui Sahoe-wa Moonhwa* 분단 반세기 남북한의 사회와 문화 (Seoul: IFES Press, 1996).

4. Geum-Soon Lee, *Buhkan Joominui Gukgyung Idongsiltae Byunhwawa Jonmang* 북한주민의 국경이동 실태 변화와 전망 (Seoul: KINU, 2005).

5. Geun-Soon Lee, *Bukhan Joominui Geujooidongsiltae mit Byunhwa Jonmang* 북한주민의 거주이동 실태 및 변화전망 (Seoul: Kinu, 2007)

6. Good Friends, *Doomangangul Gunuon Saramdul* 두만강을 건너온 사람들 (Seoul: Jungto Chulpansa, 1999, a).

7. Good Friends, *Saram dapge Salgosshipso* 사람답게 살고싶소 (Seoul: Jungto Chulpansa, 1999, b).

8. Good Friends, *Bukhansramduli Malhanun Bukhan Iyagi* 북한사람들이 말하는 북한 이야기 (Seoul: Jungto-Publisher, 2000).

9. Good Friends, *Bukhansahoe, Mooussi Byunhago Itnunga?* 북한사회, 무엇이 변하고 있는가 (Seoul: Jungto Chulpansa, 2001).

10. Good Friends, *Bukhan Sikryangnangwa Bukhan Ingwon* 북한 식량난과 북한인권 (Seoul: Jongto Chulpansa, 2004).

11. Good Friends, *Onului Bukhan, Bukhansui Naeil* 오늘의 북한, 북한의 내일 (Seoul: Jungto-Publisher, 2006):

12. Gookto Tongilwon (NUB), *Bukhan Juminsaenghwal Siltae Chosa* 북한 주민생활 실태조사 (Seoul: Gookto Tongilwon, 1989)

13. Gookto Tongilwon (NUB), *Gwisoonja Jeungunul tonghaebon Bukhancheje Byunhwa Siltae* 귀순자 증언을 통해 본 북한 체제변화 실태 (Seoul: Gookto Tongilwon, 1991).

14. Gyo-Duk Lee, Soon-Hee Im, Jong-A Cho, Gidong Lee and Young-Hoon Lee, *Saetominui Jeung-onuro Bon Bukhanui Byunhwa* 새터민의 증언으로 본 북한의 변화 (Seoul: KINU, 2007)

15. Hangook Yusung Yungooso, *Bukhan Yusungui Sarmgwa KKoom* 북한여성들의 삶과 꿈 (Seoul: Sahoe-Moonhwa Yungooso, 2001).

16. Soon-Hee Im, *Sikryangnangwa Bukhanyusongui Yukhal mit UisikByunhwa* 식량 난과 북한여성의 역할 및 의식변화 (Seoul: KINU, 2004).

17. Soon-Hee Im, *Bukhan Yusungui Sarm: Chisokgwa Byunhwa* 북한여성의 삶: 지속과 변화 (Seoul: Haenam, 2006).

18. Whan-Gu Lee, *Bookui Silsanggwa Husang* 북의 실상과 허상 (Seoul: Korean Publishing Corporation, 1985).

Appendix 3

Major Laws related to the Status of Women

1) *Sex Equality Law* (July 30, 1946)[1]

For 36 years Korean women were subjected to ceaseless humiliation and cruel exploitation by Japanese imperialism. They had no political or economic rights and were excluded from cultural, social and political life.

The medieval, feudal relations of the family added to their political and economic oppression. It was the lot of Korean working women to suffer contempt and humiliation, and remain illiterate.

With the liberation of Korea from the colonial rue of Japanese imperialism, the social position of women changed. The democratic reforms being carried out in north Korea have provided conditions for liberating women from the former inequalities in the political, economic, cultural and family life.

With the aim of sweeping away the remnants of the Japanese imperialist colonial policy, transforming the old feudal relations of the sexes and encouraging women to participate fully in cultural, social and political life, the Provisional People's Committee of North Korea decides as follows:

---

1 Kim Il Sung, Works 2: 290–292.

Article 1. Women have equal rights with men in all spheres of State, economic, cultural, social and political life.

Article 2. Women have equal rights with men to elect and be elected to the local and the supreme organ of power.

Article 3. Women have equal rights with men to work, to receive equal wages and social insurance and education.

Article 4. Women, like men, have the right to a free marriage. Unfree, forced marriages without the consent of the couple concerned are forbidden.

Article 5. Women have equal rights with men to a free divorce when circumstances arise in which the conjugal relations become too difficult and cannot be continued any linger.

The mother's right to a lawsuit against the former husband for the expense of bringing up the children is recognized. And it is provided that lawsuits for divorce and for the expense of bringing up the children shall be dealt with in the people's courts.

Article 6. The marriage ages are defined 17 for women and 18 for men.

Article 7. The evil practices of polygamy and violation of women's human rights by selling and buying them as wives or concubines, which are remnants of the medieval and feudal abuses, shall be prohibited hereafter.

The systems of licensed and unlicensed prostitution and the professional entertainer system (entertainers' associations and schools) are prohibited. Those who violate this provision shall be punished by law.

Article 8. Women have equal rights with men to inherit personal and landed property and, in case of divorce, to share the said property.

Article 9. Upon the promulgation of this law, Japanese imperialism's ordinances and regulations on the "rights" of Korean women shall become null and void. This law shall come into force from the day of its promulgation.

2) *Law on Abolition of the Persistent Feudal Customs*

(January 24, 1947) [2]

Article 1. If a man who was proposing marriage, or his parents, relatives or those related to the proposing party offered money, livestock, fortune or labor as the reward of marriage to the proposed woman, or her parents, relatives or those related to the proposed, he or they shall be put to forced labor for up to one year.

Those who received money, fortune, or labor shall be fined to the amount of money they had received.

Article 2. Those who force women to marry, or to remain in the marriage, or those who deceive or kidnap women for the purpose of marriage shall be imprisoned for up to two years.

Article 3. Those who marry a minor below the age of marriage shall be put to forced labor for up to one year.

Article 4. Those who commit polygamy or those who violate monogamy shall be put to forced labor for up to one year, or be fined up to 2,000 Won.

Appendix. To those relations already existing before the enforcement of this law shall be applied those laws in effect at the time of establishment of the relations.

---

2 *Bukhan Gwangye Saryojip* V: 791. Translated by the author.

3) *The Law on Nursing and Upbringing of Children* (1976)[3]

Chapter One. The Fundamentals of the Law of the DPRK on
The Nursing and Upbringing of Children

Article 1. In the DPRK the children represent the future of the country, are reserves of builders of communism, and successors to our revolutionary cause to carry forward the revolution.

Article 2. Bringing up children under public care is one of the major policies of the socialist state; it is an educational method based on socialist pedagogy. The DPRK rears all children in nurseries and kindergartens at state and public expense.

Article 3. Even when children are at nursery age, parents are free to raise their children at their homes, instead of sending them to nurseries.

Article 4. The Law of the DPRK on the Nursing and Upbringing of Children has inherited the brilliant revolutionary traditions created in the glorious anti-Japanese revolutionary struggle for the liberation of the country and the liberty and happiness of the people.

Article 5. The Law of the DPRK on the Nursing and Upbringing of Children is guided solely by the great *Juche* idea of the Workers' Party of Korea, a creative application of Marxism-Leninism to the reality of our country.

Article 6. The Law of the DPRK on the Nursing and Upbringing of Children contributes, through further consolidation and development of the advanced system of rearing children established generally in our country, to training all of them to be new revolutionary men of the *Juche* type, to the sacred work of emancipating women from the heavy burden of raising children, to the

---

3 *Choson Chungang Yungam* (DPRK Central Yearbook) 1977: 214–215.

vigorous acceleration of the building of socialism in the country, and to the historic cause of revolutionizing and working-classizing the whole society.

Article 7. The DPRK takes every possible care that all children may grow happily wanting for nothing under the best, up-to-date conditions for their nursing and upbringing. This benefit is firmly guaranteed by the splendid socialist system established in our country, the solid foundations of the independent national economy, and the socialist policy of the Workers' Party of Korea and Government of the Republic which consider it the supreme principle of their activities steadily to elevate the material and cultural standards of the people. The benefit increases continually with the strengthening of the nation's economic foundations.

Article 8. In the guidance and control of the nursing and upbringing of children the state follows the mass line based on the great Chongsan-ri spirit and Chong-san-ri method by which superiors help subordinates and the voluntary enthusiasm of the nursery governesses and kindergarten teachers and other people who serve with the nursing establishments is aroused through giving priority to political work.

Article 9. The DPRK raises in nurseries and kindergartens at state expense, if the parents so desire, the children of the foreigners who came to seek refuge after struggling for peace and democracy, national independence and socialism and for the freedom of scientific and cultural pursuits.

Article 10. In this law the term children means the children under school age.

Chapter Two. The Raising of Children
at the State and Public Expenses

Article 11. In the nursing and upbringing of children the state institutions and social and cooperative organizations fully meet the requirements of the *Juche* idea that makes man the central factor in all considerations and places everything in the services of man.

Article 12. The state and the social and cooperative organizations are responsible for providing everything necessary for the nursing and upbringing of children in accordance with the principle: "The best things to the children."

Article 13. The state institutions and social and cooperative organizations build modern nurseries and kindergartens at the best suited places and furnish them with good nursing and educational equipment and physical training and playing facilities.

The state institutions and social and cooperative organizations provide the nurseries and kindergartens with musical instruments, toys, publications, teaching tools, etc.

Article 14. The state institutions and social and cooperative organizations build children's parks and playgrounds in towns, villages and in all other places where there are children and furnish them with various playing facilities.

Article 15. In the DPRK all children are supplied with food from birth.

Article 16. The state institutions and social and cooperative organizations provide nurseries and kindergartens with milk, meat, eggs, fruit, vegetables, sweets and other delicatessen.

The expenses for the food supplied to nursery children and kindgarteners are borne by the state and the social and cooperative organizations.

Article 17. The state makes children's clothes, shoes and other goods as best it can, and sets their prices as high as to compensate the production costs or even lower, meeting the balance by itself.

Article 18. The state brings up in baby homes and orphanages the children who enjoy no parental care.

Article 19. The state affords special protection to the children of dead revolutionaries and patriots, of the dependants of the People's Army personnel and disabled soldiers, and pays deep attention to their nursing and upbringing.

Article 20. The State affords special protection to mothers with children. The state grants women maternity leave. Their wages, provisions and shares of distribution for the period of maternity leave are borne by the sate or by the social and cooperative organizations.

The state has all pregnant women registered in good time through maternity hospitals or other medical establishments, provides systematic medical service and midwifery to them free of charge and protects their health after childbirth.

The state assigns pregnant women to light suitable work and allows mothers with babies the suckling time during working hours.

The State reduces the working hours of mothers with many children on full pay.

Article 21. The state grants special favors both to the mothers who have two or more babies at a single birth and to the babies. These mothers are given a longer period of leave with pay after the childbirth.

The state supplies triplets free with clothes and blankets, and with milk goods for a year, grants subsidies for their upbringing till they reach school age and responsibly looks after the health of the babies and mothers by specially designating medical workers for the purpose.

Chapter Three. Cultured and Scientific Rearing of Children

Article 22. It is the loftiest duty for revolutionaries to bring up healthy and intelligent children, the flower-buds of the nation.

The state pays deep attention to rearing children in a cultured and scientific manner.

Article 23. Nurseries and kindergartens look after the children with warm motherly care and bring them up in accordance with the regulations relating to collective upbringing and to hygiene and epidemic prevention.

The children's living places are kept maintained in their rooms.

The children are well looked after hygienically and given regular physical training through the medium of air, sunshine, water, medical instruments and sports apparatuses, in keeping with their ages and constitutions, so as to promote their health.

Article 24. In nurseries and kindergartens children are given a sufficient amount of varied staple foods and snacks suited to their ages and features, in accordance with the nutrition list.

Article 25. The state provides systematic medical care to the nursery children and kindergarteners.

All the medical service for the protection and promotion of children's health is free of charge under the system of universal free medical care in force in our country.

Medical workers are assigned to all nurseries and kindergartens, medical appliances and medicine are supplied to them, and the diseases of children prevented and treated in good time by specialized medical establishments.

Article 26. The state sets up children's wards whenever there are nurseries so as to thoroughly protect the children's health and to fully guarantee the social activities of women.

The children's wards take in and treat those nursery children who are as slightly ill as hospitalization is unnecessary.

Article 27. The state sets up well-furnished sanatoria for children at hot springs and spas and on seashores and at scenic spots to promote their health.

Article 28. The state institutions and nurturing establishments analyze the children's health and development and take appropriate steps, and put child care on a scientific basis and steadily develop it.

Chapter Four. Revolutionary Bringing Up and Education of Children

Article 29. Bringing up and educating the rising generation in a revolutionary manner from an early age is an important task to guarantee the prosperity and progress of the country and the bright future of the revolution.

The state devotes primary efforts to bringing up and educating all children to be revolutionaries of the *Juche* type at nurseries and kindergartens in accordance with the principle of socialist pedagogy.

Article 30. The state educates children in such a way that they do not lose sight of our past and the South Korean people and love our socialist system and the bright future of communism.

Article 31. The state educates children in the collectivist spirit of "One for all and all for one."

Article 32. The state institutions and nurturing establishments educates children to love work and to be accustomed to work from their tender age.

Article 33. The state institutions and nurturing establishments educate children to value and take a loving care of the common property of the state and society.

Article 34. The state institutions and nurturing establishments educate children to have good manners and to form the habit of living in a cultured and hygienic way.

Article 35. The state institutions and nurturing establishments cultivate in the children rich emotions and artistic talents and develop their intellectual faculties in a many-sided way.

Nurseries and kindergartens teach the children our language, songs and dances and how to play musical instruments, and arrange diverse plays for them.

Article 36. The state gives all children compulsory one-year preschool education in the senior course of the kindergarten.

During the compulsory preschool education, the state cultivates children in the habit of revolutionary organizational life and gives them the basic knowledge enough to receive school education, such as the cultured language, how to write, how to count, etc.

Article 37. The state ensures that children are educated at nurseries and kindergartens in diverse forms and ways according to their ages and psychological features.

Chapter Five. Nursery Governesses and Kindergarten Teachers Who are Revolutionaries Fostering Reserve Forces of the Revolution

Article 38. The nursery governesses and kindergarten teachers are honorable revolutionaries who bring up children to be dependable successors to our revolutionary cause, to be a new generation of the *Juche* type.

The nursery governesses and kindergarten teachers who discharge the important and worthy revolutionary duty of rearing children, the future masters of the country, have the deep respect and confidence of the people. The state is deeply concerned for making all members of society love the nursery governesses and kindergarten teachers and give them positive help, so that they will devote all their energies to rearing and teaching the children well.

The state grants favors such as conferment of honorary titles to those working in nurturing establishments who have distinguished themselves in the nursing and education of children.

Article 39. The nursery governesses and kindergarten teachers should become genuine servants of the people, true revolutionaries who dedicate all their energies to bringing up children, the future masters of the revolution, with a high sense of honor and pride in their work.

Article 40. The nursery governesses and kindergarten teachers should arm themselves firmly with the *Juche* ides and thus establish a revolutionary world outlook and revolutionize and working-classize themselves thoroughly.

Article 41. All workers of nurturing establishments including nursery governesses and kindergarten teachers should be free from disease that may affect the health of children and should have expert knowledge for bringing up children on a cultural and scientific basis and educating them along revolutionary lines, and possess appropriate state licenses.

Article 42. The nursery governesses and kindergarten teachers should acquire noble revolutionary qualities and become genuine models for children in all respects.

Article 43. Nursery governesses and kindergarten teachers should bring up children to be strong, cheerful and well-mannered successors to our revolutionary cause.

Chapter Six. Child-Nurturing Establishments and

Their Guidance and Management

Article 44. In the DPRK the child-nurturing establishments are state or public organizations which bring up the rising generation as true revolutionaries.

Article 45. The child-nurturing establishments comprise nurseries, kindergartens, baby homes and orphanages.

The nursery is a nursing organization which rears children of pre-kindergarten age at state or public expense.

The kindergarten is an educational organization which prepares children of four to five for school education.

The baby home and orphanage are nurturing organizations which rear at state expense those children who enjoy no parental care.

Article 46. The state sets up nurseries and kindergartens rationally in residential quarters and in the vicinity of women's work places.

The state organizes and runs weekly and monthly nurseries and kindergartens on a wide scale to fully guarantee the women's public activities.

The opening of nurseries and kindergartens at places in building unfavorable for the health and growth of children is prohibited.

Article 47. The state strengthens its guidance and control of nurseries and kindergartens.

The guidance of nurseries and kindergartens is realized through central bodies of educational and health service administration and local organs of power.

Article 48. The central bodies of educational and health service administration organize and guide the whole affairs of nursing and upbringing of children.

1. To prepare the program for the nursing and upbringing of children and the regulations governing the activities of nurseries and kindergartens and

to improve and perfect steadily the content and methods of nursing and upbringing.

2. To organize and guide the work of protecting and promoting the health of children.

3. To organize and guide the work of training nursery governesses and kindergarten teachers and raising their political and practical qualifications.

4. To give technical guidance to the central bodies which run nurseries and kindergartens.

Article 49. The local organ of power organizes and guides the activities of nurseries and kindergartens in the area under its jurisdiction.

1. To guide the nurseries and kindergartens to implement correctly the program for the nursing and upbringing of children and to conduct work in accordance with the regulations.

2. To organize and guide the work of providing medical care to the nursery and kindergarten children.

3. To organize and guide the work of building nurseries and kindergartens, furnishing them with facilities for nursing and upbringing, and of providing them with material conditions including food supplies.

Article 50. The state guides the officials to go regularly to the lower units and grasp their actual conditions, help and teach them and, giving priority to political work, solve knotty problems by setting personal example, as required by the work method of the anti-Japanese guerillas.

Article 51. The nurseries and kindergartens should correctly implement the program for the nursing and upbringing of children, regularize and standardize their work and strengthen the system of assuming the responsibility for the care of children.

Article 52. The state builds up training centers for nursery and kindergarten workers and trains able nursery governesses and kindergarten teachers to meet the demands.

Article 53. The state develops scientific research work for the revolutionary education and cultured and scientific upbringing of children, and consolidates the relevant scientific research institutions and strengthens its guidance of them.

The state guides literary and art organizations to produce plenty of revolutionary literary and art works such as films, songs, dances, juvenile poems and fairy tales designed for the education of children.

Article 54. The state develops the production of articles and foodstuffs for children.

The state guides the factories and enterprises engaged in the production of children's articles and foodstuffs to steadily increase their output and raise their quality in keeping with the demands and tastes of children.

Article 55. The state sets up supply agencies for nurseries and kindergartens in the center and local areas.

These agencies should be responsible for providing children's articles and foodstuffs and other supplies necessary for their nursing and upbringing.

Article 56. The social and cooperative organizations should ensure that nurseries and kindergartens have material conditions in accordance with the standards fixed by the state.

Cooperative farms should raise many domestic animals, such as chickens, goats and milk cows, and preserve fruit and vegetables well to supply a sufficient amount of foodstuffs to their nurseries and kindergartens.

Article 57. This law is also applicable to the nursing and upbringing of children in the baby homes and orphanages and to their guidance and management.

Article 58. The nursing and upbringing of children is a concern of the whole nation, the whole society.

All civil service institutions, enterprises and organizations should tap their inner reserves and practise economy and thus increase social aid to the nurseries and kindergartens.

4) *The Socialist Family Law* (1990)[4]

Chapter One. Fundamental Principles
of the Socialist Family Law of the DPRK

Article 1. The Socialist Family Law of the DPRK contributes to making the whole society a large harmonious and unified socialist family by developing the socialist marriage and family system.

Article 2. Marriage is the foundation of formation of a family. The state protects marriage by law.

Article 3. Family is the basic unit of the society. The state pays great attention to consolidating the family.

Article 4. Guaranteeing the dignity and rights of man is the natural demand of a socialist system that puts the highest value on human being. The state protects the interests and the rights of the citizen who has no legal capacity by guardianship.

Article 5. Succession is the continuation of legal protection to private property. The state guarantees the succession rights of private property.

Article 6. Special protection for mothers and children is the consistent policy of the DPRK. The state puts priority on providing conditions that enable mothers to nurse and bring up the children healthily.

Article 7. This Law regulates the socialist marital relationship and the personal and property relations among the family and relatives.

---

4 Translated by the author.

Chapter Two. Marriage

Article 8. Citizens enjoy the right of free marriage. Marriage is allowed between a man and a woman.

Article 9. Marriage is allowed to man of age 18 and above, and woman of age 17 and above in the DPRK.

The state encourages the social spirits that youths marry after they contribute to the nation and people, the society and the collectives.

Article 10. Marriage between the blood relatives within eight times removed, and marriage between relatives by marriage within four times removed are prohibited.

Article 11. Marriage is legally recognized and protected by the state when the marriage is registered to the registration office. Conjugal relations without marriage are prohibited.

Article 12. Marriage registration of the citizens residing outside of the DPRK is done to the DPRK consulate of the country. When no DPRK consulate is available, marriage registration is to be done to the equivalent authorities of the country.

Article 13. Marriages contradicting the clauses of 8 to 10 of this law are null and void. The nullification of a marriage is decided by the court.

Article 14. The marriage that is decided null and void is regarded not happened from the beginning. However, the matters of upbringing of children are decided by the clauses 22 and 23 of this law.

Chapter Three. Family

Article 15. The consolidation of the family is an important guarantee for the healthy development of the society. Citizens shall make the family harmonious and merry.

Article 16. The relationship between the husband and wife is established by marriage.

Article 17. The husband and wife keep their original family names and first names, choose their jobs according to their wishes and talents, and participate in social and political life.

Article 18. The wife enjoys the same right as the husband in the family life.

Article 19. The husband and wife have the duty to support the spouse who loses the capacity to work.

Article 20. The relationship between husband and wife becomes extinct with divorce. Divorce should be allowed only by court decision.

Article 21. A married couple can divorce when a spouse betrays the love and trust of the marriage or when the couple finds it impossible to continue their marital life for other reasons.

Article 22. In the case of divorce, the custody of the children should be decided by the agreement of the couple with a viewpoint of the interest of the children. When the agreement is not reached, the court should decide the custody. Unless there are unavoidable circumstances, the young children under the age of three are raised by the mother.

Article 23. The party who does not bring up the children should pay the cost of the bringing up the children until the children reach to the working age. However, when the party who brings up the children does not want to receive the cost, the other party may be excused. The cost of the brining up the children is decided by the court within the range of ten to thirty percent of the monthly income.

Article 24. When the party who paid the const of the brining up the children loses the capacity of labor or when the parent who raised the children remarries and thus the children are supported by the step father or mother, the party concerned may demand the exemption of the cost of bringing up the children to the court.

Article 25. The parents and the children are related by blood. The relationship between the children born to a couple who are not married and the parents is the same as the relationship between the children born to a married couple and the parents.

Article 26. The children take the family name of the father. When the children are unable to take the family name of the father, they take the family name of the mother. The family name of a child whose parents are unknown is decided by the administrative authority of the people.

Article 27. The bringing up of the children is an important duty of the parents. The parents should do their best in the bringing up of the children so that the children become independent persons with intelligence, virtue and physics.

Article 28. The parents raise the children and represent the children under age. The children should love and respect their parents and be responsible to support the parents who lose their capacity to work.

Article 29. The relationship between the step parents and the children is the same as the relationship between the real parents and the children. When the relationship between the step father or step mother and the children is established, the relationship between the real father or real mother and the children becomes extinct.

Article 30. Citizens can adopt under age children born to other people. Those who are deprived by court decision of the right to vote, those who have disease that can harm the children, and those who have no capacity to nurse and bring up the children are denied of adoption.

Article 31. Citizens who want to adopt children should obtain consent from the real parents or the guardians of the children. The consent of the adopted children is also necessary when the children are age six or over.

Article 32. Adoption is completed when the adoption is registered to the registration office with the application of the adoptee and with the approval of the administrative authorities of the people.

Article 33. The relationship between the adoptive parents and the adopted children is the same as the relationship between real parents and the children. When the relationship between the adoptive parents and the adopted children is established, the relationship between the real parents and the children becomes extinct.

Article 34. The break-up of adoption is realized when the break-up is registered to the registration office with the agreement between the adopted children and the adoptive parents, or between the adoptive parents and the real parents or guardians of the adopted children, and with the approval of the administrative authorities of the people. When the agreement of the break-up of adoption is not reached, it is decided by the court.

Article 35. The grand parents should raise and bring up the grand children who enjoy no parental care. The grand children of adult age should be responsible to the health and life of the grand parents.

Article 36. The brothers and sisters should love, respect and instruct each other as the blood and flesh. It is the duty of the brothers and sisters who have the capacity to support the siblings who have no person to take care of them.

Article 37. Minors and those who have no capacity to work shall be supported by the members of the family who can work. When there is no family member residing together who can support them, the parents, offspring, grandparents, grandchildren or the sibling who have capacity but live separately shall support them.

Article 38. Minors and those who have no capacity to work in the Article 37 of this law shall enjoy the care of the state.

Article 39. When a family is broken because of divorce or some other reasons, personal belongings that were brought into the family by marriage or inheritance or gift to a person shall return to the person. Those properties that were obtained commonly for the use of the family shall be divided upon the agreement of the couple.

When there is no agreement, the court will decide.

Chapter Four. Guardianship

Article 40. Minors who can enjoy no parental care or those who have no legal capacity for reasons of physical defects shall be designated a Guardian.

Article 41. The grandparents or sibling can be the Guardian for minors. The spouse, parents or children, grand parents or grand children, or sibling can be the guardian for those who have no legal capacity. When there are many persons who can be the Guardian, the person who is believed to be the best for the Guardianship shall be the Guardian.

Article 42. When there is no Guardian at this law or when there is disputes in the selection of the Guardian for minors or those who have no capacity to work, the local authorities for the people's administration shall select the Guardian.

Article 43. The Guardian shall manage the properties of the guard, and represent the guard.

Article 44. The Guardian shall nurse and bring up the guard and take care of the life and health of the guard.

Article 45. The local authorities for the people's administration shall direct the Guardian for the fulfillment of the obligation as the Guardian.

Chapter Five. Inheritance

Article 46. When a Citizen dies, the properties shall be inherited by the spouse, children and the parents. When there is not spouse, children or parent, the grand children and grand parents or sibling shall inherit the property. When there is no one to inherit by the previous regulation, the relatives upon the closeness of the relationship shall inherit.

Article 47. When there are many expectant heirs with the same priority, they shall have the equal amount of the property. When some of the heirs give up the inheritance, the amount of the property for the person shall be equally divided to other heirs.

Article 48. When the expectant heir abused or deliberately abandoned the deceased, or made the condition for inheritance in deliberation shall be excluded from inheritance.

Article 49. When the legal heir expectants die before the inheritee, the children of the heir expectant shall take the position of the parent in inheritance

Article 50. A Citizen may leave his or her property to inherit by the will. However, when the will impinges the interests of the citizens who were supported by the person who leave the will, the will is null and void. The decision to nullify the will shall be decided by the court upon the request of the parties concerned or the prosecutor.

Article 51. The heirs are responsible for the debts of the deceased within the limits of the property inherited.

Article 52. A Citizen shall express his of her will to accept or give up the inheritance within 6 months. When there is nor body to inherit, or when all the heirs give up the inheritance, the properties shall go to the state. The court may decide to extend the period of the give-up or acceptance of the inheritance upon the request of the parties concerned.

Article 53. The disputes related to inheritance shall be decided by the court.

Chapter Six. Sanction

Article 54. A Citizen who bleaches this law shall be charged the administrative or penal responsibility.

Charging the administrative or penal responsibility shall be decided by the court consideration and decision.

Appendix 4

A Note on the Rape in the North Korean Penal Code

The changes in the regulations on sexual crimes in the Penal Code have been worth noting. The first Penal Code of 1950 consisted of two Volumes, twenty-three Chapters and 301 Paragraphs. It stipulated punishments to the crimes of "sexual intercourse with immature person," "forcing a woman to have sexual intercourse by violence or threat or by taking advantage of her when she is helpless, "obliging sexual intercourse to his subordinate," and prostitution and operating brothels.

1950 Penal Code[1]

Para.136 One who has sexual intercourse with an immature minor and thus injures the minor or satisfy his pervert sexual desire shall be imprisoned for up to seven years. A man who has sexual intercourse with an immature minor but does not cause the aforementioned results shall be imprisoned for up to three years.

Para.137 One who commits acts of obscenity to a minor and thus deprive the minor shall be imprisoned for up to five years.

Para.138 One who forces a woman to have sexual intercourse by violence or threat or by taking advantage of her when she is helpless shall be imprisoned for up to seven years. In cases when the woman concerned commits suicide, or where the aforementioned act is committed to an immature minor, or where the aforementioned act is committed by a gang, the offender shall be imprisoned for up to ten years.

---

1 Daeryuk Yunguso, Bukhan Pupryungchip 4 (Seoul: Naewoe News Agency, 1990): 722–752.

Para.139 One who obliges a woman who is his subordinate physically or by duty to have sexual intercourse or to satisfy his pervert sexual desire shall be imprisoned for up to five years.

The first Penal Code did not use the word rape or gang rape. Until 1950s, North Koreans did not recognize rape as violence. They regarded it a forced "sexual intercourse." The legislator did not care even what meant the word "forced." It could be suspected that "forced" required a severe injury. A slap or a punch would not be enough to "force" a woman who had been living under the instruction that virginity and chastity were valued as higher than life.

Also the Penal Code was not clear who was minor. It read only "immature" minor. How old could be immature? Further, it was necessary to construct a crime that the victim was injured and the offender satisfied his pervert desire. The age of the minor, of course, remained in consideration too. A ten year old girl might be regarded as mature. The law did not exclude the possibility.

Both the injury and the "satisfaction" of the attacker would be hard to prove. However, the bigger barrier for the protection of women and minor was not the Penal Code, but the perception of the people towards rape and sexual assault against women and minor. As in Western countries, people tended to blame the victims. "Inappropriate behavior" would be the cause of the trouble. Women should not be seen and behave very chastely when be seen. However young she might be, a woman, or a young girl, could be bad and inviting for attack.

In fact, the regulation of "forced sexual intercourse" was almost a decoration. Until the 1950s, women's chastity was so valuable that losing it was worse than death. People would recognize the assault only after a woman was found dead, with a clear sign of sexual assault. Even in the rape murder case, the family of the victim lost faces, because she lost her chastity. In this circumstance, legal protection was a rather odd idea.

In accordance with the *Socialist Constitution*, the Penal Code was rewritten in

1974. The 1974 amendment was limited only Volume Two of the Penal Code, Specific Provisions, leaving Volume One, General Provisions, unchanged. The eleven chapters of Specific Provisions of 1950 Penal Code changed into eight chapters and 130 paragraphs, making the code into twenty chapters and 180 paragraphs in total.

This new Penal Code recognized two kinds of sexual crimes against women: "rape by violence and intimidation" (Article 172) and "obliging sexual intercourse" with the woman under his responsibility (Article 173).

Article 172. (Rape): One who rapes a woman by violence or intimidation shall be imprisoned for up to five years.

In cases where the aforementioned act is committed against several women or in cases of gang rape, the offender shall be imprisoned for between five and ten years. Those whose crime is severe shall be sentenced to death or imprisoned for more than ten years.

Article 173. (Obliging a Woman under His Responsibility to Have Sexual Intercourse): One who obliges a woman who is under his responsibility at work or at other duty-bound relationship to have sexual intercourse with him shall be imprisoned for up to two years.

In cases where the aforementioned act is committed against several women or when the woman concerned becomes depraved or commits suicide, the offender shall be imprisoned for up to seven years.

This Penal Code might be a little progress from the 1950 Penal Code for the protection of women, in the sense that it distinguished rape from sexual intercourse. By this 1974 amendment, the concept of rape was first introduced in the law. It also stipulated harsher punishment for repeated rape and gang rape. However, the new Penal Code still contained many problems. First, by the law, rape is constructed only by violence or intimidation. In this context, "violence" almost always meant the life-threatening eventi. The victim's mental disability or desperate condition was not considered. The absence of consent was not even conceived. Second, the subject of rape is restricted to women. Third, the provision for the protection of minors from sexual predators was vanished. In this sense, it was rather a retreat from the 1950 code.

Under this Penal Code, the victims were to be blamed, too. When a small number of victims dared to report the assault, they had to prove the "life-threatening" degree of the violence and their resistance to the extent of death. The facts that they were dressed decently enough, cautious enough, and behaved themselves well enough were the basest thing to be proved.

North Korea amended its Penal Code again in 1987, 1990, 1999, 2004 and 2005. The second amendment of the Penal Code in 1987 was almost a new enactment. The new Penal Code consisted of single volume with eight chapters and 161 paragraphs. By this amendment, the helpless condition of the woman returned to a constructing factor for rape. And the "sexual intercourse" with a girl under the age of fifteen became punishable. It was a little progress for the protection of women and minor. The punishment changed from imprisonment to reform labor. However, basically, the concept of rape remained the same.

1987 Penal Code[2]

Para.153 A man who rapes a woman by violence or threat, or by taking advantage of her when she is helpless, or who has sexual intercourse with a girl under the age of 15 shall be committed to a reform labor institution for up to five years.

In cases where the aforementioned act is committed against several women, or in cases of gang rape, the offender shall be committed to a reform labor institution for between five and ten years.

Para.154 A man who obliges a woman who is his subordinate officially or by duty to have sexual intercourse with him shall be committed to a reform labor institution for up to two years.

---

2 Jong-Go Choi, Bukhanpop (Seoul: Parkyoung-Sa, 2001): 248–261.

In cases where the aforementioned act is committed against several women or when the woman concerned becomes depraved or commits suicide, the offender shall be committed to a reform labor institution for between two and five years.

North Korean amendments of the Penal Code in 1990 and 1999 made no change for the protection of women and girls. Even the order of the paragraphs for the crimes against women was the same (Para.153~154).

The Penal Code of 2004 was another new enactment: while the 1999 Penal Code consisted of 8 chapters and 161 articles, the 2004 Penal Code consisted of 9 chapters and 303 articles, almost double of the former one. This new Penal Code inserted a new chapter titled the Crimes against the Management Order for National Defense (Chapter 4), and made the Crimes against Socialist Culture as a separate chapter (Chapter 6).

Most of all, this new Code inserted the principle of legality – i.e., the principle of nulla poena sine lege." Until 2004, North Korean criminal court accepted analogous interpretation of penal code, which caused criticism from international society of human rights abuse. The adoption of the principle of legality was a great progress in the North Korean criminal system.

The new Penal Code reinforced the protection of private property. Punishments to robbery, stealing, intimidation, fraud, embezzlement and damage were strengthened by extending the period of imprisonment for such crimes. At the same time the new law reinforced the social order and national security. Punishments for crimes against the State and the nation were enumerated in detail and intensified. Also many articles were newly inserted for punishments of crimes against socialist economic order and socialist culture. Those who distribute or produce decadent, explicit and obscene music, dance, paintings, pictures, illustrations, films, Video tapes and CD-ROMs without prior permission were to be sentenced to imprisonment for 2 years (Article 193). Even persons watching and listening to those decadent and obscene products were subject to punishment (Article 194).

The 2004 Penal Code also made a little change in the crimes against women. It separated the crime of "sexual intercourse with minor" into a new article to enforce the protection of underage girls. However, the basic concept of rape by "violence and threat" remained intact. In order to construct a rape case, a man, using violence or threats, or taking advantage of the helpless condition of a victim, violates a female subject. The absence of consent was not considered at all. Also, the subject (victim) of rape or "sexual intercourse" is female only. "Sexual intercourse" with underage boy, or rape of a man, does not constitute rape. Basically, the North Korean *Penal Code* does not regard sexual penetration of a male subject as rape. Also, the *Penal Code* does not declare sexual intercourse with underage girl to be rape, although the punishment is the same. This pattern of constructing rape is still problematic and unable to properly protect vulnerable groups, particularly women and minors.

Other crimes against women including disgraceful sexual conduct and sexual harassment, verbal or physical, are not recognized by the Penal Code. Women remain vulnerable to verbal assault or unwanted sexual conduct. North Korea amended the Penal Code twice in 2005 for minor modifications, without changing the crimes against women.

2004 Penal Code

Article 6. (Principle of Legality) The State pursues a person's criminal responsibility only when the Penal Code clearly describes the activities as crime.

Article 293. (Rape): A man who rapes a woman by violence or threats or by taking advantage of her when she is helpless shall be committed to a reform institution for up to five years.

In cases where the aforementioned act is committed against several women or in cases of gang rape the offenders shall be committed to a reform institution for between five and ten years. Those whose crime is severe shall be imprisoned more than ten years.

Article 294. (Obliging a Subordinate Woman to Have Sexual Intercourse): A man who obliges a woman who is his subordinate officially or by duty to have sexual intercourse with him shall be committed to a reform institution for up to two years.

In cases where the aforementioned act is committed against several women or when the woman concerned becomes depraved or commits suicide, the offender shall be committed to a reform institution for between two and five years.

Article 295. (Sexual Intercourse with Minor): A man who has sexual intercourse with a girl under the age of 15 shall be committed to a reform institution for up to 5 years.

In cases where the aforementioned act is repeated the offender shall be committed to a reform institution for between five and ten years.

Outside world has been focused on the nuclear or trafficking of women in North Korea. Those issues were grave and affecting the whole world. However, it may be the time to turn the attention to the matters of "individual" disasters. Rape and sexual assault are, as many have argued, attacks to the whole female population hampering the mobility of the gender.

References

Adrian Buzo, *The Making of Modern Korea* (New York: Routledge, 2002).

Ae-Sil Kim, *Bukhan Yusungui Saenghwal Siltae* 북한여성의 생활실태 ed. by Bong-Sook Sohn (Seoul: Nanam, 1991).

Amy K. Nash, *North Korea* (Philadelphia: Chelsea House Publisher, 1999.

Andrei Lankov, *North of the DMZ: Essays on Daily Life in North Korea* (Jefferson and London: McFarland & Company, 2007).

Andrew S. Natsios, *The Great North Korean Famine* (Washington DC: USIP Press, 2001).

Balazs Szalontai, *Kim Il Sung in the Khrushchev Era: Soviet-DPRK Relations and the Roots of North Korean Despotism, 1953-1964* (Washington: Woodrow Wilson Center Press, 2006).

Bohaeng Kim, *Rodong Gajong* 로동가정 (Pyongyang: Moonye Choolpan-Sa, 1979).

"Booboo Sai-e Choogo Banun Mal," *Chollima* 천리마, April-May 1981; "*Sedaejoorul Boorusun Mal*," *Chollima*, November 1988.

Bradley K. Martin, *Under the Loving Care of the Fatherly Leader: North Korea and the Kim Dynasty* (New York: St. Martin's Press, 2004).

Bruce Cumings, *Korea's Place in the Sun: A Modern History* (New York: WW Norton & Company, 1997).

Bruce Cumings, *Korea's Place in the Sun: A Modern History* (New York: WW Norton, 1997).

Bukhan Gwangye Saryojip V.

Bukhan Yungooso, *Bukhan Chongram* 북한총람 (Seoul: Bukhan Yungooso, 1983).

Bukhan, Geu Choongkyukui Silsang 북한 그 충격의 실상 (Seoul: Chosun Ilbo-Sa, A separate-volume Supplement for *Wolgan Chosun*, Jasnuary 1991).

Cabiner Resolution No.23, "Regulations on the Working Hours of Working Mothers," 1966.9.27 decided; 1966.11.1 came into force. *Choson Chungang Yungam* (DPRK Central Yearbook) 1966/67.

Cabinet Resolution No.46, "On Reforming and Strengthening the Operation of Nurseries and Kindergartens (1964.7.1): *Choson Chungang Yungam* (DPRK Central Yearbook) 1965.

Chaguen Moonjega Anida, *Chosun Nyusung*, September 1981.

Chang-Geun Lee, *Rodong Haejong-saop Kyunghum* 로동행정사업경험 (Pyongyang: Sahoegwahak Choolpan-Sa, 1989).

Chang-Guen Lee, *Woori Dang-e uihan Rodong Haejongrironui Shimhwa Baljon* 우리당에 의한 로동행정 리론의 심화 발전 (Pyongyang: Sahoegwahak Choolpan-Sa, 1992).

Charles K. Armstrong, *Totalitarian Movements and Political Religions* 6, no.3 (London: Routledge, December 2005).

Charles K. Armstrong, The North Korean Revolution, 1945-1950 (Ithaca: Cornell University Press, 2003); Adrian Buzo, *The Guerilla Dynasty: Politics and Leadership in North Korea* (Boulder: Westview Press: 1999).

Charles K. Armstrong, *The North Korean Revolution, 1945-1950* (Ithaca: Cornell University Press, 2003).

"Chinhee Gyosaga Doesiyo (Assuming the Role of the Teacher)," *Chosun Nyusung*, December 1981.

"Choongsungui Ssiasul Ppoorisimyo (Planting the Seeds of Loyanty)," *Chosun Nyusung*, July 1982, 1982).

Choson Chungang Yongam [DPRK Central Yearbook] 1970 (Pyongyang: Choson Chungan Tongshinsa, 1970).

Choson Chungang Yongam 조선중앙연감 1949 (Pyongyang: Choson Chungang Tongshinsa, 1949).

Choson Tae Baekgwa Sajon 1 조선대백과사전1 (Pyongyang: Baekgwa Sajon Chulpansa, 1995).

Christian von Krockow, *Hour of the Women* (London: Faber and Faber, 1993).

Dae-Sook Suh, *The Korean Communist Movement 1918~1948* (Princeton: Princeton University Press, 1967).

Daeryuk Yunguso, *Bukhan Pupryungchip 4* (Seoul: Naewoe News Agency, 1990).

Daeryuk Yunguso, *Bukhan Pupryungjip 1* 북한법령집 1 (Seoul: Naewoe Tongshinsa, 1990).

Decision of the Central People's Committee (1987.8.17), *Choson Chungang Yungam* (DPRK Central Yearbook) 1982.

Elizabeth Croll, *Feminism and Socialism in China* (New York: Schocken Books, 1978).

Eui-Gak Hwang, *The Korean Economies: A Comparison of North and South* (Oxford: Clarendon Press, 1993).

Friedrich Engels, *The Origins of the Family, Private Property and the State : In the Light of the Researches of Lewis H. Morgan* (1884), in Karl Marx and Frederick Engels, *Collected Works*, Vol.26, August 1882~December 1889 (New York: International Publishers, 1990):129-276.

Good Friends, *Bukhan Sikryangnangwa Bukhan Ingwon* 북한 식량난과 북한인권 (Seoul: Jongto Chulpansa, 2004).

Good Friends, *Bukhansahoe, Mooussi Byunhago Itnunga?* 북한사회, 무엇이 변하고 있는가 (Seoul: Jungto Chulpansa, 2001).

Good Friends, *Bukhansramduli Malhanun Bukhan Iyagi* 북한사람들이 말하는 북한이야기 (Seoul: Jungto-Publisher, 2000).

Good Friends, *Doomangangul Gunuon Saramdul* 두만강을 건너온 사람들 (Seoul: Jungto Chulpansa, 1999).

Good Friends, *Onului Bukhan, Bukhansui Naeil* 오늘의 북한, 북한의 내일 (Seoul: Jungto-Publisher, 2006).

Good Neighbors (2004).

Gookto Tongilwon (NUB), *Gwisoonja Jeungunul tonghaebon Bukhancheje Byunhwa Siltae* 귀순자 증언을 통해 본 북한 체제변화 실태 (Seoul: National Unification Board, 1991).

Gookto Tongilwon, *Bukgoe Pupryungchip 2* (Seoul: Gookto Tongilwon, 1971).

Gookto Tongilwon, *Bukgoe Pupryungchip 2* 북괴법령집 2 (Seoul: Gookto Tongilwon, 1971).

Gookto Tongilwon, *Choigo Inmin-Hoeui Charyochip 2* 최고인민회의 자료집 2 (Seoul: Gookto Tongilwon).

Gookto Tongilwon, *Gwisoonja Jeungunul tonghaebon Bukhancheje Byunhwa Silta*.

"Gwijoonghan Jichim (Priceless Instructions)," *Chosun Nyusung*, July 1982: 15.

Hankuk Yusong Yunguso, *Bukhan Yusongdului Sarmgwa Kkoom* 북한여성들의 삶과 꿈 (Seoul: Sahoe-Munhwa Yunguso, 2001).

Hankuk Yusung Yungooso, *Hankuk Yusung-Sa* 한국여성사 (Seoul: Poolbit, 1992).

Hankuk Yusung Yungooso: 130-133; Hyo-Je Lee, *Hankukui Yusung Woondong: Oje-wa Onul* 한국의 여성운동: 어제와 오늘 (Seoul: Chung-Woo, 1989).

Haruki Wada, *Kin Nichisei to Manshu Konichi senso* (Tokyo: Heibonsha, 1992).

Hochin Choi, *The Economic History of Korea: From the Earliest Times to 1945* (Seoul: The Freedom Library, 1971).

Hyo-Je Lee, *Hankukui Yosongwoondong: Ojewa Onul* 한국의 여성운동: 어제와 오늘 (Seoul: Chung-Woo, 1989).

Hyukmyongui Omoni 혁명의 어머니 (Pyongyang: Inmoon Gwahak-Sa, 1978).

"Hyukmyungui Omoni Kim Jong-Suk Nyusarul Mosigo (My Memory on the Mother of Revolution, Lady Kim

Jong-Suk)," *Chosun Nyusung*, February 1982.

Hyun-Sun Park, *Hyundai Bukhansahoewa Gajok* 현대북한사회와 가족 (Seoul: Hanul Publishing House, 2003).

Hyun-Sun Park, *Hyundai Bukhanui Gajoke Gwanhan Yungoo: Gajok Jeasaengsangwa Gajokgoojorul Chungsimuro* 현대북한의 가족에 관한 연구: 가족 재생산과 가족구조를 중심으로 (Seoul: Ph. D. Thesis, Ehwa Woman's University, 1999).

Il-Ho Cho, *Chosun Gajokpup* (Pyongyang: Gyoyuksa, 1958).

Insook Nam, *Nambukhan Yusung, Geuduleun Noogooinga?* 남북한 여성, 그들은 누구인가? (Seoul: Nanam, 1992); and Dongik Suh, *Bukeso Sanun Moseup* 북에서 사는 모습 (Seoul: Bukhan Yungooso, 1987).Interview by Sejong Institute (February 26, 2003).

Jae-Han Kim, *Orini Boyuk-Gyoyang Gyunghom* 어린이 보육교양 경험 (Pyongyang: Sahoe Gwahak Chulpan-Sa).

Jong-Go Choi, Bukhanpop (Seoul: Parkyoung-Sa, 2001).

Jong-Ho Huh, *Chosun Inminui Jonguiui Chokguk Haebangjonjang-Sa 1* 조선인민의 정의의 조국해방전쟁사 1 (Pyongyang: Social Science Publishing House, 1983).

Jong-Ok Lee, "For the Implementation of the Regulation on Skills Training on-the-Job", *Rodong* 로동 (1959, no.4).

Kang Ban-Sok Nyusarul Ddara Baewooja 강반석 녀사를 따라배우자 (Tokyo: Chosun Chungnyun, 1967).

Ki-Jong Chung, *Yulbyung Gwangjang* 열병광장 (Pyongyang: Monye Chulpansa, 2001).

Kim Il Sung Speech at the Ali Arham Social Science Institute in Indonesia (1965.4.14), *Choson Chungang Yungam* (DPRK Central Yearbook) 1966-67.

Kim Il Sung, *Chojakchip 7* 저작집 7 (Pyongyang: Sahoe-gwahak chulpan-sa, 1980): 211. Author's translation.

Kim Il Sung, *Chojakchip 8* 저작집 8: 1953.8-1954.6 (Pyongyang: Chosun Rodongdang Choolpan-Sa, 1980).

Kim Il Sung, *Chojakchip 9* 저작집 9: 1954.7-1955.12 (Pyongyang: Chosun Rodongdang Choolpan-Sa, 1980).

Kim Il Sung, *Selected Works*, Vol. 1 (Pyongyang: Foreign Languages Publishing House, 1971).

Kim Il Sung, *On the Revolutionization and Working-Classization of Women* (Pyongyang: Foreign languages Publishing House, 1974).

Kim Il Sung, *Segiwa Dobulo* 세기와 더불어 (Kim Il Sung Memoir: With the Century), Vol. 7 (Pyongyang: Choson Rodongdang Chulpansa, 1996).

Kim Il Sung, *Works* 1 (Pyongyang: Foreign languages Publishing House, 1980).

Kim Il Sung, *Works* 2 (Pyongyang: Foreign languages Publishing House, 1980).

Kim Il Sung, *Works* 4 (Pyongyang: Foreign Languages Publishing House, 1980).

Kim Jong Il, *Sunchip 8* 김정일선집 (Pyongyang: Chosun Rodondang Choolpan-Sa, 1998).

Kuksa Pyunchan Wiwonhoe, *Bukhan Gwangye Saryojip V: Pupjepyun* 북한관계사료집V: 법제편 (Seoul: Kuksa Pyunchan Wiwonhoe, 1987).

Kukto Tongilwon, *Choigo InminHoeui Jaryojip* 1 최고인민회의 자료집 1(Seoul: Kukto Tongilwon, 1988).

Kwang-Woon Kim, *Bukhan Jongchisa Yungu 1: Gundang, gunkuk, gunkunui yuksa* 북한 정치사 연구 I: 건당, 건국, 건군의 역사 (Seoul: Sunin Publishing, 2003).

Kyung-Hye Lee, *Nyusung Moonje Haekyul Kyunghum* 녀성문제해결경험 (Pyongyang: Sahoegwahak Choolpan-Sa, 1990).

Kyungja Jung and Bronwen Dalton, *Asian Survey 46* (2006, no. 5).

Let's Follow the Model of Lady Kang Ban-Suck 강반석 녀사를 따라배우자 (Tokyo: Chosun Chungnyun, 1967).

Mao Tse-Tung, *Selected Works 1* (Peking: Foreign Languages Press, 1967).

Marion P. Spina, *On Korea: Academic Paper Series*, Vol. 1 (Washington DC: KEI, 2008).

Minju Choson (The party organ of the WPK), 1953.6.1.

Miryang Youn, *Bukhanui Yusung Chongchaek* 북한의 여성정책.

Miryang Youn, "Yusungui Chiwiwa Yukhal," *Bukhanui Sahoe Moonhwa* 북한의 사회문화 ed. by Bukhan Yungoo Center, Sejong Institute (Seoul:, Hanul, 2006).

Myung-Rim Park, *Hankuk Jonjaengui Balbalgwa Giwon II: Giwongwa Wonin* 한국전쟁의 발발과 기원 II: 기원과 원인 (Seoul: Nanam, 1996).

Nicholas Eberstadt and Judith Banister, *The Population of North Korea* (Berkeley : Institute of East Asian Studies, University of California, Center for Korean Studies, 1992).

Moon-Soo Yang, *Pigyo Kyungje Yungu* 12, no. 2 비교경제연구 (Seoul: Korean Association of Comparative Economic Studies, 2005).

Ohn-Jook Lee, *Bukhan Yusungui Saenghwal Siltae* 북한여성의 생활실태, ed. by Bong-Sook Sohn: 1991).

On the Revolutionization and Working-Classization of Women.

Robert K. Sawyer, *Military Advisors in Korea: KMAG in Peace and War* (Washington DC: Department of the Army, 1962).

Roxane Witke, *Women in China: Studies in Social Change and Feminism*, ed. by Marilyn B. Young (Ann Arbor: Center for Chinese Studies, The University of Michigan, 1973).

Ryuksa Yunguso, *Choguk Haebangjonjang Siki Balhyundoen Hoobang Inmindeului Hyukmyungjok Saenghwalgipoong* 조국해방전쟁시기 발현된 후방인민들의 혁명적 생활기풍 (Pyongyang: Social Science Publishing House, 1976).

Sang-Jin Ko, *Chulhak Yungoo* 철학연구 (Pyongyang: Gwahak Baekgwasajon Chulpansa, 1999, no.1).

Sang-Yong Kim, *Buphak Yungoo* 법학연구 Vol. 13, No. 2(Seoul: Law Study Institute, Yonsei University, June 2003).

Sejong Institute, *Bukhanui Sahoe Munhwa* 북한의 사회문화, Sejong Yungoo Chongsoe 7 (Seoul: Hanul, 2006).

Si-Rim O, *Sin Saimdang kwa Chanyo Kyoyuk* 신사임당과 자녀교육 (Seoul: Minyesa, 1986).

Soon-Hee Im, *Bukhan Yusungui Sarm: Chisokgwa Byunhwa* 북한여성의 삶: 지속과 변화 (Seoul: Haenam, 2006).

Stephan Haggard and Marcus Noland, *Famine in North Korea: Markets, Aid, and Reform* (New York: Columbia University Press, 2007).

Stephan Haggard and Marcus Noland, *Hunger and Human Rights: The Politics of Famine in North Korea* (Washington DC: US Committee for Human Rights in North Korea, 2005).

Sung-Bo Kim, *Sajingwa Grimuro Bonun Bukhan Hyundaisa* 사진과 그림으로 보는 북한현대사 (Seoul: Yuksa Yunguhoe, 2004).

Sung-Hee Sohn, Gwanrip Hansung Yuhakgyoui *Sullip gwajonggwa Gyogwa Gwajong Yungoo* 관립 한성고등여학교의 설립과정과 교과과정 연구(Seoul: MA Thesis at the Ewha University, 2004).

Tae-Ho Park, *Chosun Inminui Jonguiui Chokguk Haebangjonjang-Sa 3* 조선인민의 정의의 조국해방전쟁사 3

(Pyongyang: Social Science Publishing House, 1983).

Tae-Young Lee, *Bukhan Yusung* 북한여성 (Seoul: Sil-Chun Moonhacksa, 1988).

Toikoo, Keiko, *Travel Sketches of North Korea*, Jiusiki Eijia Publisher, Tokyo, 1982.

Tokanfu, *Tokanfu tokei nenpo* (Annual Statistical Report of the Residency-General of Korea 1910. Re-quoted from Theodore Jun Yoo, *The Politics of Gender in Colonial Korea: Education, Labor, and Health 1910-1945* (Berkeley: University of California Press, 2008).

Tongil Yungoowon, *Whitepaper on Human Rights in North Korea* (Seoul: Korean Institute for National Unification, 2003).

Un Rim, *Bukhan Kim Il Sung Wangjo Bisa* 북한 김일성왕조 비사 (Seoul: Hankuk Yangsheo, 1992).

UNICEF, *Nutrition Assessment 2002, DPR Korea*

Vipan Chandra, *Imperialism, Resistance, and Reform in Late Nineteenth Century Korea: Enlightenment and the Independence Club* (Berkeley: Institute of East Asian Studies, University of California, 1988).

Wan-Joo Bang, *Choson Gaegwan* 조선개관 (Pyongyang: Foreign Languages Publishing House, 1987).

Whan-Gu Lee, *Bookui Silsanggwa Husang* 북의 실상과 허상 (Seoul: Korean Publishing Corporation, 1985).

Woo-keun Han, *The History of Korea*, tr. by Lee, Kyung-shik (Seoul: Eulyoo-Gak, 1970).

Yang Zhaoquan, "Comrades Kim Il Sung," quoted in Charles K. Armstrong.

Yongrin Moon, "Gyoyook Chejewa Chedo," *Bukhangaeron* 북한개론 (Seoul: Ulyoo-Sa, 1990): 393.

Yoonok Chang with Stephen Haggard and Marcus Noland, *The North Korean Refugee Crisis: Human Rights and International Response*, ed by Stephen Haggard and Marcus Noland (Washington DC: US Committee for Human Rights in North Korea, 2006).

Yosup Chung, *Hankuk Yusong Woondong-Sa* 한국여성운동사(Seoul: Iljogak, 1971).

Young-Ja Park, *Bukhanui Gundaehwa Gwajonggwa Yusungui Yukhal* (1945-1980s) 북한의 근대화 과정과 여성의 역할 (1945-1980년대): 공장과 가정의 정치사회와 여성노동을 중심으로 (Seoul: Ph.D Thesis, Sunggyunwan University, 2004).

Young-Ja Park, *Bukhanui Geundaehwa Gwajong-gwa Yusungui Yukhal, 1945-1980 Nyundae* 북한의 근대화 과정과 여성의 역할, 1945-1980년대: 공장과 가정의 정치사회와 여성노동을 중심으로 (Seoul: Ph. D Thesis, Sunggyungwan University, 2004).

Yusung Gaebalwon (Research Institute on Women's Development), B*ukhan Yusungui Chiwi-e Gwanhan Yungoo* 북한여성의 지위에 관한 연구: 여성관련 법 및 정책을 중심으로 (Seoul: Yusung Gaebalwon, 1992).

"Yusungui Onowa Kyoyang The Language of Women and Civility," *Chosun Nyusung*, January 1990.

Index

A

Agriculture, 279
Ancestor worship, 16
Andrew Natsios, 201
Anti-capitalistic revolution, 276
Anti-feudal, revolution, 276
Anti-feudal democratic revolution, 53
Anti-imperialist, 53
Anti-Japanese struggle, 40
Anti-Japanese Women's Association, 146
Anti-revolutionary, 191
Anti-sectarianists struggle, 114, 115
Arch of Triumph, 127
Arduous March, 8, 128, 196, 200, 271, 284
Aristocracy, 30
Armistice, 131
Association for the Restoration of Fatherland, 72
Axis of Evil, 204

B

Baby-boomers, 156
Bagger(hua-zi), 223
Bean-curds a day, 263
Birth control, 160
Body Mass Index(BMI), 236
Bolshevik revolution, 44
Book of Rites, 55
Boolyo-Boolgoolui Hyukmyung Toosa Kim Jong-Suk
Dongjirul Hoesanghayu, 148
Bosung Market, 246
Bourgeois capitalist, 45
Bourgeois culture, 69
Bourgeois revisionists, 120
Breadwinner, 5
Bureaucratic power, 30
Bush admistration, 204

C

Cabinet resolution, 129
Capitalism, 54
Capitalists, 249
the Central Committee, 202
Central plan, 270
Centralization and collectivization of the economy, 114
Chanyanghoe(praising club), 29

Chinese Communist Party(CCP), 45, 46
Chollima, 153, 173
Chosun(Chosun Dynasty), 16, 30, 33, 77, 200
    custom, 34
Chosun Association for Women's Education, 41
Chosun Chungang Yungam, 180
Chosun Farm Workers' Union, 181
Chosoun Scout, 181
Chosun Trade Union, 181
Chun Yun-Ok, 182
Chuson Yusung, 149
Civil Code, 81, 277
    North Korean Civil Code, 209
Citizen Registration System, 244
Clinton administration, 199
Coalition for the Amendment of the Family Law, 83
Collectivism, 209
Collectivization of the agricultural sector, 115
Colonial
    authority, 31
    rule, 30, 35
    power, 33
Comfort women(jugun-ianfu), 38, 39
Commander-in-chief, 150
Communism, 40, 116
Communists, 152, 276
Communist revolution, 6
Communist party, 158
Concubine, 19
Confucianism, 26
    Confucianization, 16
    Confucian tradition, 7, 278
Conference, 181
Constitution, 276
Construction work, 191
Coronation, 198
Counter-revolutionary, 156
Cultural policy(bunka seigi), 31
    cultural politics, 43
Custody, 157
Cut off, 198

D

Daily Rodong, 234
Daytime Lightbulbs, 264, 285
Dear Leader, 199
Decade of Organizational Flood, 40

Women in North Korea
From Revolution to Markets

First edition   30 November 2023
Second edition   15 December 2023
Author   Miryang Youn
Publisher   Jaegyo Lee

Designe   Ja-young Park
Produce   Jikyung Munhwa

Publisher   Good Plus Communications
Publication Registration   7 May 2013 No. 2013-000136
Address   2th Floor, 21, Bugahyeon-ro 22-gil, Seodaemun-gu, Seoul, Republic of Korea
Tel   82-2-6080-9859
Fax   82-0505-115-5245
E-mail   goodplusbook@gmail.com
Facebook   www.facebook.com/pages/goodplusbook

ISBN   979-11-85818-56-6 (03340)